Business and Entrepreneurship in Saudi Arabia

Business and Entrepreneurship in Saudi Arabia

Opportunities for Partnering and Investing in Emerging Businesses

EDWARD BURTON

WILEY

Published by John Wiley & Sons, Inc., Hoboken, New Jersey.
Published simultaneously in Canada.

For general information on our other products and services or for technical support, please contact our Customer Care Department within the United States at (800) 762-2974, outside the United States at (317) 572-3993 or fax (317) 572-4002.

Wiley publishes in a variety of print and electronic formats and by print-on-demand. Some material included with standard print versions of this book may not be included in e-books or in print-on-demand. If this book refers to media such as a CD or DVD that is not included in the version you purchased, you may download this material at http://booksupport.wiley.com. For more information about Wiley products, visit www.wiley.com.

Library of Congress Cataloging-in-Publication Data is available:

ISBN 9781118943960 (Hardcover)
ISBN 9781119296188 (ePDF)
ISBN 9781119296171 (ePub)

Cover Design: Wiley
Cover Images: (top) © Kingdom of Saudi Arabia, Royal Commission for Jubail & Yanbu; (bottom) © Saudi Desert Photos by TARIQ-M/ Getty Images, Inc.

Printed in the United States of America.
10 9 8 7 6 5 4 3 2 1

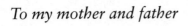

To my mother and father

Contents

Preface

This book is about business in the Kingdom of Saudi Arabia and how change occurring within the Kingdom is transforming how business is done. It is about Saudi Arabia's business community and the importance and relevance the Kingdom's economy and its industrial and commercial centers have to global business. But, more importantly, it is about the people, companies, and business environment that make doing business in Saudi Arabia such a unique and rewarding experience.

I have spent most of my professional career assisting American enterprise in the trade of their goods and services, and placement of their capital investments in markets around the world. During the course of this vocation, I have gained knowledge in the art and science of evaluating foreign markets for business and learned what to look for when identifying countries representing the best prospects for gaining and growing market share for American businesses. I have found no market more thought-provoking nor engaging than the Kingdom of Saudi Arabia.

There have been numerous books written about Saudi Arabia over the past 25 years. However, a cursory review of those works show their subject matter primarily centers on oil, internal, regional and international politics, the Kingdom's economy, or its social questions of the day. To be sure, studies of these topics are valuable to a rounded understanding of Saudi Arabia. But the dearth of books dedicated to the subject of commercial affairs inside the Kingdom has assumed a deafening quality given Saudi Arabia's importance to the world. And, there are reasons for the absence of credible literature on the subject.

Culturally, Saudi Arabia has often been labeled a closed society. Many who approach the market for business comment on the insular nature of the Kingdom's culture, which in turn casts upon it a facade of inscrutability and impenetrability. For those electing not to spend the time to get to know the country and its people, an inevitable feeling of enduring challenge characterizes doing business there. However, with modest and sincere effort, the Kingdom's enormous market opportunities and an enriched experience with its businesses eagerly await those who wish them. It is for this reason, and my enduring respect and admiration for the Saudi business community I have written this book.

I lived and worked in Saudi Arabia for three years. Considering there are American "long-termer" expatriate workers with more than 30 years in the Kingdom, I am always on guard against exaggerating my familiarity with the Kingdom. However, I believe that for one to have some sense of the Kingdom's vitality, exceptionality, and promise, one must spend significant sustained periods within its borders. I gained my sense of the Kingdom through those three years serving as commercial attaché in the American embassy in Riyadh as well as almost 10 years now as president and CEO of the U.S.-Saudi Arabian Business Council. Through these unique and valued professional appointments, I have been fortunate to have gained the trust, confidence, and support of some of the Kingdom's most respected and esteemed business people. Owners and senior management of small, medium-sized, and large Saudi companies have enthusiastically supported bringing this book to market because their story is not being told. It has only been through the privileged access afforded me over the years that this book and its glimpse into the Kingdom's private world of business were made possible.

The chapters of this book are summarized as follows:

A current view of Saudi Arabia's economic strength and rapidly expanding industrial complex is given in Chapter 1. The period between 1938 and 1970, from the discovery of oil to the nation's first formal economic development effort and onset of industrial expansion, is given significance since this is when many of the Kingdom's well-known businesses were established. The chapter examines the Kingdom's national economic development plans, especially the first and most recent ones, and looks at historical efforts by the Saudi government to integrate the Kingdom's business sector into serving the nation's development goals. The chapter examines the question whether adequate coordination between and among the public and private sectors has attended implementation of these plans. Two of the most important topics of influencing economic development, Saudi Arabia's pursuit and achievement of membership in the World Trade Organization (WTO) and its relentless drive toward economic diversification from an oil-based economy is covered in this chapter. This assessment includes a special focus on how the business community has met the challenges of increased foreign competition and more demanding regulatory environment since the Kingdom's accession to WTO membership in December 2005.

Chapter 2 scrutinizes Saudi Arabia's rush to innovation and the creation of a knowledge-based economy, as well articulated in its ninth national development plan. A discussion of the Saudi national science, technology, and innovation plan, promulgated by King Abdulaziz City for Science and Technology (KACST) in furtherance of its charter, is presented and its impact assessed. The chapter appraises the Kingdom's efforts to construct a permanent milieu for the nation's growing cadre of researchers, developers, and innovators. The chapter offers a general survey of major research and development projects underway in Saudi Arabia and offers examples of cutting edge studies in the applied industrial sciences. Work being done in this area by world-renowned institutions such as King Abdullah University for Science and Technology (KAUST) and its industry collaboration program (KICP), King Saud University (KSU) and its Riyadh Techno Valley, and KACST, particularly its Nanotechnology Centre of Excellence and BADIR program are highlighted. The chapter looks at the state of patent applications in the Kingdom and highlights the important work being done by the nation's patent authorities, the Saudi Patent Office (SPO), and the National Patent Office (NPO). Given that the operational condition, efficacy, and performance of a country's patent registration system is often a useful barometer on the health of innovation among its brightest people, useful figures are presented as to the demographics on the origin of patentable innovations within Saudi Arabia.

Chapter 3 assesses the enduring legacy of Saudi Arabia's family-owned businesses (FOBs). The chapter affords the reader a rare and brief look inside several of the Kingdom's best known and respected family establishments and appraises the historical significance of these businesses. Observing their humble beginnings in business, in some cases being the nation's first start-ups through vendor and supplier contracts with the precursor to Saudi Aramco back in the 1940s, 1950s, and 1960s, Chapter 3 delves into the role they continue to play in the Kingdom's commercial and industrial development. This chapter examines the transformation of these businesses into globally diversified commercial entities. We look at the challenges faced by these companies as they transition their corporate leadership from first to second generation, and from second to third generation as younger family members are integrated to their businesses. With an average of five children born to Saudi families, when the time comes to pass on control of a family business from a matured founder to a founder's relatives, there are often familial conflicts and thorny legal issues with which to contend, particularly when the death of a founder occurs.

This chapter also examines questions such as: What happens when an older generational leader or group of family leaders of a company, who were the guiding and authoritarian forces behind its growth and success over decades, begin to exit the day-to-day control of the company to make way for younger generational family owners and managers? This chapter devotes a portion of commentary on the corporate governance practices followed by Saudi FOBs and what that means for co-investors with these firms. This chapter presents the views of second- and third-generation Saudi FOB members on what changes in generational leadership means for Saudi FOBs from their perspectives.

Chapter 4 presents entrepreneurship in Saudi Arabia today from the perspectives of those engaged in business. The chapter looks at the definition of "entrepreneur" and what it means to be one in Saudi Arabia today. Examining the early definitions of the term "entrepreneur" from Irish-French economist and himself the quintessential entrepreneur, Richard Cantillon, and the views of Jean-Baptiste Say, the celebrated French economist and businessman who was among the earliest to attempt to define the word 200 years ago, this chapter looks at Saudis who have their own start-ups and established enterprises that have grown with aid from some of the Kingdom's governmental and private-sector-funded support entities and institutional incubators. We look at these business owners and how they chose their own paths to Saudi Arabia's commercial class.

Chapter 5 further explores what it means to be a Saudi entrepreneur facing the challenges and pursuing the rewards that differ greatly from those of the traditional path of one seeking long-term employment within government bureaucracies. This chapter surveys the great push to promote and assist startups and new growth businesses in the Kingdom by government institutions, chambers of commerce, and private enterprise. Instructional and funding programs such as Endeavor, Riyadah, the Centennial Fund, and the specialized approach to start-up promotion of TAQNIA will be viewed in Chapter 5.

This chapter further examines the phenomena of Saudi entrepreneurship and turns a discerning eye on understanding the motivational forces behind it. We take a look at what drives the entrepreneur in Saudi Arabia to break the stereotypical sedentary, often perceived apathetic Saudi youth more interested in social diversion than helping to advance the Kingdom's development interests through their own labor, ingenuity, and achievement. Where does the desire for self-achievement come from? Does the desire for Saudis to invent, improve, and apply new technologies or make "the next big thing" spring from the same fervor possessed by Steve Jobs as the phrase "fire in the belly" was reminted for him and other innovators in the high-tech industry? Because many Saudis and non-Saudis question whether young Saudis possess the same drive and passion for success older generations of Saudis undoubtedly exhibited in building their family owned businesses many decades ago, this chapter looks at whether today's Saudi business person has the same fire and passion for personal and commercial achievement. The chapter gives examples of how those engaged in promoting entrepreneurship see evidence of a strong spirit of excellence and a will to create and commercially prosper possessed by aspiring Saudi business people.

Chapter 6 recaps important themes in this book with a particular emphasis on what is on the horizon for business in the Kingdom. A view of the Kingdom's Tenth Development Plan (2015–2019) maps out the next five years of the country's growth plans. Chapter 6 presents the opportunities for business between Saudi and American companies that serve the mutual commercial and economic interests of both countries. The chapter will view some of the recent strategic alliances and partnerships between Saudi businesses and foreign investors that are shaping the competitive business environment in Saudi Arabia today.

At the outset, it is important for the reader to appreciate that I am an American on the outside looking in on Saudi Arabia. I say "on the outside" because I believe unless you are Saudi, it is impossible to have the genuine experience of knowing and appreciating all of the tremendous challenges and tectonic shifts one has to deal with on a daily basis in Saudi Arabia and truly view those changes for what they really mean. So, in my pursuit of authoring a balanced book on business in the Kingdom, I am presenting and filtering the commentary of others that hopefully serve as useful examples of alternative approaches to solving some of the Kingdom's challenges in working with and supporting the Saudi private sector. In the end, however, contextually, these are Western, and in particular, American perspectives. Notwithstanding these perspectives, one can be assured the Saudi-American relationship remains one of the most important sovereign-to-sovereign relationships either nation maintains with the world's nations.

American President Barack Obama has visited the Kingdom of Saudi Arabia in June 2009, in January and March 2015, and then again in April 2016. And since taking their respective offices in the Obama administration, Secretary of State John Kerry and Secretary of Commerce Penny Pritzker have had their own official visits to Saudi Arabia. These were no routine diplomatic courtesy calls. Most experts, analysts, and followers of U.S.-Saudi relations agree that the Kingdom and the United States have reached a historic crossroad in their 80-year-old relationship. Until January 23, 2015, all prior visits to the Kingdom by President Obama and the emissaries of his cabinet dealt with the late King Abdullah Bin Abdulaziz Al Saud. Upon King Abdullah's death, announced Friday, January 23, 2015, Saudi Arabia was launched into a period of profound and unprecedented transformation.

On January 23, 2015, the Custodian of the Two Holy Mosques, His Majesty King Salman Bin Abdulaziz Al Saud, ascended the throne of the Kingdom of Saudi Arabia. On April 29, 2015, King Salman appointed His Royal Highness Prince Mohammed Bin Naif Bin Abdulaziz Al Saud crown prince and first deputy prime minister. The late King Abdullah had already appointed HRH Prince Mohammad Bin Naif Minister of the Interior on November 5, 2012. And, in a move that caught most Saudi analysts off guard and surprised many, His Majesty King Salman Bin Abdulaziz Al Saud appointed his son, His Royal Highness Prince Mohammed Bin Salman Bin Abdulaziz as deputy crown prince, putting him third in line to the throne after Deputy Crown Prince and Interior Minister Mohammed Bin Naif.

The appointment of His Royal Highness Prince Mohammed Bin Salman, 30 years old, as deputy crown prince, was also accompanied by His Royal Highness's appointment as minister of defense, making him one of the youngest ministers of defense in the world. Although the actions taken by His Majesty King Salman in conveying to His Royal Highness Prince Mohammed Bin Salman his appointments and new responsibilities were quite substantive, they also held great symbolism for many Saudis of younger generations. For the first time, the Kingdom signaled to the world, and most importantly to Saudis themselves, that its leaders were fully cognizant of the importance of the contributions to be made to the future of the country by its younger generation.

On September 4, 2015, at the invitation of U.S. President Barack Obama, the Custodian of the Two Holy Mosques, His Majesty King Salman Bin Abdulaziz Al Saud, along with his son, Deputy Crown Prince Mohammad Bin Salman Bin Abdulaziz Al Saud, and the Saudi ministers of foreign affairs, finance, commerce, and health, paid an official state visit to the United States and met with President Obama at the White House. The dimensions and depth of the Saudi–U.S. relationship have expanded and deepened greatly over the last 80 years. The relationship certainly continues to withstand a seemingly constant stream of threatening geopolitical storms. These official meetings, and even unofficial back channel communications between the two nations, have served in the long run to bolster and fortify the relationship between them.

The United States has been one of the most important trade and investment partners of Saudi Arabia since the creation of the modern Saudi state. The United States recognized the Kingdom of Hejaz and Nejd and its Dependencies on May 1, 1931. The name of the country was changed to the Kingdom of Saudi Arabia by decree on September 18, 1932. Diplomatic relations were established on February 4, 1940.[1]

Of course, between U.S. recognition of the Kingdom in 1931 and the establishment of diplomatic relations with the Kingdom in 1940, there was a very significant occurrence inside the Kingdom ... the 1938 discovery by the Standard Oil Company of California of the first commercial oil field and its famous first productive well, "Dammam No. 7." Although it took the Kingdom 42 years to acquire complete ownership of what has become the world's largest oil company, it was during these years that the bedrock of the U.S.–Saudi bilateral relationship was formed ... commerce between the two countries.

There have been peaks and valleys in this relationship, often caused by geopolitical winds blowing throughout the Middle East that have bolstered and tested commercial relations. Less than three years after the United States established its first diplomatic presence in the Kingdom with the opening of the American Legation in Jeddah on May 1, 1942, U.S. President Franklin Roosevelt had his celebrated meeting with Saudi King Abdulaziz Al Saud aboard the USS Quincy on the Great Bitter Lake near the Suez Canal on February 14, 1945. During their visit, President Roosevelt and King Abdulaziz discussed the ending of World War II, a portion of their nations' mutual commercial interests, and from the Saudi perspective, the discouraging momentum toward the partitioning of Palestine.

Today, as the Kingdom faces regional armed conflicts, prosecutes a war in Yemen as it works to achieve a responsible peace with all parties, comes to grips with the ghastly rise of ISIS (the Islamic State of Iraq and Syria—also known as ISIL or DAESH), articulates its continual consternation over the world community's irresolution of the ever-present Palestinian-Israeli issue, the September 4, 2015, meeting in Washington between His Majesty King Salman and President Barack Obama must have been viewed as oddly reminiscent of the 1942 meeting between King Abdulaziz Al Saud and President Roosevelt on the Great Bitter Lake, or at the very least, a lamentable case of déjà vu.

The White House reported that when President Obama and His Majesty King Salman met in September 2015, they discussed a range of issues. Among a host of subjects, the White House Office of the Press Secretary reported in its press release of September 4, 2015, that the two leaders discussed, it stated:

> *The President noted the Kingdom's leadership role in the Arab and Islamic world. [T]he two parties affirmed the need to continue efforts to maintain security, prosperity and stability in the region and in particular to counter Iran's destabilizing activities.... [T]he two leaders noted the on-going military cooperation between the two countries in confronting ISIL/DAESH, in working to protect the sea-lanes and in confronting piracy.... [T]he two leaders underscored the importance of confronting terrorism and violent extremism. They expressed their continued commitment to the security cooperation between Saudi Arabia and the United States, including joint efforts to counter al-Qaeda and ISIL/DAESH. They noted the importance of their cooperation to stem the flow of foreign fighters, to counter ISIL's hateful propaganda, and to cut off terrorist financing streams.... [O]n Yemen, the*

two parties stressed the urgent need to implement relevant United Nations Security Council resolutions, including UNSCR 2216, in order to facilitate a political solution based on the GCC Initiative and the outcomes of the National Dialogue.... [R]egarding the Palestinian-Israeli conflict, the two leaders underscored the enduring importance of the 2002 Arab Peace Initiative, and underlined the necessity of reaching a comprehensive, just and lasting settlement to the conflict based on two states living side-by-side in peace and security.... [2]

Despite the thorny foreign policy matters facing the two nations, one of the most reassuring qualities of the U.S.–Saudi bilateral relationship is the ability of both nations to continue trading and investing with each other at levels that over time always trend higher. Over the 80-plus years of the relationship, there have been serious ruptures, rebalances, and repairs of the two nations' political and strategic cooperative bonds.

I took note of one such unofficial bilateral flap on a March 2016 trip I made to the Kingdom when it seemed as though everyone had an opinion of a magazine interview with President Obama in a cover story of *The Atlantic* titled "The Obama Doctrine," in which he seemed to many Saudis as depicting them as having benefited from America's political and military engagements in the Middle East with marginal contributions from them at best. It seemed to upset so many that most Saudis with whom I spoke during my March 2016 visit to Riyadh viewed with high skepticism the fourth planned visit to the Kingdom by President Obama the following month. When President Obama arrived in Riyadh on April 20, 2016, he received what the world press characterized as a chilly reception. Nevertheless, photos of the president being greeted by Saudi King Salman at Al-Auja palace show a respectful and cordial reception.

Unfavorable political agitations and incidents will likely continue between the two nations with varying degrees of harm. The business relationship, however, continues to manage to maintain its remarkable strength. In recent years, a number of analysts have predicted the decline and even the outright demise of the Saudi–U.S. strategic bilateral relationship. They often point to the Kingdom's decided shift toward the East and particularly China. Yet, in terms of trade and investment, the United States remains one of the Kingdom's most important trading partners. Many Saudis believe the United States is the Kingdom's most important partner for business and is unlikely to be supplanted in the near future.

When U.S. Commerce Secretary Penny Pritzker arrived in Saudi Arabia in March 2014 with a trade delegation of 21 U.S. companies just before President Obama's visit that month to Saudi Arabia, the bilateral commercial relationship enjoyed between the two countries was at the top of the list of issues to be discussed with senior leaders.

At a luncheon in honor of Secretary Pritzker and her trade delegation to the Gulf Region, co-hosted by the U.S.–U.A.E. (United Arab Emirates), U.S.–Saudi Arabian,

Figure P.1 Joint Business Council Luncheon for The Honorable U.S. Secretary of Commerce Penny Pritzker, Washington, DC, W Hotel, February 27, 2014
From left to right: Ambassador Patrick Theros, president and managing director of the U.S.-Qatar Business Council; H.E. Ahmad Al-Sobae, deputy chief of mission to the U.S. embassy of the State of Qatar in Washington D.C.; H.E. Adel Al-Jubier, minister of foreign affairs of the Kingdom of Saudi Arabia and at the time of this photograph Saudi Arabian ambassador to the United States; H.E. Penny Pritzker, U.S. secretary of commerce; H.E. Yousef Al-Otaiba, U.A.E. ambassador to the United States; Danny Seabright, president of the U.S.-U.A.E. Business Council; and Edward Burton, CEO and president of the U.S.-Saudi Arabian Business Council. Photo Credit: Courtesy of the United Arab Emirates Embassy in Washington, D.C.

and U.S.–Qatar Business Councils, held on February 27, 2014 (see Figure P.1), Secretary Pritzker remarked on her March 2014 mission itinerary to the three countries and the importance of the Saudi market by stating:

> *From the UAE, we will travel to Riyadh. As you know, America's bilateral ties with Saudi Arabia date back to the 1930s when U.S. companies discovered oil. In the ensuing decades, this relationship has become our anchor in the Gulf. (And we all look forward to President Obama's second visit to Saudi Arabia in just a few weeks.)*
>
> *In September 2013, I spoke at the third U.S.-Saudi Business Opportunities Forum in Los Angeles—the previous two were held in*

Atlanta and my hometown of Chicago. Each event had more than 1,000 businesses attending who are excited about this market. My remarks at the Los Angeles Forum centered on the historical importance of the U.S.-Saudi bilateral commercial relationship and the many trade and investment opportunities in the Kingdom in sectors such as housing, manufacturing, education, and infrastructure. There were over 300 in attendance for the L.A. Forum's first panel discussion entitled "Special Session: An Introduction to Doing Business in Saudi Arabia."[3] The interest in the Saudi market attending that gathering was avid, and for good reason.

Figure P.2 USSABC Luncheon for The Honorable U.S. Ambassador to Saudi Arabia Joseph Westphal, Riyadh, Intercontinental Hotel, September 17, 2014 From left to right: Edward Burton, USSABC president and CEO; Mubarak Al-Khafrah, chairman, National Industries Corporation (Tasnee) and chairman, Saudi Arabian Hollandi bank and current USSABC vice chairman; Honorable Joseph Westphal, U.S. ambassador to Saudi Arabia; His Excellency Tawfig Al-Rabiah, Saudi minister of commerce and industry; Mohamed Al-Mady, president, General Organization for Military Industries Corporation and former Saudi USSABC co-chairman; Dr. Basheer Al-Ghuraydh, USSABC secretary general and executive director.
Photo Credit: U.S.-Saudi Arabian Business Council.

Figure P.3 USSABC Welcoming Reception for incoming Saudi Co-Chairman
Abdallah Jum'ah, Riyadh, Al Mashreq Hotel, March 15, 2015
From left to right: Dr. Basheer Al-Ghuraydh; USSABC secretary general and
executive director; Mohamed Al-Mady, president, General Organization for
Military Industries Corporation and former Saudi USSABC co-chairman; Abdallah
Jum'ah, chairman, Saudi Arabian Investment Bank and current USSABC Saudi
co-chairman; Peter Robertson, former vice chairman of the board, Chevron and
current USSABC U.S. co-chairman; Sheikh Abdulaziz Al-Quraishi, founding
USSABC Saudi co-chairman and board member emeritus; Mubarak Al-Khafrah,
chairman, National Industries Corporation (Tasnee), chairman, Saudi Arabian
Hollandi bank and current USSABC vice chairman; Edward Burton, USSABC
president and CEO.
Photo Credit: U.S.-Saudi Arabian Business Council.

In 2014, the U.S. exported $18.68 billion worth of American goods to Saudi
Arabia, and in the first three months of 2015, U.S. exports to the Kingdom reached
$4.54 billion.[4] As in the U.A.E., there are numerous opportunities for American
firms to serve as partners in infrastructure projects in Saudi Arabia. The Kingdom is
looking to invest $1 trillion in current and future projects, and American firms can
offer world-class expertise in project management, architectural, and engineering
services. Our businesses want to participate in projects ranging from the Riyadh
Metro to renewable energy initiatives to rail development. See Figures P.2and P.3.

NOTES

1. U.S. Department of State, Office of the Historian, "Guide to the United States' History of Recognition, Diplomatic, and Consular Relations, by Country, since 1776: Saudi Arabia," http://history.state.gov/countries/saudi-arabia#diplomatic_ relations.
2. The White House, President Barack Obama, Office of the Press Secretary, "Joint Statement on the Meeting between President Barack Obama and King Salman Bin Abd al-Aziz Al Saud," September 9, 2015, https://www.whitehouse.gov/ the-press-office/2015/09/04/joint-statement-meeting-between-president-barack-obama-and-king-salman.
3. U.S.-Saudi Business Opportunities Forum, Los Angeles, CA, September 16, 2013, "Special Session: An Introduction to Doing Business in Saudi Arabia," link to panel video: https://vimeo.com/74694009.
4. United States Census Bureau, *Trade in Goods with Saudi Arabia,* http://www .census.gov/foreign-trade/balance/c5170.html.

Acknowledgments

Without the trust and mutual respect I enjoy within the Saudi and American business communities, this book would not have been written. It is with sincere appreciation and gratitude that I acknowledge the comity and collegial interaction I continue to enjoy with the many Saudi and American owners, principals, senior executives, and entrepreneurs of companies of all sizes, histories of operations, and sectors. I would also like to acknowledge the U.S.-Saudi Arabian Business Council (USSABC), its co-chairmen, Mr. Abdallah Jum'ah, USSABC Saudi co-chairman, and former chief executive officer and vice chairman of Saudi Aramco, and Mr. Peter J. Robertson, USSABC U.S. co-chairman and former vice chairman of the board of Chevron Corporation, as well as the entire USSABC board of directors. I would also like to thank the USSABC executive directors: Ms. Susanne Lendman, executive director and chief of staff in our U.S. office, and Dr. Basheer Al-Ghuraydh, secretary general and executive director of the USSABC Riyadh office and recent member of the Majlis Ash Shoura.

The U.S.-Saudi Arabian Business Council was established in December 1993 to improve the mutual knowledge and understanding between the private sectors of the United States and Saudi Arabia, and to promote bilateral trade and investment. Throughout its 20-year history, and with its office in Riyadh, our Business Council has been known as the premier U.S.-based bilateral business promotion entity working within the Saudi and American business communities, advancing the interests of its companies. Through the outstanding leadership of its co-chairmen and board of directors, and extensive market knowledge and experience of its staff, the USSABC facilitated thousands of business connections and successful business transactions between U.S. and Saudi firms.

I would like to extend a heartfelt word of thanks to Sheikh Abdulaziz Al-Quraishi, Dr. Abdulrahman Al-Zamil, chairman of the council of Saudi chambers of commerce and industry, as well as his brother, Mr. Khalid Al-Zamil, who I am proud and fortunate to have as a member of the USSABC board of directors, for the support and encouragement they have given me during this entire endeavor. They have given up some of their time to offer me advice and their thoughts on some of this book's subject matter. Sheikh Abdulaziz Al-Quraishi especially has helped with offering his suggestions and recommendations for improvements to some portions of my manuscript. Given the importance and stature of all of them in the Kingdom, their willingness to support this project has great value to its objectives. I offer a special thanks to Mr. Richard Debs, advisory director of Morgan Stanley, member of its international advisory board, and chairman of Morgan Stanley Saudi Arabia, for his invaluable encouragement to me in this project and commentary on my manuscript. And, a special thanks to Lyn Doverspike for her encouragement and support.

About the Author

Edward Burton has actively advised thousands of companies engaged in international trade and investment in markets around the world for over 35 years. He currently serves as chief executive officer and president of the U.S.-Saudi Arabian Business Council, the premier U.S.-based private-sector organization promoting trade and investment between the United States and the Saudi Kingdom. Mr. Burton has counseled hundreds of Fortune 500 companies as well as thousands of small and middle-tier firms during the course of his professional career. Having lived and worked in Saudi Arabia as an American diplomat in the U.S. embassy in Riyadh, and the U.S. consulates in Jeddah and Dhahran, Mr. Burton has a unique insider's knowledge about the country, its business community, and how business gets done in the Kingdom.

Mr. Burton is a frequent speaker at roundtables and panel discussions across the United States, Saudi Arabia, and the Gulf Cooperation Council (GCC) on Saudi Arabia's trade relations. He has had numerous television interviews and articles published by recognized industry magazines such as *Fortune, Offshore* magazine, *Water World,* and *Nuclear Power International.*

Mr. Burton has accumulated over 27 years of experience in trade promotion and international business development. Before joining the Business Council, Mr. Burton served as the commercial attaché at the American embassy in Riyadh, Saudi Arabia. He managed a staff of 27 officers, commercial specialists, and other local direct hire personnel serving offices in the cities of Riyadh, Jeddah, and Dhahran. He was responsible for all U.S. Foreign Commercial Service (USFCS) operations in Saudi Arabia and had oversight of all USFCS management, administrative, and fiscal matters in the U.S. embassy and consulates in the Kingdom. He also supervised USFCS operations in Manama, Bahrain, through a partnership arrangement with the U.S. embassy in Manama. Mr. Burton was also appointed directly by former U.S. Commerce Secretary Donald Evans to serve as the USFCS regional coordinator for the agency's Iraq reconstruction regional initiative.

Earlier in his career, Mr. Burton was the U.S. Department of Commerce Network Director of the U.S. Export Assistance Center (USEAC) in Philadelphia and as such had primary management responsibility for USEAC offices in seven northeast U.S. states. Before joining the U.S. department of commerce, he served former New Jersey Governor Christine Todd Whitman as the State of New Jersey's international trade director.

Mr. Burton holds a bachelor of arts degree in political science from the University of Charleston and a doctor of jurisprudence degree from the Dickinson School of Law. He practiced law in New Jersey with the law firm Cooper Levenson. He also received certified international trade and management training at the Thunderbird School of International Business and the Harvard Business School of Publishing.

Introduction

There are many, many Saudi business people whom I greatly admire, few more than Sheikh Abdulrahman Al-Jeraisy, chairman of the Jeraisy Group, one of Saudi Arabia's most well-known and accomplished businessmen. His story and rise to the Kingdom's upper echelon of the Saudi corporate community is both instructive and illustrative of where Saudi Arabia has been and where it is going.

Surely young Abdulrahman Al-Jeraisy could barely contain his sense of excitement and wonderment since the decision by his family was finally made to have him travel from his ancestral home in Raghbah to begin a young boy's life in the capital city of Riyadh with his uncle, Mohammad Bin Abdulrahman Al-Jeraisy. At the age of seven, he began the two-day journey to Riyadh by camel from Raghbah, 75 miles northwest of the capital city. The year was 1940. The trip to the city that would help define many of his personal and professional successes is one that has been made by scores of original founders, first-generation owners, and leaders of many of Saudi Arabia's most recognized family-owned businesses. The arduous journey from noble and humble villages and towns across Saudi Arabia, usually by camel or donkey in those days, but sometimes by car or truck, was one taken by many of today's corporate and government leaders whose names are instantly recognizable to those familiar with the Kingdom. So, the story of Sheikh Abdulrahman Al-Jeraisy, one of Saudi Arabia's most well-known and respected businessman, and the sights and sounds experienced during his journey to Riyadh is a notable one. It is noteworthy not only because of the compelling contrasts between modest beginnings and great achievements in business and in life over many decades for one man, but also because it is illustrative of the rapid rise of the city that young Abdulrahman walked through as a boy and the city Riyadh has become. Sheikh Abdulrahman Al-Jeraisy is one of many men in Saudi Arabia who have built some of the world's most successful family-owned businesses from scratch whose foundations have been built on dedication to Allah, family, and hard work. The captains of industry atop most of the Kingdom's family-owned businesses discussed in this book share these common values.

As he moved closer to Riyadh, young Abdulrahman and his traveling companions seemed to be elevated from the vastness of the desert landscape, wadis (valleys, ravines, or channels that are dry except in the rainy season), and the foreboding pervasiveness of barren rock mountain ranges to a hilly dominated expanse of green trees and gardens drawing closer. They passed the date farms and orchards that led to the city of Riyadh. Soon, young Abdulrahman saw the great mud wall that encircled the city. The sights and sounds of the city, the circulation of people through its narrow streets, lines of merchant kiosks, and multi level dwellings soon dominated all that was visible. In 1940, the year of Abdulrahman's journey to Riyadh, the city had been the official capital of the Kingdom of Saudi Arabia for only eight years.

Riyadh's modern history is closely associated with two dates, 1902 and 1932. The first, 1902, was the year in which King Abdul Aziz Bin Abdul Rahman Al-Saud reclaimed the city and launched his three-decade effort to unify the tribes of the Arabian peninsula. The second, 1932, saw the establishment of the modern Kingdom of Saudi Arabia and the beginning of a new era when the city was elevated to the status of capital city of a nation, covering most of the peninsula. The three intervening decades were a period of slow but steady growth for the city. The Riyadh of 1902 was no more than a mile across. It consisted of the Masmak, the citadel that was also the seat of government, a large mosque, a spacious marketplace, and several hundred houses, all built of mud brick. The entire city was surrounded by a thick mud wall ranging as high as 25 feet. The city's famous date gardens were mainly located outside the walls. Sheikh Abdulrahman recounts the story of his youth in Riyadh that when the end came for Isha prayer, the night-time and last of the daily prayers recited by practicing Muslims, the city would shut itself for the night by closing the main city gates to those outside.

The Riyadh of the time of young Abdulrahman's arrival is not the Riyadh of today. In 1940, there were no overhead electricity transmission lines, no power stations, or state power regulator. No light bulbs were to be found in most Saudi homes, mosques, or commercial establishments. If one had looked in earnest, electricity could have been found in some of the palaces of the royal family. Electrical power generation and the mass distribution of electricity came to the Kingdom and Riyadh in 1951 with the establishment of the Kingdom's first public utility, the Riyadh Electricity Company. Responsible for building this power infrastructure were American companies Bechtel (then known as Bechtel Brothers McCone) and Thomson-Houston Electric Company (a merged entity with Societe Alsacienne de Constructions Mecaniques, which formed the French headquartered company Alsthom, today known as Alstom, which built the first gas turbine in 1951.) Following the European Union's final approval, General Electric, an American global powerhouse in the Saudi market, acquired Alstom in late 2015.

At the time of Sheikh Abdulrahman's journey to Riyadh, the capital had fewer than 30,000 inhabitants and an economy that was primarily composed of merchant and agrarian commerce and local government. Today, the city of Riyadh has 5.7 million people and a population growth rate of 4 percent per annum. Its economy is one of the most industrially diverse in the Middle East, with real estate, manufacturing, medicine and health care, the service sector, and government contributing the most to the city's gross domestic product, estimated to be more than US$16 billion (60 billion Saudi riyals). Massive infrastructure projects are poised to transform the already cosmopolitan Arabian Gulf city into the most powerful business center in the Middle East. And the region is taking notice. Perhaps best captured in the regional business publication *The Gulf,* the magnitude of commercial activity, which included almost 3,000 projects valued at US$18.7 billion (70.3 Saudi riyals [SR]) scheduled for implementation in the Riyadh region throughout 2014, was stated as follows:

Infrastructure projects dominate spending. Some Saudi riyals (SR) 57 billion worth of power projects comprising 10 power generation facilities, 62 power transmission projects, and 19 power distribution projects. Meanwhile, SR 823 million worth of water network schemes are being implemented. Transport networks are also being overhauled to relieve pressure on the city's choked arteries and efficiently connect the various economic clusters currently being built or in the pipeline across the city. The most eye-catching transport scheme is the $16 billion underground metro system, construction work on which is due to start later this year. The huge project will be complemented by new roads, railways, and airport projects, the value of which will be SR24 billion in 2013/14 alone. The ADA (Ar-Riyadh Development Authority) notes that some SR 43 billion is being spent on financial and technological cities, hotels, offices, and industrial cities during this period. Arguably the most high profile of these projects is the hugely ambitious King Abdullah Financial District (KAFD), a massive real estate project whose glass tower blocks now dominate the skyline of North West Riyadh.

We will revisit Sheikh Abdulrahman Al-Jeraisy and the Jeraisy Group in Chapter 3. For now, however, let us acknowledge that the rapid rise of the Saudi capital has been at pace with the rise and modernization of the Kingdom itself. We will view more evidence of this in our first chapter.

CHAPTER 1

The Kingdom's Modern Economy and Economic Might

THE MODERN SAUDI ECONOMY AND THE NATIONAL DEVELOPMENT PLANS

From the moment Standard Oil of California (SoCal), through its subsidiary California-Arabian Standard Oil Company (CASCO), struck oil from famous well Dammam No. 7 in Dhahran in 1938, the trajectory of the Kingdom's development and fortunes has never strayed far from the flow of the black liquid gold. Throughout its modern history, oil revenues have allowed Saudi Arabia to achieve an unimaginable level of economic development within a seemingly fleeting period of time.

In 1945, before mass-generated and distributed electricity came to the Kingdom, before Saudi Arabia had a national monetary regulator and the country's official currency had been minted (just 10 years before), and before the nation's road systems were built, its finances were in disarray and the world's powers expected it to slide into bankruptcy. Through direct subsidies and revenues from oil production, the United States and the United Kingdom kept the Saudi Kingdom from economic ruin. It was the exceptional leadership of His Majesty, Ibn Saud, and that of his sons and a cadre of able advisors that formed the masonry substructure upon which all future national gains would be built. The careful, methodical, and prescient approach to managing the Kingdom's state and economic affairs is what helped transform the nation from a primarily agrarian and trading nation into the nineteenth-largest economy in the world that it is today. Before the discovery of oil, 90 percent of Saudi Arabia's population subsisted as nomads and peasant farmers.

To understand how the Kingdom's economic and financial affairs are managed today, one must grasp and appreciate the fiscally conservative approach its chief financial stewards have always taken. Insight in this regard comes from Dr. Mohammed Al-Jasser, the former minister of economy and planning (MoEP) and former governor of the Saudi Arabian Monetary Agency. Dr. Al-Jasser is now the secretary general of the Strategic Partnership Office of the Council of Economic and Development Affairs (CEDA). In a speech he gave at the Saudi Arabian General Investment Authority's (SAGIA) Seventh Annual Global Competitiveness Forum (GCF) on January 19, 2014, then economy and planning minister Al-Jasser stated:

> *I would not be divulging a secret when I tell you that Saudi policy making is a very patient process that takes a long-term view. Policy makers in this country first determine where the long-term interest of the country lies. Then they work diligently and patiently toward that goal. Short-term conditions may change from time to time and may put tremendous pressure on us to change course, but we generally try to keep our eye on the ball and resist short-term temptations.*[1]

Since the 1930s, the production of oil and its revenues to the Kingdom heavily influenced economic planning. In large measure, because of the underdevelopment of its infrastructure and regional political issues, the period between 1930 and 1970 saw inconsistent growth in the Kingdom's oil production and export capacity. World War II disrupted the development of the oil industry in Saudi Arabia. Until 1945, Saudi Arabia recorded total revenues of less than US$4 million per year. However, by 1949, revenues climbed to US$85 million, approximately 60 percent coming from the production and export of oil.[2]

In 1970, however, Aramco was still a foreign controlled company. It began to expand the production of oil several times greater than pre-1970s levels. As the industry's production and infrastructure began to take off and oil revenues grew at faster rates, the Saudi government moved to establish a formal strategic planning process to ensure the integration of all aspects of the Kingdom's human, natural, and fiscal resources, institutions, and its economic and social interests into the deliberative process in shaping the nation's medium and long-term development goals.

The first Five-Year Development Plan was approved in 1970. Since then, there have been a total of nine such plans adopted and implemented. See Table 1.1.

Although economic planning in Saudi Arabia was given thoughtful attention by King Abdulaziz Al-Saud, it was his son, King Faisal Bin Abdulaziz Al-Saud, who brought a new level of depth, range, and analysis to bear on planning the growth of the nation. Having taken over complete management of a badly mishandled economy and virtually all aspects of governance from his half-brother Saud Bin Abdulaziz in 1964, King Faisal

Table 1.1   Chronology: Kingdom of Saudi Arabia Five-Year Development Plans

First Development Plan	1970–1975 G	(1390–1395 AH)
Second Development Plan	1975–1980 G	(1395–1400 AH)
Third Development Plan	1980–1985 G	(1400–1405 AH)
Fourth Development Plan	1985–1990 G	(1405–1410 AH)
Fifth Development Plan	1990–1995 G	(1410–1415 AH)
Sixth Development Plan	1995–2000 G	(1415–1420 AH)
Seventh Development Plan	2000–2005 G	(1420–1425 AH)
Eighth Development Plan	2005–2010 G	(1425–1430 AH)
Ninth Development Plan	2010–2015 G	(1431–1436 AH)
*Tenth Development Plan:	2015–2020 G	

*Tenth Development Plan is currently being considered by the Saudi government and is expected to be a new part of a 15-year transformational period for the Saudi economy.
G = Gregorian Calendar; AH = Islamic Calendar, also referred to as the Hijri Calendar.

began an unprecedented period of carefully planned economic expansion and government growth. King Faisal acquired the expertise of imported Western technocrats and experts who assumed positions alongside Saudis in government entities around the Kingdom. The beginning of this period witnessed a dramatic increase in the number of expatriate workers in Saudi Arabia, a phenomenon that the Kingdom is still grappling with today. Correcting the imbalance of an over reliance on foreign labor in the place of a higher number of employed Saudis is one of the greatest economic and social challenges facing the country, in this century or the last.

The president of the Kingdom's central planning organization, Hisham Mohiddin Nazer, submitted the first Five-Year Plan to King Faisal on August 16, 1970 (13/6/1390 AH). The rationale, objectives, and goals of the current, Ninth Year Development Plan (2010–2015) are reminiscent and elementally similar to those articulated in President Nazer's submission to King Faisal in 1970. He stated the plan objectives as:

The general objectives of economic and social development policy for Saudi Arabia are to maintain its religious and moral values, and to raise the living standards and welfare of its people, while providing for national security and maintaining economic and social stability. The objectives will be achieved by:

1. Increasing the rate of growth of gross domestic product
2. Developing human resources so that the several elements of society will be able to contribute more effectively to production and participate fully in the process of development

3. Diversifying sources of national income and reducing dependence on oil through increasing the share of other productive sectors in gross domestic product.[3]

In viewing the similarities between the themes, rationale, and objectives of the First Development Plan and the most recent, the Ninth Development Plan, the comparisons between the Kingdom's economic and industrial profile during the 1970–1975 period of the First Plan and the 2010–2015 period of the Ninth, throws a strong light on the vision, foresight, and analytical powers the nation's planners have possessed since early in the creation of its modern economy.

During the preparation of the First Development Plan leading up to 1970, the Kingdom faced an economic crisis unlike the economic turmoil facing it during the writing of the Ninth Development Plan, but a crisis nevertheless. Because of the nation's poorly managed economy by King Saud and the inexperienced close family members he appointed to key government positions, during the late 1950s and early 1960s, the Kingdom's finances were in very bad shape. Its currency was on a steep decline against all of the currencies of its trading partners. It was a nation whose market was flooded with foreign goods and possessed of virtually no global exports other than oil. The national debt had been on a steadier upward incline since King Saud assumed the throne from his father Ibn Saud in November 1953. And, as more foreign workers took up residence in Saudi Arabia for work, an increasing amount of the nation's wealth continued to escape the country as expatriated earnings.

One must consider Saudi Arabia had virtually no heavy industry leading up to the 1970s. And, besides oil production, its basic economic output came from light manufacturing, construction, agriculture, and merchant trading and services. When the most recent National Development Plan, the Ninth, was drafted, the nation had a different economic profile. When surveying its industrial and economic might today through the lens of the Ninth Year Development Plan, one gains an appreciation over how close the Kingdom has adhered to its core values in deliberating its future. In its preface, the Ninth Development Plan stated:

> *The Ninth Development Plan is based on five main themes, together forming an integrated framework for furtherance and acceleration of balanced comprehensive development in the coming few years, as well as for laying the foundations for sustainable development in the long run. These five themes are: continuing efforts to improve the standard of living and quality of life for citizens, development of national human resources and their employment, restructuring of the Saudi economy, balanced development among regions, [and]*

enhancement of the competitiveness of the national economy and Saudi products in both the domestic and external markets. In addition, the Plan focused on numerous other issues, such as continued expansion and maintenance of infrastructure, acceleration of the pace of economic and institutional reform, and the privatization program, promotion of technological and informatics development, as well as raising economic efficiency and productivity in the public and private sectors, development of natural resources, especially water, and development of environmental protection systems.[4]

The challenges faced by Saudi fiscal authorities during the drafting of the Ninth Plan were numerous: a global financial recession in full swing, an alarmingly high Saudi unemployment rate and a steady inflow of foreign workers, an onerous and growing rate of inflation, higher costs of materials, supply, and labor for major priority construction projects, and a growing influx of foreign goods and commercial competitors challenging locally produced goods and domestic companies.[5] Nevertheless, in preparing the Ninth Development Plan, the Kingdom had a strong foundation upon which to build a successive plan.

During the Eighth Development Plan, 2005–2010 (1425–1430), the Kingdom experienced an annualized rate of growth in an already high level of investment of about 11.2 percent. This contributed to an increase in the average ratio of investment to real GDP from 21.1 percent in 2004, the last year of the Seventh Development Plan 2000–2005 (1420–1425 AH), to 28.1 percent.[6] Because of historically high world oil prices for oil that had not ameliorated until 2008, the Kingdom's coffers were well cushioned to weather the global economic meltdown.

In moving ahead with the Ninth Plan, the Ministry of Economy and Planning listed its expected accomplishments of the Plan as follows:

During the next five year (2010–2014), the Ninth Development Plan aims to realize an average annual GDP growth rate of 5.2 percent at constant prices of 1999. This would result in increasing the average per capita GDP at constant prices from $12,320 (SR 46,200) in 2009 to approximately $14,186 (SR 53,200) in 2014.[7]

The Ministry's expected deliverables at the macroeconomic level were listed as:

- Growth in merchandise and services exports at an average annual rate of 4.5 percent, thus bringing their share of GDP to about 35.7 percent by the end of the Plan in 2014.

- Growth in merchandise and services imports at an average annual rate of 7.7 percent, to bring their share of GDP to around 67.6 percent by the end of the Plan in 2014.
- Growth in final consumption (government and private commodities and services at an average annual rate of 5.4 percent, to constitute around 90 percent of GDP in 2014.
- Increasing the share of national manpower in total labor force (Saudization rate) from 47.9 percent in 2009 to approximately 53.6 percent in 2014 by providing 1.1 million job opportunities to labor market entrants.
- Reducing the unemployment rate among the national workforce from around 9.6 percent in 2009 to about 5.5 percent by the end of the Plan in 2014[8] (See Table 1.2.).

Judged against its stated economic indicator goals in Table 1.2, in assessing the effectiveness of the Ninth Development Plan, the Kingdom may be seen as having gone a long way toward achieving its goals. Although expecting to bring down the unemployment rate from 10.5 percent in early 2010 to 5.5 percent within a five-year period may have appeared a tad ambitious, they were not far off. The Saudi Department of Central Statistics and Information (CDSI) reported that the unemployment rate in 2013 was 5.6 percent, a figure that held fast into the first quarter of 2014.[9] And, more to the thrust of this book, the key indicator of how much more the Saudi private sector is playing a role in contributing to the growth in Saudi

Table 1.2   Main Indicators of the Ninth Development Plan (2010–2014)

Indicators	Average Annual Growth Rate (%)
Real GDP	5.2
Gross Fixed Capital Formation	10.4
—Oil Sector	7.9
—Private Sector	11.8
—Government Sector	5.2
Merchandise and Services Exports	4.5
—Non-oil Exports	10.0
Merchandise and Services Imports	7.7
—Final Consumption	5.4
Rate of Saudization (%)*	53.6
Unemployment Rate %*	5.5

*By end of the Plan.

GDP is equally impressive. The Saudi private-sector's contribution to GDP at constant prices for 2012 was recorded by the CDSI at 58.8 percent.[10] In February 2014, banking sector analysis of this activity for the month of January 2014 confirmed a strong Saudi private-sector performance. The Saudi British Bank (SABB) published the results of the headline "SABB HSBC Saudi Arabia Purchasing Manager's Index (PMI) for January 2014," a monthly report issued by SABB and Hong Kong Shanghai Banking Corporation (HSBC). In it, the bank reported the Kingdom's non-oil sector activity grew at an accelerated rate for the third successive month to its highest rate since October 2012 because of elevated production and new orders.[11]

Saudi companies are growing more, producing more, and exporting more non-oil goods than ever before. At the end of 2013, non-oil exports achieved a record high after recording months of moderate gains. Intermediate and tertiary chemicals, plastics, and base metals make up the bulk of non-oil exports. The Saudi non-oil private sector was the main growth driver for the Saudi economy in 2013, registering growth of 5.5 percent, compared to a 0.6 percent contraction in the oil sector because of reduced production out of the Kingdom and lowering world oil prices. In August 2014, SABB reported their PMI results for July 2014 in which the Saudi non-oil sector achieved the fastest pace of growth since September 2012, in sharply improving environments of operating conditions.[12] The SABB Emerging Markets Index (EMI), an SABB/HSBC report taken from PMI surveys, reported for August 2014 a 17-month high in the growth of the non-oil sector on backs of stronger output, employment, and new orders.

Does the growth and success of the Saudi private sector owe an overwhelming debt to the Kingdom's development planners? How integrated has the Saudi private sector been into the Kingdom's push for development and diversification away from a purely oil-based economy?

Having worked in both government and the private sector, I am acutely aware of the disconnect that often occurs between government, when it envisions positive change for its constituents and then creates and uses methods to pursue such change, and the private sector, which is often compelled to adhere to new policies as unwitting or reluctant agents of change. On more than one occasion working for government, I witnessed the creation of government-redesigned programs and services without the slightest input from the government workers and their managers on the ground charged with delivering and executing the new initiatives. In these instances, on many occasions there was also a complete lack of consultation with the constituents themselves, private-sector companies for whom the new programs, procedures, and services were being created. Planning for change and the effort put into its execution are always best accomplished through collaboration and close consultation between both the affected and those affecting. In Saudi Arabia today, there is ample evidence to suggest that the Saudi government has achieved and continues to maintain a sincere and active engagement with the country's private sector. There appears to be real collaboration and coordination between government and business on numerous fronts when it comes to the expansion and diversification of the Saudi economy and the development of a knowledge-based economy.

THE PRIVATE SECTOR'S ROLE IN NATIONAL DEVELOPMENT AND NON-OIL GDP

When examining the question of whether the Saudi private sector has been adequately incorporated into the economic development plans of the Kingdom, it is instructive to review how the Saudi government has interacted with the community and their pronouncements concerning their role.

Since oil revenues began streaming into the Kingdom in the 1930s, the private sector has been the beneficiary of patronage in the form of contracts doled out by King Abdulaziz and his successors. In part to reward loyalty to his leadership during the challenges faced while he was unifying the country, and in part to grow nascent manufacturing and trading communities across the Kingdom eager to capitalize on the government's spending priorities, the king and his sons succeeding him, awarded contracts to what were then primarily small Saudi businesses to construct government buildings, roads, build bridges, schools, and airports, and to supply goods and services to a young nation. With the exception of the larger merchant firms of Jeddah and a few in the western province, many of the old family-owned businesses began operations and expanded between the 1930s and 1960s as a result Aramco contracts, partnerships with foreign firms in fulfillment of government contracts, and through other government spending that had knock-on effects on the developing Saudi economy. Although business leaders were rarely offered government jobs or asked to help steer economic policy decisions, the business community's value as perceived by the nation's rulers and their economic planners was growing.

At the time the first Five-Year Development Plan was delivered, the Saudi government said about economic change and the role of the private enterprise:

> *The commitment of Saudi Arabia to a free economy derives from the teachings of the nation's religious code and its long-standing social traditions. It is supported by growing evidence that economic and social change cannot be imposed on the country by the actions*

of the government alone, but must come about through increasing participation of all elements of society in both the process of development and its benefits. Only by continuously encouraging private enterprise—large and small companies, family businesses, and individuals—to pursue those activities that they can undertake more effectively than government agencies, will the economy be able to benefit to the full from the ability and initiative of all of its people.[13]

The Ninth Development Plan echoed the First Development Plan when positioning the private sector in high prominence in setting the Plan's main directions toward shaping its economy. Under its "Main Directions" section, the Plan stated its objectives as:

[The] objectives further include development of national human resources and raising their efficiency, enhancing contributions of the private sector to the development process, supporting the move toward a knowledge economy, raising the rates of growth and performance efficiency and competitiveness of the Saudi economy in an international environment dominated by globalization and heightened competition based on science and technology achievements.[14]

SO, HOW HAS IT ALL WORKED OUT?

Governments have always made decisions that affect businesses and businesses have always had to comply with any requirements emanating from those decisions. It is when those decisions lead to laws and regulations that, in their view, are unnecessarily in a state of discordance with making profits that businesses voice concern. It is also when the implementation of those laws and regulations is clouded by uncertainty in the application and process that the business community often registers its dissatisfaction. Normally, businesses voice dissent less with the laws and regulations themselves, as opposed to how they are applied and over what turn out to be unintended consequences borne by them.

Some within Saudi Arabia's business community express a desire to see more cohesiveness and coordination between what is viewed as a growing government bureaucracy tasked with moving the nation forward and themselves. There are numerous private and publicly funded entities that are created almost every year in Saudi Arabia tasked with championing the interests of economic development, modernization, entrepreneurship, and commerce. These new entities will often have specific economic mandates or support certain constituent groups within the Kingdom essential for contributing to sustained growth in favor of constituencies such as small and medium-sized businesses (SMEs) or education and technical training.

A recent example has been the creation of a new joint public-private investment company to direct investments in the industrial and manufacturing sectors in the government's continuing efforts to further diversify the Saudi economy. In April 2014, the international newspaper Asharq Al-Awsat reported a statement it had taken from the minister of finance of the Kingdom of Saudi Arabia, His Excellency Dr. Ibrahim Al-Assaf, reporting his government's intention to establish the Saudi Arabian Company for Industrial Investment, a joint venture (JV) between the Saudi finance ministry's public investment fund (PIF), Saudi Aramco, and global chemical manufacturing giant SABIC (Saudi Basic Industries Corporation).[15] Time will reveal how much this new entity will collaborate with the wider Saudi business sector in executing its mission and achieving its goals. I have, however, enjoyed a brief working experience with the PIF's secretary general, His Excellency Abdul Rahman Al-Mofahdi, and I am aware of his appreciation of the business community and the value of their input. I harbor no doubts this new entity will show its value to the growth of the Saudi industrial and manufacturing sectors in swift fashion.

The subject of Saudi Arabia's efforts to privatize its state-owned enterprises and its accession to the World Trade Organization (WTO) offer additional insight into the integration of Saudi private business into realizing the economic development aspirations of the nation.

Privatization was certainly on the Saudi government's mind when it articulated the possibilities of business undertaking activities performed by government agencies and doing so more effectively. This reference to privatization appeared in the first Five-Year Development Plan, but a full 27 years were needed for the Kingdom to take action, which it did by forming a committee to coordinate and oversee the large-scale privatization of select industries. In 1997, a ministerial committee was formed to define the government's objectives and the principles of a privatization program, study strategies and modalities in the creation and implementation of such a program, and select the best industries in which the government held interests, tagging them for eventual sale.

In 1999, the supreme economic council (SEC) was created by royal decree No. A/111, dated August 29, 1999 (17/5/1420 AH). The council of ministers, a body of sitting cabinet members formed by King Abdulaziz Al Saud in 1953, through Council of Minister Decision No. 257, dated February 4, 2001 (11/11/1421 AH), later charged the SEC with the responsibility of supervising the Kingdom's new privatization program and to monitor and report on its implementation. In addition to finalizing the list of enterprises and their activities to be sold off, the council was also made responsible for crafting the process for implementation and setting a timetable for auctioning off the government's businesses. On June 4, 2002, the SEC issued Decision No. 1/23 (32/3/1432 AH), in which was adopted an official strategy of privatization. It later approved 20 industry sectors that would be privatized:

(1) Water and Sewage; (2) Desalination; (3) Telecommunications; (4) Aviation Services; (5) Railways; (6) Roads, including management, operations, maintenance, and construction; (7) Airport Services; (8) Postal Services; (9) Grain silos and Flour Mills; (10) Seaport Services; (11) Services for industrial cities; (12) Government shares in corporations; (13) Government shares in joint investment companies with Arab and Islamic countries; (14) Government-owned hotels; (15) Sports clubs; (16) Municipal services; (17) Educational services; (18) Social services; (19) Agricultural services; and (20) Health services.[16]

As an entity created to spur economic activity in the Kingdom, the SEC was to last 15 years. However, on January 29, 2015, by royal decree, His Majesty King Salman Bin Abdulaziz Al-Saud eliminated numerous councils and commissions, including the SEC. On the same day, the SEC was replaced by the Council of Economic and Development Affairs (CEDA), also commonly known as the Economic Development Council). Deputy Crown Prince and Defense Minister Mohammed Bin Salman Bin Abdulaziz Al-Saud became the council's head. The other appointed members of the Council of Economic and Development Affairs that day were the minister of justice; minister of petroleum and mineral resources; minister of finance; minister of water and electricity; minister of labor; minister of housing; minister of hajj; minister of economy and planning; minister of commerce and industry; minister of transport; minister of communications and information technology; minister of social affairs; minister of municipal and rural affairs; minister of health; minister of civil service; minister of culture and information; minister of agriculture; minister of education; and ministers of state and members of the council of ministers Dr. Musaid Bin Muhammad Al-Eiban, Dr. Essam Bin Saad Bin Said, and Mohammed Bin Abdulmalik Al-Shaikh.[17]

In responding to queries from a WTO working group on the Kingdom's accession to WTO membership, the Saudi negotiating team reported on the objectives of the privatization program, stating: "Although the percentages of private ownership had not been set, the end result of the process, in each case, would be to ensure a continued increase in the share of the private sector and to expand its participation in the national economy by adopting the best available modality, including transferring certain types of economic activities to the private sector."[18]

When it was first created, the SEC held much promise for the Saudi private sector's input into the crafting of economic policy, particularly as it would affect private sector participation in how that policy played out. In the royal decree that created the SEC, a provision was made to form a 10-person advisory board that comprised non-government "highly qualified and experienced experts in economic and directly related fields" to offer "opinions and recommendations concerning issues related to the national economy."[19] Among the stated "objectives of economic policy" cited in article (1) of the royal decree creating the SEC, the last three objectives listed speak to the importance the Saudi government placed on privatization and heightening engagement of the private sector in the Kingdom's global trade and investment realities and aspirations. Objectives 10, 11, and 12 of article (1) of royal decree No. A/111 are listed as:

(10) Increasing capital investment and domestic savings in the national economy in an effective manner, supporting the government's privatization program, and developing the offset program

(11) Increasing the participation of the private sector in developing the national economy through the government's privatization program

(12) Strengthen the economy's ability to react effectively and flexibly to changes in the international economic environment.

In over 10 years since the Kingdom's privatization plan was adopted, progress in executing sales of state-owned assets have been slow and episodic. A month before accession to WTO, Saudi WTO negotiators identified the following enterprises in the Kingdom as "state-owned or controlled" and with "special or exclusive privileges":

(1) Saudi Arabian Basic Industries Corporation (SABIC—70 percent government-owned; 30 percent privatized; (2) Saudi Telecom Company (STC)—created as a public joint-stock company out of the old Ministry of Post, Telephone and Telegraph (MOPTT) in preparation to privatize these services, with 70 percent of STC shares owned by the government; 20 percent of shares owned by the general public; and 10 percent owned by the General Organization for Social Insurance (GOSI) and Pension Fund; (3) National Commercial Bank (NCB), a joint-stock company, with 69.30 percent owned by the government and the remaining stock owned privately; (4) Saudi Real Estate Company (SREC) 64.60 percent government-owned through the public investment fund; (5) Saudi Arabian Oil Company (Saudi Aramco) a wholly owned government enterprise; (6) Saudi Arabian Mining Company

(Ma'aden), a closed joint-stock company, wholly owned by the government with scheduled phases of privatization planned; (7) Saudi Arabian Airlines (SAUDIA), wholly owned by the government, having privatized a 30 percent stake in its catering operations in 2012, with privatization planned of its remaining four units (cargo, maintenance, aviation academy, and ground services over the next couple of years; (8) Saline Water Conversion Corporation (SWCC) a wholly owned government enterprise; (9) Saudi Railways (SRO) a wholly owned government entity; (10) National Company for Cooperative Insurance (NCCI) 30 percent owned by the government and 70 percent owned by the general public; (11) Grain Silos and Flour Mills Organization (GSFMO) wholly owned by the government; and (12) Specialized Financial Institutions (SFIs) all wholly owned: (a) Saudi Arabian Agricultural Bank (SAAB), (b) Saudi Industrial Development Fund (SIDF), (c) Public Investment Fund (PIF), (d) Real Estate Development Fund (REDF) and Ministry of Finance Lending Program.[20]

In addition to the sell-offs identified in the preceding list, the Kingdom has also sold to the general public a 19 percent ownership interest in the Saudi Electric Company (SEC), a joint-stock company; 74 percent owned by the government and 7 percent owned by Saudi Aramco with total government ownership therefore amounting to 81 percent; and a 57 percent interest in Saudi Arabian Fertilizer Company (SAFCO), with 43 percent interest held by SABIC. There have been other services that the government has allowed to be taken over by the private sector. Areas such as municipal water supply, medical and health care services, electricity, including generation, distribution, and transmission, and telecommunications have all experienced various stages of privatization. There is evidence that private-sector participation in previously government-dominated enterprises have increased. In the medical and health care industry, for example, last year the ministry of health announced that the government's composition of the Saudi health care market decreased from 80 percent two years ago to 60 percent in 2013.

There were businessmen on the SEC advisory board from the beginning, as there is today. The most recent additions to the advisory board occurred in March 2014. There remains, however, a sentiment in some parts of the Saudi business community that there could be more input from them into the setting of economic policy and to the creation and explanation of clearer incentives to business in order to foster greater Saudi private-sector investment into privatization opportunities. Business will always want government to take their interests into consideration when setting policy and creating new laws. The Kingdom's accession to WTO is often used as an example by private enterprise.

In the years leading up to December 2005, before Saudi Arabia became a member of WTO, there was great trepidation within the Kingdom from many quarters over how WTO membership would affect the Saudi business community. During the import substitution years of the 1960s and 1970s when a significant degree of Saudi protectionism was in force through relatively high tariff barriers for imported goods, emerging Saudi companies enjoyed considerable growth as their foreign competitors faced 10 to 30 percent tariffs on goods they brought to the Saudi market. During this period, Saudi local industry experienced stability and growing prosperity as well as increased business with foreign investors. Many firms also bolstered their annual turnover through the awards of government contracts, particularly those engaged in construction and vendor/supplier activities. Preferences were given to sourcing from local vendors, suppliers, and contractors before WTO accession. One might easily refer to those times as the halcyon days of Saudi local industry. The Saudi WTO commitments to lower import tariffs to be in line with maximum tariff rates set by the world body changed many aspects of doing business in Saudi Arabia and also met with considerable skepticism and resistance.

One has only to canvas media coverage of Saudi Arabia/WTO related matters in the year or two leading up to 2005 to glean the anxiety and apprehension felt by many within the nation's business community. The *Arab News*'s daily newspaper, *Al-Madinah*, quoted Fawaz Al-Tuwaijeri, a Saudi businessman engaged in the agricultural sector, as saying the Kingdom's accession to WTO would have a negative effect on its industrial and agricultural sectors. The businessman was quoted as, saying: "Farmers will not receive most of the incentives they receive now."[21] The newspaper also quoted Abdul Nasser Al-Nahdi, another Saudi businessman engaged in agriculture and industry as saying: "At least 60 percent agricultural and industrial projects, especially the small ones, face bankruptcy following WTO accession as they will not be able to compete with international firms."[22]

Saudi negotiators for the Kingdom's WTO membership well recognized the challenges presented to Saudi businesses by accession. Shortly after the Kingdom became a WTO member in March 2006, Fawaz Al-Alami, chief Saudi WTO negotiator, forecast a 13 percent growth in non-oil Saudi exports as a result of WTO membership. He cautioned the Saudi business community, however, particularly Saudi family owned businesses, against an over reliance on the Saudi local markets for the bulk of their turnover. A *Saudi Gazette* newspaper article reporting on a paper Mr. Al-Alami delivered at a March 2006 conference on Saudi family businesses, quoted the negotiator as saying that out of the Kingdom's 14,762 companies, more than 45 percent were family owned and managed businesses, possessing $66 billion in fixed assets and a combined turnover worth $32 billion. He stated that approximately 77 percent of these businesses rely on representation of foreign brands. Saudi Arabia, he noted, imports 95 percent of its consumable goods, with only 10 percent produced in the local Saudi market.[23]

At times, it may have seemed to Saudi businesses that the government was tone deaf when it came to their concerns over the flood of foreign competition that was predicted to overrun the domestic markets upon which their businesses were built. Many in business looked on while the Saudi government continued to enact laws and regulations that prepared Saudi Arabia for the kind of commercial environment required by the WTO for membership. In the years just prior to WTO accession, the Kingdom enacted 42 laws, 19 of which were directly related to core WTO agreement requirements. There were meetings between Saudi government negotiators from the ministry of commerce and industry, the Saudi Arabian General Investment Authority (SAGIA—the Kingdom's one-stop shop for investors in Saudi Arabia), and the individual businesses and collectively with the various chambers of commerce and industry and their subcommittees throughout the country.

Notwithstanding, a concerted effort on the part of the Saudi government to give notice of the proposed changes and solicit business commentary, at least one government official intimately involved in negotiating WTO accession for the Kingdom conceded to me that engagement with the business community was not what it could have been in regard to the frequency of contact and incorporating their input into fashioning negotiating positions on key WTO subjects. Given the longstanding culture of governance in Saudi Arabia, which has been very much driven by the monarchial infrastructure and its supporting executive bodies and agencies such as the council of ministers, their ministries, and agencies, it is not surprising that business was always seeking clarity when contemplating their business environment in a post-WTO world.

Five years after WTO accession, the Kingdom began to implement the fifth and final phase of tariff reductions required under the terms of their WTO membership. The Kingdom committed to, and began to implement in December 2010, cuts involving approximately 122 items that included chemical and plastic products and consumer goods. Customs duties that had ranged between 7.6 percent and 20 percent were slashed to between 5.5 percent and 6.5 percent. Duties on 10 importable agricultural products were also reduced from 25 percent to 15 percent.

The Kingdom and its leadership remain confident over adhering to its commitments under the terms of its WTO membership, optimistic over reaping the benefits of its membership, and capitalizing on translating those benefits toward the further diversification of its economy and social development through a greater participation of the private sector and increased foreign direct investment. Speaking at a Ministry of Commerce and Industry (MOCI) and WTO organized training seminar on WTO regional agreements, held May 14 and 15, 2013, in Riyadh, the daily newspaper *Arab News* quoted His Excellency, Commerce and Industry Minister Tawfiq Al-Rabiah, in referencing WTO agreements, as saying: "Such agreements within the WTO framework contribute to the expansion of foreign markets for local products besides increasing trade with partners of the Kingdom. In its quest to attain a high economic status, the Kingdom has been striving to make agreements that would open up new markets for its exports apart from creating mutual trade exchange."[24]

Saudi Arabia hailed the recent conclusion of the WTO Ninth Ministerial Conference, held in Bali, Indonesia, December 3–7, 2013, and the joint ministerial declaration that ensued. The decisions that were made during the meeting were intended to engender a more efficient and productive world trade system, allow developing nations more options for achieving food security, and improve conditions of trade for least-developed nations and facilitate higher levels of their development. The daily *Arab News* quoted His Excellency, Commerce and Industry Minister Tawfiq Al-Rabiah as saying: "It's a historic accord. It will enable Saudi exporters to supply their goods in targeted markets at shorter times and lesser cost. Saudi Arabia has always been trying to apply modern customs procedures, using advanced technology."[25]

In retrospect, the death knell sounded by many within the Saudi business community leading up to WTO accession was probably hyperbolized to an extent. Although on an individual company basis some Saudi enterprises have been negatively affected, there is much evidence to suggest that WTO accession for the Kingdom has brought a big boost in the nation's transparency, particularly as perceived and experienced by foreign companies seeking entry to and expansion within the Saudi market. There is also evidence that WTO is serving to assist in the diversification of the Saudi economy and foster greater global competitiveness for the nation. Numerous examples can be given whereby the Kingdom's WTO membership has strengthened a Saudi business and investment environment conducive to an increase in foreign direct investment levels. There are numerous examples of foreign investors in the Saudi market that have augmented their commitments to technology transfer, sharing of industrial processes, and funding of proprietary innovation applications within the Kingdom.

Today, diversification remains the Kingdom's chief tool in achieving a balanced economy and broad-based development of its society. The pursuit of growth of Saudi Arabia's non-oil sector has been a high priority for many decades. In the First Development Plan, Saudi planners well acknowledged the over-dependence on oil as the primary economic driver. In 1970, identifying the Kingdom's best hope of funding further needed economic development, the Plan stated:

> *The economy of Saudi Arabia today is dominated by four main characteristics: its dependence on oil; its commitment to a free economy; its manpower problems; and its rapid progress in all sectors over the last decade. [D]ependence on oil is the obverse of the advantages derived from the abundance of oil. Rapid expansion of oil production has provided the Kingdom with both government revenues and foreign exchange to finance development. However, economic growth in Saudi Arabia has been primarily a product of this one sector rather than the substantial development of agriculture, mining, and manufacturing that is normally responsible for such growth. Moreover, it has led to the situation where further development of the economy over the coming decades is mainly dependent on growth in revenues and foreign exchange earnings from oil, a situation that must gradually be changed by diversifying production, exports, and sources of government revenue.[26]*

In the preface of the Ninth Development Plan, the Kingdom recognized that after more than a 40-year period of planned economic development, it had reached a critical juncture in its history. After acclaiming the achievement of a "quantum leap" from one of the world's lesser-developed economies to one with a well-established industrial base and one counted as the ninth-largest economy in the world, in the Ninth Development Plan Saudi planners proclaimed the Kingdom's intention to double down on continued economic diversification.

We will discuss the Kingdom's Tenth Development Plan and the more far-ranging expected National Transformation Plan (NTP) in Chapter 6. A strong and recent sign of the Saudi government's intention to modernize and streamline its approach to the nation's economic development activities, however, has been the demise of the Supreme Economic Council.[27]

THE KINGDOM'S PATH TO ECONOMIC DIVERSIFICATION

Early recognition of the Kingdom's need to diversify its economy away from one fueled by oil revenues to an economy reliant on a diversity of income sources and a pliantly absorptive capacity for domestic and foreign direct investment was present well before the framing of the First Development Plan. Growth of the Saudi non-oil sector before the First Development Plan was sporadic and anemic, but was obviously present. It was after the First Development Plan that the Saudi government's decision to pursue an economic development policy based on massive industrial development and diversification became unequivocal and resounding. The growth of this important segment of the Saudi economy has always been coupled with government spending and direct investments. During the 1960s and 1970s, Saudi government involvement with the private sector in producing goods for domestic and international consumption experienced its most meaningful beginnings.

After its creation in 1968, the blended lubricant manufacturer, Petromin, built a steel rolling mill in Jeddah in partnership with private sector entities and businesses in various parts of the Kingdom. In the mid-1970s, the Royal Commission of Jubail and Yanbu began the construction of a downstream industrial complex the likes of which the world had not ever seen before, and still ranks today as the largest civil engineering industrial project in the world. Throughout its existence, its achievements in raising the petroleum downstream industrial output of the Kingdom have been done in collaboration with domestic Saudi and foreign corporate investments.

As the eminent scholar and educator, Mr. Mohamed A. Ramady, pointed out in his seminal book *The Saudi Arabian Economy*, in the early 1970s the Saudi government confronted a number of decisions that would determine the direction of its economy for decades to come.[28] The path at that time and preceding the First Development Plan had been sustained by public expenditures in feeding large-scale oil production. With the oil embargoes of 1967 (June to September) and 1973 (October 1973 to March 1974), the swelled coffers of the Saudi treasury led to consistent balance of payment surpluses and sparse incentives to seek out alternative domestic energy solutions or diversity of national exports.[29]

At a critical developmental point in time for the Kingdom, it elected to adopt a large-scale industrialization and diversification program. As a result of this undertaking, there is no question that the Saudi business community benefited enormously from what has been a sustained period of government expenditures lasting more than 40 years. There have also been admirable successes in the government's efforts to diversify its economy following implementation of the First Development Plan in 1970. The creation of the industrial complexes in Jubail and Yanbu, vast countrywide transportation infrastructure development, and the improvement of government administrative and program delivery systems have all contributed to the growth of the economy in many areas.

In the 25 years from 1970 to 1995, the non-oil sector's share of GDP increased from 46 percent to just over 70 percent, tripling GDP to US$ 125.1 billion reflecting a growth rate of 8.6 percent in current prices.

By 2002, non-oil GDP had reached US$186 billion, although the percentage of non-oil contribution to GDP had experienced a trough from the high 1970-to-1995-period levels.[30] By 2002, 10 years later, the private sector's contribution to real GDP reached 49 percent, experiencing growth of 8.3 percent. Ten years hence, in 2013, the Saudi ministry of finance issued a statement on the Kingdom's national budget for 2014. In that statement, the ministry gave an assessment of 2013 performance and reported on that year's estimated GDP growth:

> *According to the Central Department of Statistics and Information (CDSI), GDP is estimated to reach SR 2,794.8 (US $745.3) billion in current prices in 2013, reflecting a growth rate of 1.54 percent. The private sector is estimated to grow by 9.38 percent, whereas the oil sector declined by 3.83 percent in 2013. In real terms, GDP for 2013 is estimated to grow by 3.8 percent, compared to 5.81 percent last year. The oil sector is estimated to decline by 0.61 percent while the government sector is estimated to grow by 3.73 percent and the private sector by 5.5 percent in 2013. The private sector's contribution to GDP is expected to exceed 58.75 percent. All components of non-oil GDP recorded positive and healthy growth in 2013. Specifically, the non-oil industrial sector is estimated to grow by 4.72 percent; construction by 8.11 percent; transport, storage, and communications sectors by 7.2 percent; wholesale, retail, restaurants, and hotels by 6.16 percent; and finance, insurance, and real estate by 4.86 percent.[31]*

Visually, the division of GDP composition by sector is striking. When combing the sectors that make up most of the Saudi private sector in Figure 1.1, one can see the construction, real estate, transportation, financial services, and the retail and wholesale services sectors leading the way of growth for the Saudi economy. The dominance of mining, petroleum, and natural gas production remains, however, the engine of the Saudi economy and the key to its vitality over the years.

Countercyclical measures taken by the government over time have given strong support to what has been one of the most vibrant of all G-20 national economies. Although the Kingdom has avoided deficit spending to sustain this level of potent fiscal support, the government's expansionary strategy and increasing annual expenditures on industrialization and government functions have been viewed by some as unsustainable given declining oil revenues. The government also appears to be reining in the pace of its spending.

Revenues and spending for 2014 were expected to exceed budgeted income and outlays as had occurred for the previous decade. For the first time

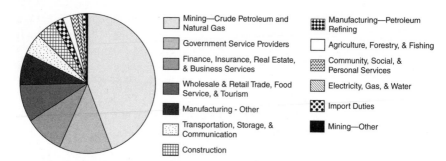

Figure 1.1   KSA GDP Composition by Industry Sector
Source: Kingdom of Saudi Arabia, Central Department of Statistics and Information.

since 2005, however, the government forecasted a balanced budget for 2014 rather than the usually expected surplus.

As Mohamed Ramadi noted in his book, *The Saudi Arabian Economy: Policies, Achievements, and Challenges,* concerning the industrialization promotion strategies:

> [T]*he negative factors that have crept into this strategy over time are now causing the most concern. As will be discussed later, issues of mismatch between domestic labor supply and market needs, the continuing strain on balance of payments due to large expatriate labor remittances, institutionalized inefficiencies and, despite diversification, continuing reliance on oil and oil derivative exports are features of the Saudi economy today. Most of these problems are inherited from the earlier development plans.*

As Ramady accurately perceived, although the Saudi government may have understood the risks of the development policies they were pursuing, the magnitude and long-term consequences Mr. Ramady listed may not have been fully synthesized. The "mismatch between domestic labor supply and market needs" listed by Professor Ramady deserves special mention.

Before 1970, the percentage of Saudi citizens engaged in the workforce was well over 80 percent and the percentage of foreign workers was approximately 18 percent. The displacement of Saudis by expatriate workers as a result of industrialization policies implemented by the Kingdom, however, has been prolific. In 1985, the population of Saudi Arabia was 13,273,000. The number of foreign residents in the Kingdom that year was estimated to be 4,563,000, with a total foreign workforce of 3,522,700.[32] By 1995, the makeup of the workforce was 40 percent Saudis and 60 percent foreigners.

According to the CDSI, Saudi Arabia's population reached 30 million in 2013, representing a 2.7 percent increase over 2012, when the population was pegged at 29.2 million. Expatriates in the Kingdom accounted for approximately one third of the population, at 9.7 million. In November 2014, a senior Saudi labor ministry official reported that there were more than 8.2 million expatriates working in the private sector, compared with 1.4 million Saudis.[33] Over two million are estimated to be illegal migrant workers. The task of shedding the Saudi workforce of excessive numbers of foreign workers has been going on in earnest for at least 25 years.

The Saudization of the Kingdom's workforce has been one of the most difficult and quarrelsome issues the Saudi government has had with the Saudi private sector over the years. "Saudization," a term that has come to mean the formal Saudi government policy requiring increasing levels of employment of Saudi citizens with a corresponding diminution of expatriate workers in the workforce has been around in one form or another for at least four decades. The Saudi government has instituted various levels of rigorous enforcement and extended leniency, depending on how the adverse effects from the policy have affected the economy and the private sector.

As mentioned earlier, the industrialization strategies of the Saudi government was done in collaboration and participation of the private sector. Businesses across the Kingdom wielded a relatively unobstructed hand in the importing the foreign labor they needed to get plants built, roads constructed, and services delivered. This partly explains why the business sector has reacted contentiously to what has been the most intensified crackdown on migrant workers and reducing the Kingdom's dependence on foreign labor in its history of Saudization.

For decades, the Saudi government has sought to impose a fixed requirement that the Saudi private sector should have on average between 20 percent and 75 percent of its workforce composed of Saudi citizens, depending on the type of industry and commercial sectors. Various levels of incentives and disincentives have been employed to encourage the private sector to comply with hiring quotas. Finally, on September 10, 2011, the "Nitiqat" indigenization program, the latest version of Saudization, came into effect. After a year and a half period of implementation, dissatisfied with the private sector's pace of displacement of Saudi workers for expatriates, the Saudi government began to take tough action in restyling, reshaping, and implementing Nitiqat.

The Saudi government began issuing warnings to migrant workers early in 2013, urging them to take advantage of an amnesty program that afforded them the opportunity of legalizing their immigration status through a set process, thereby avoiding the consequence of arrest and deportation. Four million foreign laborers are believed to have used the amnesty program and left the Kingdom.

Following the seven-month amnesty program and in the aftermath of the crackdown that continued well into 2014, hundreds of thousands of illegal workers were deported, an estimated 33,000 people were arrested and untold numbers have gone into hiding. To those in the business community using such labor pools, the enforcement measures have meant no workers available to them in fulfilling contracts to provide garbage removal, janitors to clean schools and other public and private places of business, and a growing scarcity of construction laborers. The National Committee of the Council of Saudi chambers of commerce have considered the reporting of tens of thousands of construction contracts postponed or canceled as a result of the foreign worker crackdown.[34]

Most in the business community are in agreement and empathize with the government's efforts to increase Saudi employment by replacing foreign workers with qualified Saudi workers. Most business people also understand the need to keep as much of the expenditure of wages earned inside the Kingdom actually spent within the country. Some even view the importance of the new laws in patriotic terms and perceiving them as good for the Kingdom's future and economic longevity. Most recognize that the outflow of foreign worker remittances is a serious problem for the Kingdom. According to the World Bank, $26.6 billion was sent out of Saudi Arabia destined for the native lands of the Kingdom's foreign workers, ranking it as the second-highest remittance-sending country in the world after the United States, which stands at $123.23 billion.[35]

Compounding the challenges faced by businesses on top of the migrant crackdown has been the creation of the Nitiqat system. The color-coded compliance program categorizes compliant companies that have achieved varying levels of required employment of Saudis into Premium, or Green, Yellow, and Red. The Green category is for those entities that have achieved the highest required levels of employed Saudis and therefore affords the most flexibility in meeting their ongoing foreign expatriate employment needs. The lowest, unsatisfactory, level of Saudi employment is the Red category, and punitive measures noncompliant entities may face are the prohibition against hiring new expatriate workers, renewing employment contracts of existing workers, and a greatly reduced capacity to open new operations by low-status companies within the country. See Table 1.3.

Moreover, the evolving nature of the Nitiqat system and proposed laws under its rubric, including the possible incurring of punitive fines for noncompliance, continue to cause consternation among the Kingdom's businesses. One new law proposed by the Saudi Ministry of Labor that would restrict the stay of foreign workers to seven years and discourage them from bringing their families to Saudi Arabia during their work contract produced an outcry from businesses across the country. The *Arab*

Table 1.3 Nitiqat (Zones) Program in a Nutshell, U.S.–Saudi Arabian Business Council (USSABC)

Compliance-Related and Disciplinary Zones			
Excellent Zone	**Green Zone**	**Yellow Zone**	**Red Zone**
VIP category	Very good category	Poor compliance	Noncompliance
Incentives:	Incentives:	Punitive Measures:	Punitive Measures:
▪ Can hire anybody from any part of the world ▪ Easier visa processing ▪ Can change professions of their workers even to those that are restricted to Saudis ▪ **Grace Period:** One year	▪ Can apply for new visas once every two months ▪ Can change their foreign workers' profession except to those restricted to Saudis ▪ A six-month respite after the expiry of their zakat and revenue certificates	▪ No new visas ▪ Restrictions in renewing or transferring visas ▪ No control on workers who can switch over to premium zone companies ▪ **Grace Period:** Nine months to improve employee status	▪ Banned from change of profession, transfer of visas, issuance of new visas and opening files for new branches ▪ **Grace Period:** Six months to improve employee status

News reported that Saudi businesses and economists opposed the proposed regulations and charge that if implemented, the law would have the effect of rendering 70 percent of the Kingdom's private companies into the Red category of the "Nitiqat" system.[36]

Although the Saudi Ministry of Labor announced in April 2014 that the Nitiqat program has doubled the number of jobs for Saudis since it was introduced three years ago, from 723,894 to over 1.46 million, the program's implementation remains deeply problematic for the business sector in the Kingdom.[37] Some Saudi companies have reported much lower profit margins on higher labor and administrative costs associated with compliance with the "Nitiqat" system. There have also been well-publicized reports of some businesses hiring Saudis, "any Saudis," simply to satisfy what is accepted in practice as a quota system.

The employment of Saudi citizens in official company positions, without any expectation of them actually doing the work associated with those positions, merely to satisfy imposed quota requirements from the "Nitiqat" system has become known as the "Fake Saudi Worker" syndrome. Saudis of all skill sets and conditions in life, including those with physical disabilities, have been reported as having been hired for positions but never afterward showing up for their jobs.

Many dynamics are at work with the restructuring of the country's labor sector and the pressures on the Saudi private sector to comply with the new laws are constant. The fact that Saudis have historically preferred government employment to private sector jobs because of their relatively higher pay scales, fewer required work hours, and liberal compensation packages continues to sustain an imbalance in job opportunities between the two sectors. Both Saudi companies and foreign-owned firms find that one of their biggest challenges in doing business in the Kingdom is securing qualified and skilled labor. I have spoken to a number of business owners who have related incidents within their own companies of job vacancies for skilled jobs that have gone unfilled because of a lack of Saudi applicants.

Comprehensive diversification of the Saudi economy remains elusive to the Kingdom. The economy is still heavily dependent on oil revenues. Although expansionist economic diversification has created jobs, it has not created them fast enough. Current statistics reflect a growth rate that should record a Saudi population of 37.2 million by the year 2020.

In its "IMF Country Report" on Saudi Arabia, based on its regular Article IV bilateral consultations, the International Monetary Fund (IMF) signaled concerns about the Kingdom "dealing with demographic pressures," particularly the challenge of employing a growing population of young Saudis entering the workforce. Fifty percent of the Saudi population is below the age of 25. As the IMF report points out: "Despite total employment growth averaging near 8.5 percent, Saudi employment growth was 4.6 percent in 2010–2012."[38] The IMF Country Report described the policy discussions between the IMF and Saudi authorities on the demographic and labor issues by stating:

> *Demographic pressures due to a rapidly growing and young population are posing a challenge for policy makers in terms of creating jobs, addressing housing needs, and managing the demand on the natural resources of the country. Reforms are under way to address some of these challenges. Meanwhile, the global oil market is likely to be less favorable for Saudi Arabia in the next few years than it has been over the past decade. In this context, discussions focused on two main areas: (i) policies to address economic and social issues—high unemployment, housing, and rising energy consumption, and (ii) maintaining macroeconomic stability while sustaining strong non-oil growth.[39]*

The IMF reports on insightful admonitions during the Article IV consultations concerning the uncertainties of the global oil market and its future influences on funding for improving Saudi employment and diversifying its economy. The subject of shale gas development in the United States is increasingly given by influential Saudis as an example of an oil market development spurring new urgency for it to speed up economic diversification.

The torrential expansion and gains made within the U.S. unconventional gas industry experienced tremendous growth over the last eight years. As of 2012, unconventional gas production reached an estimated 18 percent of global gas production, the majority coming from the United States and Canada. Shale gas output increased by a factor of 13 over the last decade, to reach just under one-half of total gas production in 2010. As of 2013, however, shale gas output was still concentrated in the United States.[40] The United States and Canada account for virtually all of the shale gas produced commercially in the world today.

Although only occurring less than a decade ago, the rapid expansion of the shale oil and gas industries in the United States has been labeled a "game changer" for the economic future of the United States and its energy trading partners. Nowhere in its relationships with trading partners does this have the potential for new realities than between the United States and its historical energy trading partner, Saudi Arabia. It is now estimated that the United States will displace Saudi Arabia as the world's biggest oil producer somewhere between 2015 and 2020. With its energy ascendancy in full arch, U.S. dependency on petroleum from the Middle East's oil producers has fallen significantly over the last few years. Historical increases in U.S. light oil production from shale and tight rock formations have significantly encroached upon the Kingdom's revenues from sales of its lighter grade crude to American markets.[41]

The largest individual publicly known Saudi investor in the United States, His Royal Highness Alwaleed Bin Talal Bin Abdulaziz Al-Saud, has been vocal in expressing his concern over the rise of shale gas production in the United States and the perceived threat he believes it poses to Saudi Arabia's economic stability. In His Royal Highness's public pronouncements, Prince Alwaleed has urged the Kingdom's leaders to intensify the diversification of the country's economy and find new alternatives to oil as the nation's chief foreign exchange earner. Speaking on the need for economic diversification, the prince has been quoted as stating: "It is a pivotal moment for any oil-producing country that has not diversified. Ninety-two percent of Saudi Arabia's annual budget comes from oil. Definitely, it is a worry and a concern."[42]

In an open letter by His Royal Highness addressed to the Kingdom's former Minister of Petroleum and Mineral Resources, Ali Al-Naimi, the *Wall Street Journal* quoted Prince Alwaleed in commenting on Saudi Arabia's over-reliance on crude production, saying the Kingdom is: "facing a threat with the continuation of its near-complete reliance on oil, especially as 92 percent of the budget for this year depends on oil."[43]

In public statements, the former Minister of Petroleum and Mineral Resources, Ali Al-Naimi, stated the Saudi government's position that the U.S. shale gas revolution does not pose a threat to Saudi Arabia, and it will not reduce its oil output merely in reaction to what is happening in the United States and other countries that are pursuing shale gas plays. In 2015, Saudi Arabia came under heavy criticism for increasing its production of crude in order to damage rival shale gas producers, primarily from North America, so as to maintain its global market share as oil prices continued its precipitous fall. Cognizant of the criticism, Minister Al-Naimi spoke at the annual major IHS CERAWeek oil conference in Houston, Texas, where he brought a message of conciliation to a national industry group that saw its share of job loss, idling of wells, loan defaults, and bankruptcies in 2015 and 2016. His Excellency told the audience gathered to hear his keynote speech that Saudi Arabia was not at war with shale gas producers and that everyone in the global industry should trust the market to work.

The countercyclical approach employed by the nation's fiscal leaders have served it well and have led most in the world financial community to laud the Kingdom's fiscal conservatism and management of its economy. These strategies were outlined by the former Saudi minister of economy and planning, Dr. Muhammad Al-Jasser, during the U.S.-Saudi Business Opportunities Forum, our U.S.–Saudi Arabian Business Council organized in Atlanta, Georgia, in December 2011. Speaking at that conference, the largest of its kind on U.S.-Saudi commercial relations, Minister Al-Jasser stated:

> We have for many years used a countercyclical approach, i.e., paying down our government debt during the upswing of the cycle, and in our case the upswing cycle is higher oil revenues, be it through prices or quantities or both, and running budget deficits during the downswings in order to cushion the economy so it does not go into a tailspin as when oil prices sometimes do.... The result was that we were able to shirk the global recession of 2008–2009, and briefly run a budget deficit in 2009.[44]

As the Kingdom enters 2016 under its new leadership, it continues to pursue a more diversified economy. There is no question that its macroeconomic and fiscal policies have stood the test of time. The question of whether the areas of growth emphasized in prior National Development Plans for the country have sufficiently accelerated diversification fast enough remains.

Although at this writing the full Tenth Development Plan is not available, the government has released the objectives of the Tenth Development

Plan (2015–2020). They contain a number of familiar themes: "Transition to a knowledge-based economy and a knowledge society" [Third Objective]; "Expand the absorptive capacity of the national economy" [Fourth Objective]; "Raising the value added of natural resources in the national economy, diversifying their sources" [Sixth Objective]; and "Developing the SMEs Sector and increasing its contribution to GDP" [Seventh Objective].[45]

Moreover, the Tenth Development Plan will be part and parcel of what the Saudi government is calling its National Transformation Plan (NTP), which is to be a more detailed strategy than the broad instructive documents as the Kingdom's development plans have been served. The NTP will put muscle and sinew toward the direction and growth of the Saudi economy. It is being developed by CEDA through the leadership of Deputy Crown Prince and Defense Minister Mohammed Bin Salman Bin Abdulaziz Al-Saud and a handful of advisors. The aim of the NTP was discussed by the deputy crown prince during his September 4, 2015, visit to the United States. The goal of placing the stability of the Saudi economy beyond the risks of the inevitability oil price fluctuations is the main factor driving the formulation of the NTP.

In discussing the Tenth Development Plan and the Kingdom's plan for a long-term national transformation policy, Mr. Osama Mansouri, an advisor to the minister of economy and planning, was quoted as saying to the Oxford Business Group: "The first five years of the Tenth Development Plan mark the start of the 15-year transformation of the Saudi economy into a knowledge economy. On a macroeconomic level, the government has declared its intention to pursue fiscal and monetary policies that 'contribute to the fiscal stability, stimulate economic growth, and support social welfare.'"[46]

It is clear that the Tenth Development Plan and the overarching NTP will be one of the most significant developments in the Saudi Arabian government's plan to reshape the nation's economy. Under the strong hand of His Royal Highness Deputy Crown Prince Mohammed Bin Salman Bin Abdulaziz Al-Saud, the CEDA has been busy at work crafting the NTP. Other than the need to accelerate the diversification of the Saudi economy and move it away from an overwhelming reliance on oil, little is known about what might be expected when the NTP is formally announced and its contents and implementation plans made public. The first public comments about the NTP came from a Saudi official of ministerial rank in March 2016 when His Excellency Abdullatif Al-Othman, governor of the Saudi Arabian Investment Authority (SAGIA). Al-Arabiya quoted Governor Al-Othman as saying the CEDA has approved approximately 133 recommendations to improve business competitiveness. The proposals on which CEDA deliberated center around eight main pillars of the private sector and will include measures on transparency and consistency of laws. Al-Arabiya quotes the governor as saying: "They are very low hanging fruit, but major initiatives that will be announced within the next six months. You will see major decisions on very critical issues that are of interest for both local and international investors."[47]

From the beginning, Saudi Arabia's development plans have always looked at the preceding plan as a way to identify and build upon its successes. We are not able to look at the details of the Kingdom's Tenth Development Plan or the NTP at this writing. However, viewing the Ninth Development Plan, we see it possessed the unmistakable hallmark of a shift in focus and government attention on the human capital and innovative potential of the country in carrying it forward.

In listing its objectives for the Ninth Development Plan, several objectives stand out in terms of how the Saudi government was planning to achieve new directions for the economy. A number of these objectives merit specific mention when considering the business community's participation in driving the Kingdom toward diversification and more opportunities for all:

> *Third Objective: To achieve sustainable economic and social development by accelerating the rate of economic growth and social welfare; Seventh Objective: To diversify the economic base horizontally and vertically, expand the absorptive and productive capacities of the national economy and enhance its competitiveness, and maximize the return on competitive advantages; Eighth Objective: To move toward a knowledge-based economy and consolidate the basis of an information society; and Ninth Objective: To enhance the role of the private sector in socioeconomic and environmental development and expand domains of private investments (domestic and foreign) and public-private partnerships.*[48]

Perhaps more than any other listed within the Ninth Development Plan, in regard to diversification of the economy and the role of the private sector, these objectives point clearly to the priorities that have been pursued over the life of this plan. And, based on my observations of what the Kingdom's leadership has been doing over the past four years, gives a good indication of how it might proceed in the way of priorities through the next 10 or so years. Innovation and further building of a knowledge-based economy took firm root in the Ninth Development:

> *A knowledge-based economy is defined as "an economy that is capable of knowledge production, dissemination and use; where knowledge is a key factor in growth, wealth creation and employment,*

and where human capital is the driver of creativity, innovation, and generation of new ideas, with reliance on information and communication technology (ICT) as an enabler." Moreover, there is a positive correlation and mutual interaction between the "knowledge society" and the "knowledge-based economy." In addition, "knowledge" has become a critical requirement for enhancing competitiveness of countries in the twenty-first century.[49]

No close observer of Saudi Arabia could have missed the country's big investments in education, training, and focus on the human side among its national treasures. The shift toward constructing a knowledge-based economy has been distinctive and has diffused many activities and programs of both the government and the Saudi private sector. The rush to innovation and the creation of a more diversified economy using the nation's growing technological prowess is the subject of the next chapter.

NOTES

1. His Excellency Dr. Mohammed Al-Jasser, Minister of Economy and Planning in Seventh International Competitiveness Forums, http://www.mep.gov.sa/themes/GlodenCarpet/index.jsp (January 19, 2014).
2. Kingdom of Saudi Arabia, Ministry of Planning, Riyadh, Third Development Plan for the Kingdom of Saudi Arabia, 1980–1985 (1400–1405 AH), 8.
3. Kingdom of Saudi Arabia, Central Planning Organization, Riyadh, the Development Plan for the Kingdom of Saudi Arabia, 1970–1975 (1390–1395 AH, 23.
4. Kingdom of Saudi Arabia, Ministry of Economy and Planning, Riyadh, Ninth Development Plan for the Kingdom of Saudi Arabia, *Preface,* 2010–2015 (1431–1436 AH), iii.
5. Kingdom of Saudi Arabia, the Ministry of Economy and Planning, Riyadh, Brief Report on the Ninth Development Plan, 2010–2014 (1431/32–1435/36 AH), 11, 12.
6. Kingdom of Saudi Arabia, Ministry of Economy and Planning, Riyadh, Ninth Development Plan for the Kingdom of Saudi Arabia, 2005–2010 (1431–1436 AH), 2.
7. "Brief Report on the Ninth Development Plan," 23, 24.
8. Ibid., See Figure 1.2, Main Indicators of the Ninth Development Plan (2010–2014).
9. Central Department of Statistics and Information (CDSI), "Latest Statistical Releases, Key Indicators: Unemployment Rate 2013," http://www.cdsi.gov.sa/English.
10. Central Department of Statistics and Information (CDSI), "Latest Statistical Releases, Key Indicators: Private Sector's Contribution to GDP at Constant Prices for 2012," http://www.cdsi.gov.sa/English.

11. "SABB HSBC Saudi Arabia Purchasing Manager's Index—Press Release—Compiled by Market," Saudi Arabian British Bank (SABB) Hong Kong Shanghai Banking Corporation (HSBC), March 4, 2014.

12. "SABB HSBC Saudi Arabia Purchasing Manager's Index—Press Release—Compiled by Market," Saudi Arabian British Bank (SABB) Hong Kong Shanghai Banking Corporation (HSBC), August 5, 2014.

13. Kingdom of Saudi Arabia, Central Planning Organization, Riyadh, the Development Plan for the Kingdom of Saudi Arabia, 1970–1975 (1390–1395 AH), 21.

14. Kingdom of Saudi Arabia, Ministry of Economy and Planning, Riyadh, Ninth Development Plan for the Kingdom of Saudi Arabia, *Main Direction of the Ninth Development Plan*, 2005–2010 (1431–1436 AH), 25.

15. Mohamed Al-Bishi, "New Saudi Company Will Spearhead Industrial Investment—Finance Minister," Asharq Al-Awsat, April 20, 2014, www.aawsat.net/2014/04/article55331408.

16. Supreme Economic Council Decision No. 1/23 of 23/3/1423 AH (June 4, 2002).

17. Royal Embassy of Saudi Arabia, Public Affairs, "King Salman Abolishes Numerous Councils and Commissions," January 29, 2015, https://www.saudiembassy.net/latest_news/news01291505.aspx.

18. World Trade Organization, "Report of the Working Party on the Accession of the Kingdom of Saudi Arabia to the World Trade Organization," WT/ACC/SAU/61 (05–5141), November 1, 2005, 15.

19. Royal Decree No. A/111 dated August 29, 1999 (17/5/1420 AH), Article (3).

20. World Trade Organization, "Report of the Working Party on the Accession of the Kingdom of Saudi Arabia to the World Trade Organization," WT/ACC/SAU/61 (05–5141), November 1, 2005, 18.

21. *Arab News*, "WTO Entry to Boost Foreign Investment," September 12, 2005, http://www.arabnews.com/node/272872 (Accessed April 24, 2014).

22. *Arab News*, "WTO Entry to Boost Foreign Investment," ibid.

23. Saudi in Focus, "45% of Saudi Firms at Risk from WTO," March 15, 2006, http://saudiinfocus.com/en/forums/topic/45-of-saudi-firms-at-risk-from-wto.

24. *Arab News*, "Kingdom Keen on Fully Utilizing WTO Deals," May 15, 2013, http://www.arabnews.com/news/451669.

25. *Arab News*, "$1 Trillion WTO Deal: Saudi Exporters to Reap Benefits," December 9, 2013, www.arabnews.com/news/489241.

26. Kingdom of Saudi Arabia, Central Planning Organization, Riyadh, the Development Plan for the Kingdom of Saudi Arabia, 1970–1975 (1390–1395 AH), 21.

27. Royal Embassy of Saudi Arabia, Public Affairs, "King Salman Abolishes Numerous Councils and Commissions," January 29, 2015, https://www.saudiembassy.net/latest_news/news01291505.aspx.

28. Mohamed A. Ramady, *The Saudi Arabian Economy: Policies, Achievements and Challenges* (Springer Science + Business Media LLC, 2010); Kindle File, (*Part 2, The Development Process; 2. Reforms and Economic Planning, National Economic Planning: The Framework, Strategic Choices*).

29. Ibid.

30. Royal Embassy of Saudi Arabia, "About Saudi Arabia: Development Plans," May 6, 2014, www.saudiembassy.net/about/countryinformation/economy_global_trade/development_plans.aspx.

31. Kingdom of Saudi Arabia, Ministry of Finance, Riyadh, "Press Release, Recent Economic Developments and Highlights of Fiscal Years 1434/1435 (2013) and 1435/1436 (2014) December 23, 2013," Economic Developments 1. Gross Domestic Product (GDP), 4.
32. Source: United Nations, Department of Economic and Social Affairs, Population Division, "World Population Prospects: The 2012 Revision."
33. *Zawya/Saudi Gazette,* "Over 8m Expats in Private Sector," November 7, 2014, https://www.zawya.com/story/Over_8m_expats_in_Saudi_Arabias_private_sector-ZAWYA20141107053918/#utm_source=zawya&utm_medium=web&utm_content=latest-news&utm_campaign=free-homepage.
34. *The National,* "Saudi Arabia Moves Towards a Future without Expatriate Workers," March 18, 2015, www.thenational.ae/opinion/saudi-arabia-moves-towards-a-future-without-expatriate-workers.
35. The World Bank, "Remittance Data: Bilateral Remittance Matrix 2012," http://econ.worldbank.org/WBSITE/EXTERNAL/EXTDEC/EXTDECPROSPECTS/0,,contentMDK:22759429~pagePK:64165401~piPK:64165026~theSitePK:476883,00.html#Remittances (Accessed May 8, 2014).
36. *Arab News,* "New Labor Proposals Opposed," January 23, 2014, www.arabnews.com/news/513836.
37. *Arab News,* "Nitiqat Program Generates 1.5 Million Jobs for Saudis," April 30, 2014, www.arabnews.com/news/563416.
38. International Monetary Fund, "IMF Country Report No. 13/229," Saudi Arabia 2013 Article IV Consultation, July 2013, 11.
39. "IMF Country Report No. 13/229," ibid.
40. International Energy Agency, "Frequently Asked Questions: Natural Gas," 2014 OECD/IEA (Accessed April 7, 2015).
41. Wael Mahdi, Bloomberg News, "U.S. Shale Oil Output May Impact Saudi Light Grades, Jadwa Says," December 17, 2013, www.bloomberg.com/news/2013-12-17/u-s-shale-oil-output-may-impact-saudi-light-grades-jadwa-says.html.
42. Joao Peixe, "Prince Alwaleed Warns Shale Revolution Threatens Saudi Economic Stability," Oil Price.com, November 20, 2013, http://oilprice.com/Latest-Energy-News/World-News/Prince-Alwaleed-Warns-Shale-Revolution-Threatens-Saudi-Economic-Stability.html.
43. Summer Said and Benoit Faucon, "Shale Threatens Saudi Economy, Warns Prince Alwaleed; Investor Says Kingdom's Economy Increasingly Vulnerable," *Wall Street Journal,* July 29, 2013, http://online.wsj.com/news/articles/SB10001424127887323854904578635500251760848.
44. U.S.-Saudi Arabian Business Council (USSABC), "U.S.-Saudi Business Opportunities Forum," Atlanta, GA, December 6, 2013, USSABC YouTube Channel: https://www.youtube.com/watch?v=v33_FhNwfXQ.
45. Kingdom of Saudi Arabia, Ministry of Economy and Planning, "Objectives of the Tenth Development Plan (2015–2019)," http://services.mep.gov.sa/themes/BlueArc/index.jsp;jsessionid=7926AFCDA3E8FA7B31210CAABFE08914.beta?event=View&ViewURI=/inetforms/themes/clasic/article/articleView.jsp;jsessionid=7926AFCDA3E8FA7B31210CAABFE08914.beta&Article.ObjectID=119.

46. Oxford Business Group, *The Report: Saudi Arabia 2015, Saudi Arabia–Economy,* "Saudi Arabia's New Development Plan Shows Clear Commitment to Education and the Private Sector," www.oxfordbusinessgroup.com/analysis/long-game-new-development-plan-shows-clear-commitment-education-and-private-sector (Accessed March 27, 2016).

47. *Al Arabiya Economy* (English), "Saudi Policy-Making Body Approves Economic Reforms," March 22, 2016, http://english.alarabiya.net/en/business/economy/2016/03/22/Saudi-policy-making-body-approves-economic-reforms.html.

48. Kingdom of Saudi Arabia, Ministry of Economy and Planning, Riyadh, Ninth Development Plan for the Kingdom of Saudi Arabia, *Preface,* 2010–2015 (1431–1436 AH), 26–27.

49. Ibid., Chapter 5, "Knowledge Based Economy," 5.1, 87.

CHAPTER 2

Innovation in Saudi Arabia

The Kingdom's March Toward the Future

EVALUATING INNOVATION IN SAUDI ARABIA:
THE GLOBAL INNOVATION INDEX AND THE IMPORTANCE
OF INTERNATIONAL MARKET ENGAGEMENT

Saudi Arabia's journey toward a national culture of advancement in technology and innovation has roots in the illustrious past of Islamic research and discovery. Invention and worldwide impactful contributions to science are nothing new to the Islamic world. During the Abbasid dynasty, 750 to 1258 A.H., Islamic culture, arts, and scientific advancement reached its apex. The vertex of this pinnacled legacy of achievement was the undeniable fact that the world's economy at that time benefited enormously from the furtive and creative minds of Islamic theorists, scholars, and scientists resident in the dynasty's capital, Baghdad. Lavish donations and contributions given to fund the scientific pursuits of Muslim intellectuals from Baghdad and throughout an Islamic empire stretching from Asia to Southern Europe helped to advance an already flourishing economic, commercial, and trading imperium.

It is doubtful a return to the golden age of seventh-century Islamic world preeminence of intelligentsia and innovation is what the Kingdom had in mind when its ministry of economy and planning submitted the Ninth Development Plan incorporating the notion of a knowledge-based economy as one of the document's prime directives. However, it is quite clear Saudi leaders wished to engender the Kingdom with the same widespread economic benefits the Islamic world derived from innovation 14 centuries ago by the Abbasids.

In explaining the importance of a knowledge-based economy and the direction intended for the Saudi economy over the following 15 years, the Ninth Development Plan stated:

For many years, the Kingdom has been laying the foundations of a knowledge-based economy capable of keeping abreast of, capturing, and indigenizing the accelerating development in knowledge and technology, as well as generating and disseminating knowledge internally. Such an achievement would then lead to restructuring of the national economy, raising the productivity of the various economic sectors, establishing new activities and services based on knowledge, enhancing competitiveness of the national products in domestic and external markets, generating new competitive advantages, developing the natural resources and rationalizing their use for sustainable development, and building a highly skilled knowledge workforce. In order to strengthen and consolidate this aim, the Ninth Development Plan devotes its eighth general objective and seventh implementation mechanism to this aim.[1]

To have been a country with no mass-generated and distributed electricity 64 years ago and then to have passed in an orderly, deliberate, and earnest fashion into becoming a nation in which some of the world's most advanced interdisciplinary research is being conducted is no small feat. The experience of the Kingdom in its creation of a national superstructure based on technology and innovation is broad-based in terms of those within its society being affected. The effort is also noteworthy because of its status as a developing country. In fact, comparatively speaking, countries in the Middle East lack the standing and recognition for innovation and the advancement in technology enjoyed by many countries with developed and developing economies around the world. Saudi Arabia, however, fares better than most in the Arabian Gulf.

The Global Innovation Index (GII) is an annual statistical analysis and publication co-produced by Cornell University, the World Intellectual Property Organization (WIPO), and the French-based graduate business school, INSEAD, which reports on a broad notion of innovation using specific metrics and measuring "the climate and infrastructure for innovation and on assessing related outcomes."[2] Using a comprehensive and complex series of input and output data indices, the GII arrives at the Innovation Efficiency Ratio or more simply, "the ratio." This ratio is obtained from measuring such critically important innovation factors, drivers, and influencers as private- and public-sector institutions, human capital and research, existing technical and general infrastructure, the relative sophistication of financial market forces available for supporting the innovative environment and the sophistication of the business (inputs), and knowledge and technology factors such as how knowledge is created and diffused within society and its impact, as well as the creative fruits of innovation such as tangible assets, intangible yields such as online activity, and other things like goods and services (outputs). The GII then uses these ratios to calculate averages yielded by the analyses for each country.

The GII is known as a useful tool to lend critical analysis to a country's approach to creating, or in the instances of some nations recrafting, the ecosystems essential to the vitality and longevity of a nation that consistently produces innovations efficiently and sustainably.

Out of the 142 nations measured in the 2013 GII's *Global Innovation Index Ranking*, Saudi Arabia ranked 42nd, behind its GCC neighbor the United Arab Emirates (38th) and ahead of Qatar (43rd), Bahrain (67th) and Oman (80th). A respectable position to be sure. However, the GII further evaluates and ranks each country through a series key indicators and pillars that identify a country's economic size, geographical region, and the core of its capabilities and internal infrastructure supporting its ecosystem for innovation. The GII categorizes these rankings and a country's strengths and weaknesses in the Country/Economy Profiles section.[3] In viewing these rankings, a critical question arises within this chapter concerning Saudi Arabia, given its inclusion in the GII as a "high income" country and its stature as the 19th largest economy in the world as a member of the G-20: Are there areas within the GII-ranked indices in which the Kingdom might improve so as to further its standing among nations and evince a heightened state of a culture of innovation? Given Saudi Arabia's quest to achieve a knowledge-based economy, this question deserves examination. There are a number of the strengths and weaknesses identified for Saudi Arabia in the GII that prove instructive on this question.

The GII arrives at its innovation efficiency ratio by measuring critical pillars of inputs and outputs within subindices. The GII pillar inputs are: institutions, human capital and research, infrastructure, market sophistication, and business sophistication. Its pillar inputs are knowledge and technology outputs and creative outputs. Saudi Arabia achieved overall high rankings within the creative outputs pillar (24th), market sophistication pillar (38th), human capital and research pillar (39th), infrastructure pillar (41st) and business sophistication input pillar (46th). However, the Kingdom had relatively low rankings in the knowledge and technology outputs pillar (78th) and institutions pillar (77th).

Within the knowledge and technology outputs pillar, Saudi Arabia received very low-ranked scores in indicators that highlight the Kingdom's pronounced need to aid its business sector in the area of promoting the nation's exports. Weaknesses were identified within the knowledge diffusion subpillar (111th) and among its indicators were the percentage of high-tech exports minus re-exports (115th) and the percentage of communications, computer, and information services exports (114th). The knowledge creation sub-pillar also received a relatively low rank (71st) for a high-income nation, and its domestic resident patent application indicator (79th), which examined patent applications filed by the Kingdom's domestic residents through the Saudi Patent Office (SPO) and the Patent Cooperation Treaty (PCT), which was flagged as a weakness within its ecosystem.

Despite placing high in the creative outputs pillar (24th), primarily due to strengths in the Kingdom's intangible assets in ICT and business modeling, the overall scoring in this pillar also masks some revealing weaknesses. Within the creative goods and services sub-pillar (84th), an identified weakness in the percentage of creative goods exports indicator registered a ranking of 104th out of the 142 countries ranked. Although Saudis are among the most Internet-engaged societies in the world, the Kingdom fell within a low rank in the online creativity subpillar (77th). All of this points to an overarching innovation ecosystem that has some strong basic governmental and procedural backbone, but may lack a nuanced supportive system that achieves a direct and positive impact to the Saudi entrepreneur and businessperson. In a country whose business community relies heavily on the export and import of commodities, goods, and services, supporting Saudi businesses (new or established) in engaging international markets is of critical importance.

Besides the benefits stemming from the December 2013 WTO Bali accord referred to in the previous chapter, there have been a number of Saudi government programs and initiatives designed to stimulate stronger export sales of national goods and services to the world's markets.

In 1999, the Saudi Fund for Development (SFD), the Kingdom's main development financing fund since its creation in 1975, began financing the loan, surety, and insurance operations of non-oil Saudi exports. The Saudi Export Program (SEP), created pursuant to royal decree, began operations at the beginning of 2000 with the following objectives:

- Develop and diversify Saudi non-oil exports by extending credit facilities and insurance.
- Maximize the competitiveness of Saudi exporters by providing credit facilities to foreign buyers.
- Motivate Saudi exporters to explore and enter new markets by mitigating risks associated with international trade transactions such as nonpayment.

- Encourage and enhance the involvement of Saudi exporters in projects that are funded or managed by the Saudi Fund for Development.
- Maximize technical cooperation, joint financing, and reinsurance arrangements with most international and regional banks and institutions engaged in trade finance.[4]

To qualify for the program, the minimum value of the export transaction financed under the program is US$27,000 (SR 100,000), and the exported goods should be of Saudi origin or have local value added content of more than 25 percent. Although the beneficiaries of the program are primarily intended to be Saudi companies, foreign companies manufacturing in and exporting from the Kingdom are also eligible to apply for export financing and the other SEP offerings. Foreign private-or public-sector buyers of Saudi goods and services are also eligible to apply to the SEP. The SEP also extends direct funding through supplier credits that assist Saudi exporters in extending required credit to their foreign importers. If a Saudi business or foreign investor in the Kingdom is engaged in a project outside Saudi Arabia that requires Saudi goods or services, the SEP will provide local buyer credits permitting those goods or services to be sourced in the Kingdom and used in the execution of the project outside the Kingdom. In 2004, just a few years after granting its first loan facilities, the SFD board of directors approved financing for 22 non-crude oil export operations with a total value of approximately US$93 billion (SR 350 billion). By 2004 and since its inception, the SFD board had approved 51 applications for trade finance and export credit facilities, with a total value of US$309 million (SR 11.6 billion).[5]

When a nation attempts to grow its technological prowess and fortify the capacity of its private sector to innovate, commercialize inventions, and increase exports, one of the proven ways to do this is by ensuring optimal avenues for cross-border trade and investment. For those with experience in international trade, the old adage "investment follows exports" is a familiar one and axiomatic in its application. This is not always the case, and much depends on the motivations and intentions of the new-to-market exporter. For Saudi Arabia these days, if a U.S. exporter seeks a trading relationship with the Saudi market, a long-term strategy for market engagement is the only viable path to pursue. The sharing of technology or some type of knowledge transfer will invariably figure into the relationship if the effort is to be meaningful to the interests of the company and to those of the Kingdom. In regard to attracting emerging U.S. technologies into the Kingdom and supporting growth in capacity for innovation within Saudi companies, the facilitation of bilateral trade between the United States and Saudi Arabia should be viewed as an essential and elemental tool.

Under the leadership of His Excellency, Saudi Minister of Commerce and Industry, Tawfiq al-Rabiah, assistance to small and medium-sized enterprises has taken center stage. In 2013, Minister Al-Rabiah began work in establishing an export promotion entity whose responsibilities would be to aid the nation's exporters in entering markets around the world. I had the privilege of sitting down and speaking with Minister Al-Rabiah about the entity that he had in mind to take Saudi non-oil exports to new, higher levels. We discussed the nature of the work such agencies of the U.S. government and other nations do in service to their exporting communities. We even discussed possible names for the planned organization. It was evident from my conversation with the minister that he had a clear vision of how the government should be serving the international market interests of Saudi exporters.

The Ministry of Commerce and Industry (MOCI) has diplomats in Saudi embassies advancing the commercial interests of the Kingdom in its critically important markets. As president and chief executive officer of the USSABC, I continue to have the privilege of working with the diplomats in the commercial sections of the royal Saudi embassy in the United States and their consulates in New York City, Houston, and Los Angeles. In a market the size of that of the United States, fielding inquiries and channeling requests from the many Saudi and American businesses for information and the opportunity to connect across borders is a daunting daily responsibility. The Saudi consul generals and the MOCI commercial officers in the United States do a decent job in coping with the enormity of the task of assisting Saudi exporters and promoting U.S. investment in the Kingdom. However, the new export promotion entity Minister Al-Rabiah was to create was meant to go beyond the basics. Since much of the Saudi government's efforts in export promotion is geared toward increasing non-oil exports, and since large Saudi companies tend to dominate the oil and hydrocarbon downstream sectors, my impression was that this new export promotion entity would intuitively benefit the country's SMEs.

The Saudi Export Development Authority (SEDA) was created under the MCI. Mr. Ahmad Al-Hakbani, a former senior official with the Saudi Industrial Property Authority (MODON), was named its first secretary general. Mr. Al-Hakbani would later become a deputy minister in the MOCI. Upon assuming the post of SEDA's secretary general, he immediately began work setting up SEDA and staffing the new organization. I met with Secretary General Al-Hakbani and had an extended discussion concerning the promotion of Saudi exports and what would constitute best practices for a government entity such as SEDA as it seeks to fulfill its mission. I told him I was of the opinion that although it is not perfect, I considered the American system of assisting U.S. exporters into foreign markets a prime example of how a nation effectively champions the interests of its exporting community. At the top of this structure is the U.S. Department of Commerce (USDOC), the International Trade Administration (ITA), and its U.S. and Foreign Commercial Service (most commonly known as "the Commerce Service"). From its offices in more than 100 U.S. cities and within U.S. embassies and consulates in 75 countries around the world, the Commercial Service serves American exporting companies in providing technical and substantive trade data and assistance with market entry and expansion strategies every day.

Having worked in international trade for many years working in the private sector, running the State of New Jersey's international trade office, and working for the USDOC's ITA and its Commercial Service, I have a profound appreciation for the important work international trade professionals perform in expanding the market horizons of U.S. businesses around the world. It has also given me a better understanding of how the benefits of a well-rounded bilateral commercial relationship between trading nations can be shared more fully if clarity of purpose exists between them. Although not a substitute for careful economic planning, a measured and expanded trading relationship between two countries can lead to greater sharing of technology through induced private-sector relationships such as joint ventures, strategic alliances, technology licensing, mergers and acquisitions, and research and development agreements.

Governments have a critical role to play in contributing to welcoming environments conducive to business wherein companies from trading and investing nations are supported in their efforts to make new business linkages with local businesses that lead to the sharing of knowledge. This is one of the best ways to inspire a knowledge-based economy. Only by creating a community of knowledge that recognizes less the national borders that separate and focuses more on collectively exceeding the current bounds of technical knowledge can a sustainable knowledge-based economy exist and flourish for a nation. From my experience, helping more U.S companies to export to the Saudi market, and assisting more Saudi companies to export to the United States, contributes to the creation of this "community of knowledge" and in turn strengthens the Kingdom.

Although the USDOC keeps statistics on actual export deals it facilitates between U.S. companies and their foreign customers, the amount of technology transferred to the Kingdom through U.S.–Saudi joint ventures and Saudi commercial patents inspired by U.S. technologies are incalculable. The United States and its business communities continue to contribute to the positive direction innovation is taking inside the Kingdom. Other nations are partnering with Saudi Arabia contributing to the growth in its storehouse of innovations and inventions. Saudi Arabia continues to make impressive investments in shaping its environment of innovation and both the private and public sectors in the country are determined participants. Within the private sector, some of the biggest and best-known companies are helping to contribute to this milieu. With the massive spending the Saudi government has devoted to its public-sector institutions in the area of technology building, however, a look at some of the Kingdom's foremost public institutions leading the advancement of technology building and dissemination is merited.

Before proceeding further with the subject of the state of innovation in Saudi Arabia, a brief mention should be made of the difference between innovation and invention.

INNOVATION VERSUS INVENTION

When it comes to actualizing the development of technological advancement within the Kingdom, much of the discourse within Saudi Arabia has experienced a decided inclination toward emphasizing innovation as opposed to the concept of invention. In what constitutes the foundational document for the Kingdom's future science and technological development and the precursor for all subsequent industry-specific sector and sub-sector development plans from a technological viewpoint, the national science and technology policy speaks heavily as to the path to growing innovative capacity yet mentions the word "invention" only a couple of times. I think it is important throughout this discussion of Saudi Arabia's pursuit of a knowledge-based economy and the nurturing of its knowledge-based industries (KBI) that we be mindful of the distinction between "innovation" and "invention."

Most technology historians and experts agree that invention is not the same as innovation. To put it simply, invention is always in the first instance and what follows in terms of improvement of the original is some form of innovation. One of the world's greatest twentieth-century business management theorists and authors, and the inventor of the concept of "management by objectives," Peter F. Drucker, highlighted in his book *Innovation and Entrepreneurship,*[6] what has been observed by economists as the "invention of invention." Drucker observes that it was during the onset of World War I when the so-called inventor emerged from his and her dark and occluded laboratories to a world that began to recognize their research as having an impact on the world as it was known. From articles fashioned for war to the new industrial processes of the day, and then beyond to miraculous medical discoveries, the names of inventors began to receive sustained and worldwide notoriety.[7]

Inventors were known then, as they are today, for opening the doors of the intangible to the possibilities of the tangible through the diligence and perseverance in applying their intellect and ideas to the problems and questions of the day. Although the actualization of invention may occur with the emergence of the new thing itself, particularly in the mechanical engineering of machinery, actualization, or the practical application of an invention, is recognized as transpiring through the process of innovation. The examination of existing inventions and then taking those ideas and making something tangible of it that benefits some or all of the world is what innovators do. To put it another way, invention is the luminous spark. Innovation, however, is the fire ... the flame that may burn in many different directions and to untold heights.

Drucker offers another explanation of how innovators take what exists and bring forth things from them new resources with economic benefit. Drucker said:

> *Entrepreneurs innovate. Innovation is the specific instrument of entrepreneurship. It is the act that endows resources with a new capacity to create wealth. Innovation, indeed, creates a resource. There is no such thing as a "resource" until man finds a use for something in nature and thus endows it with economic value. Until then, every plant is a weed and every mineral just another rock. Not much more than a century ago, neither mineral oil seeping out of the ground nor bauxite, the ore of aluminum, were resources. They were nuisances; both render the soil infertile. The penicillin mold was a pest, not a resource. Bacteriologists went to great lengths to protect their bacterial cultures against contamination by it. Then in the 1920s, a London doctor, Alexander Fleming, realized that this "pest" was exactly the bacterial killer bacteriologists had been looking for—and the penicillin mold became a valuable resource.*[8]

Another important point Drucker makes is that innovation does not have to be a "thing." Many examples exist through which innovators have taken existing systems in the realms of social engineering, industrial production, and business management, hospital management, and health care service delivery systems, as well as mass media and communications and created new value, resources, and ways of doing things, as a result actualizing and expanding the original idea or creative system.

The applied inherent talents, abilities, collective skill sets, sustained focus, and the drive and determination of a nation's people established an optimal pursuit of excellence in technological achievements. These attributes have always been possessed by the Kingdom and they are serving it well as it develops the kind of knowledge-based economy necessary for sustained prosperity. Of course, it is useful to have a clear plan and dedicated fiscal resources devoted to the execution of a plan. The goal of moving the country from one dependent on its natural resources to one whose future is anchored by commercially exploitable and expandable ingenuity, innovation, and invention has motivated its leaders to produce a myriad of plans and initiatives.

Later in this book, we will return to Peter Drucker and his particular views on the role of the entrepreneur in innovating within economies and societies. The point to keep in mind when one considers innovation in Saudi Arabia is that Drucker believed that innovation is not an economic or a social term, but technical terminology. These technical terms encompass the multi faceted phenomena in which there is a transmutation from an old value experienced within an economy or society through resources the old value created when it emerged, to a new value with novel resources to be used by a seemingly always-expanding populace. In *Innovation and Entrepreneurship,* Drucker stated: "Systematic innovation therefore consists in the purposeful and organized search for changes, and in the systematic analysis of the opportunities such changes might offer for economic or social innovation."

TECHNOLOGICAL AND SCIENTIFIC DISCOVERY IN SAUDI ARABIA

In the life of a nation, all journeys to unvisited horizons are best undertaken with a good road map. The course charted by the Kingdom to fulfilling its aspirations of becoming a country positively transformed by its scientific and technological innovative achievements is summarily embodied in "The Comprehensive, Long-Term, National Science and Technology Policy" (NSTP). This document, spanning the period 2001 to 2020, offers official guidance in the principles it sets forth and that the Kingdom is following to have science, technology, and innovation (STI) serve the people. According to its 1986 foundational charter, KACST was directed to propose a national policy for the development of science and technology and to devise the strategy and plans necessary to implement them. The arrival of the NSTP document was the culmination of three years of deliberations among stakeholders, including more than 500 participants from research, academia, the private sector, government, and nongovernmental organizations. The Kingdom of Saudi Arabia was the first country in the region to undertake the creation and implementation of a national policy on science and technology. KACST, the premier Saudi entity at the forefront of the advancement of Saudi Arabia into the ranks of the world's knowledge-based economies, collaborated with the MoEP in authoring NSTP. It was adopted by the council of ministers on July 8, 2002.

As adopted, the NSTP contains 10 strategic principles that establish broad areas of concentration and affords stakeholders that support the Kingdom's gains in science, technology, and innovation a reference point and methods for ensuring an integration of effort. As a reference point, the plan also serves as both a catalyst and an aid in promoting the effective realization of the objectives and goals of the Kingdom's national development plans. The 10 strategic principles provide an unambiguous narrative of Saudi leaders' thinking in regard to how the dynamism of Saudi Arabia's economic, societal, and cultural forces go forward together in serving the common goal of making it one of the world's strongest competitive nations in science, technology, and innovation. The NSTP strategic principles were meant to aid the long-term process of transitioning the Kingdom to a knowledge-based society.

As with many stated policies, programs, and agendas created and promulgated by the Kingdom, one must keep in mind one of the primary motivations of the country's leaders in directing the development and advancement of the country is being guided by the teachings, values, and principles of Islam. The validity of laws, regulations, and initiatives are often judged by it. Having such policies and programs adhere to and being in consonance with Saudi and Arab cultural values are also important considerations. As a lead-in to the enumeration of the NSTP strategic principles, KACST states: "The Science and Technology National Policy (STNP) is based upon the teachings, values, and principles of Islam that encourage learning, education, and perfection of work. The Plan also draws upon the Arab and Islamic cultural heritage." [9]

What is equally evident about the NSTP as a policy, and indeed what is clear about the development of this policy since its adoption and the many policy documents generated in its wake, is the recognition of how integral the private sector is to its success.

In the NSTP, there are 10 explicit references to the private sector and role it can and should play in the development of science, technology, and innovation. Five out of the 10 strategic principles comment specifically on how the science and research and development communities, government, and the private sector should be interacting among themselves to bring about greater awareness of the importance science, technology, and innovation are to society. The principles state a policy wherein the Saudi private sector is motivated "to assume a leading role in the implementation and management of scientific and technological activities" and "to invest in and support the activities of [the] science, technology, and innovation."

The Fifth Strategic Principle states: "Promoting, developing, and diversifying the financial support sources allocated for the activities of the national science, technology, and innovation system in a way that guarantees performing its tasks properly, through the following policies," goes on to call for the creation of methods to increase research and development resources from various sources, including the companies, so that it comprises 1.6 percent of the Kingdom's GDP by the year 2020. [10]

The Fifth Principle also calls for the development of "mechanisms" and "approaches" to motivate private-sector institutions to "invest in and support the activities of [the] science, technology, and innovation.[11]

The NSTP was the antecedent of numerous development plans plotting the way forward for the advancement of specific knowledge-based industries, the protection of national security interests, the improvement of science and research-based educational curricula, and the commercialization of scientific and technological discoveries made in the Kingdom. After the NSTP's adoption in 2002, the National Science, Technology, and Innovation Plan (NSTIP) was developed to aid in the execution of the policies set forth in the NSTP. A critical component of the NSTIP is the establishment of programs designed to strengthen strategically important technologies to the Kingdom. In doing so, the NSTIP developed eight strategic programs for the advancement of a long-term national strategy to build a knowledge-based economy and society through the creation of a globally competitive science, technology, and innovation ecosystem by the year 2015. The ultimate stated goal of the Kingdom to become one of the advanced nations in science, technology, and innovation by 2025 is aided by the NSTIP.

The Kingdom's approach to the development of an enhanced science, technology, and innovation environment is both long-term based and centered on its institutions and stakeholders. A review of any of the Kingdom's development plans and policy pronouncements pertaining to its goals of achieving the status of one of the top globally competitive knowledge-based economies will reveal many references to the interface between and among its public, private, and academic institutions and sector participants. These stakeholders are viewed as integrally important in the formation of national innovation systems essential to ensuring positive economic and societal change throughout the Kingdom. National gains in science and technological skill and ability are not the ultimate goal here. More is required for such gains and the creation of an ever-expanding national base of knowledge leading superior innovation. In its Strategic Technology Program Summary document, KACST and MoEP stated:

> [I]t is widely understood that science and technology is an important element of innovation, but that not all innovation is based in science and technology—much innovation comes through improvements to business processes or new ways to deliver services. Technological innovation requires not just research and development, but a whole system of supporting institutions and policies. It has become well understood that a society's capacity for innovation depends on the strength and interactions of many institutions and the effectiveness of a variety of policies.[12]

The NSTP and the NSTIP policy, program, and implementation documents are uniform in their conceptual understanding of how government should interact with the private sector. In affirming the important role the private sector plays in the process of delivering impactful and nationally beneficial innovation, NSTP and NSTIP prime documents also recognize some limitations of business in moving the national agenda for a knowledge-based society forward. The summary document goes on to say:

> *[A] well-functioning national innovation system is recognized as the key to a nation's capacity to maintain sustainable innovation-based economic growth. The national innovation system's approach stresses that the flow of technology and information among people, enterprises, and institutions are key to the innovation process. While private firms are responsible for getting most new products or services into applications and into the marketplace, firms require connections to markets, knowledge, people, and capital from outside of their organization, leading to key roles for governments and universities.*[13]

We have discussed early on the role government can play in opening up markets to striving entrepreneurs and SMEs, especially export markets, for a nation's goods, services, and exportable innovations. We will discuss later the critical issue of access to capital from within the Kingdom and tapping into internationally sourced funding available to assist in the growth of the Kingdom's new and innovative businesses. A well-rounded discussion of innovation in Saudi Arabia would be wholly lacking, however, without referring in some detail to those public academic and research institutions that arguably are among the greatest agents of change in the nation's STI ecosystems.

KING ABDULAZIZ CITY FOR SCIENCE AND TECHNOLOGY (KACST)

KACST was established in 1977 as the Saudi Arabian National Centre for Science and Technology (SANCST), but renamed in 1985. There is no public academic or research institution in Saudi Arabia that has proven itself more as the most important positive agent of change over as much of a sustained period in the country's history than KACST. One could argue that the research conducted in the field of oil and gas by Saudi Aramco over last few decades produced some of the greatest changes for the Kingdom's economic prosperity and the global energy industry. I believe, however, that the Kingdom's historical record since 1977, the year that KACST was founded, shows KACST has exceedingly contributed to the progressive transformation of the Kingdom's capabilities to affect new scientific, technological, and innovative change across a wide swath of industries. Within the industrial, agricultural, and service sectors mandated to its developmental pursuits, the record contains an impressive array of accomplishments. KACST summarizes its main responsibilities and objectives as follows:

Main Responsibilities

1. Propose a national policy for the development of science and technology and develop strategies and plans necessary to implement them.
2. Coordinate with government agencies, scientific institutions, and research centers in the Kingdom to enhance research and exchange information and expertise.
3. Conduct applied research and provide advice to the government on science and technology matters.
4. Support scientific research and technology development.
5. Foster national innovation and technology transfer between research institutes and industry.
6. Foster international cooperation in science and technology.

Strategic Objectives

- A sustained planning mechanism for all scientific disciplines.
- Scientifically knowledgeable and capable government agencies.
- A developed R&D infrastructure with fully functioning centers of excellence in all scientific disciplines.
- Strong interaction between the private sector and research centers.
- Regional leaders in patent ownership and issuance. Advanced incubator systems and output.
- World leaders in strategic technologies, including water and oil and gas.
- Enhanced interaction networks between all scientific agencies.[14]

The officials selected to manage critically important institutions such as KACST have been of exceptional quality. KACST's formal structure is headed by a supreme council followed by the president of KACST, His Excellency Dr. Mohammed Ibrahim Al-Suwaiyel. KACST President Dr. Al-Suwaiyel, who served the Kingdom as a vice president of KACST before the appointment to his first term as president in 2007, has skillfully guided the journey of KACST from an institution whose primary role began as an issuer of research grants, repository of science and technology databases, and Internet provider, to one of the region's most prolific generators of funded advancements in science, technology, and innovation.

There are two office branches reporting to the office of the president that are critically important to the successful fulfillment of KACST's mission. Besides the office of the president, the offices of vice president for research institutes, headed by His Highness Prince Dr. Turki Bin Saud Mohammed Al-Saud, and vice president for scientific research support headed by the Most Honorable Dr. Abdulaziz M. Alswailem, the primary drivers for the realization of the myriad of KACST project goals and objectives.

KACST is at once the nation's regulator, promoter, primary scientific, and technology researcher, funding agency and chief policy executor. As KACST president, Dr. Al-Suwaiyel described the agency in a January 3, 2011, interview with Muslim science: "[T]oday, it has become the office of the science advisor, the de facto science ministry, the national laboratories, and the key science funding body in the Kingdom. It is kind of like OSTP, science ministry, national laboratories, and National Science Foundation (NSF) in the United States combined."[15]

President Dr. Al-Suwaiyel made reference to the Office of Science and Technology Policy (OSTP) in the United States. This office, established by the U.S. Congress in 1976, advises the president of the United States and senior officials within the Executive Office of the President on the effects of science and technology on domestic and international affairs. The 1976 congressional act authorizing the OSTP to lead interagency efforts to develop and implement sound science and higher education communities, and other nations toward this end.[16] On its website, the agency states its mission is "threefold; first to provide the president and his senior staff with accurate, relevant, and timely scientific and technical advice on all matter of consequence; second to ensure that the policies of the executive branch are informed by sound science; and third, to ensure that the scientific and technical work of the executive branch is properly coordinated so as to provide the greatest benefit to society."[17]

OSTP's initiatives include such disparate subjects as combating climate change, improving science, technology, engineering, and mathematics education, and promoting open data and technical information sharing to "spurring innovation." The OSTP also has broad authority and responsibility in the process of budgeting and crafting priorities of U.S. research and development funding of federal agencies engaged in R&D activities. It is this dual function KACST and OSTP share in common within their respective countries that makes Dr. Al-Suwaiyel's reference to OSTP so appropriate. Despite the differences in dollar value in the levels of national funding, the work of KACST and OSTP (in addition to other U.S. government funding agencies such as National Science Foundation (NSF) and the U.S. Department of Energy's National Laboratories) in selecting projects that receive funding and advising their most senior leaders of their governments as to how society benefits from the advances in STI flowing from funded R&D is quite similar. Nevertheless, it should be noted that the OSTP is a small part of the U.S. tech community whereas the stature of KACST within Saudi Arabia is comparably much larger.

The Kingdom of Saudi Arabia is firmly positioned among the world's nations that are using advancements in science and technology to confront some of the most challenging problems a country must face. Food and water shortages, inefficient mass energy consumption (over half of electricity generation in Saudi Arabia comes from oil—consuming over a quarter of its annual oil production), structural economic overdependence on oil, and intractable youth unemployment are all national issues the answers to which Saudi officials look partially to advances in STI to provide. The array of program initiatives and policy tools KACST brings to bear in the pursuit of contributing to the resolution of these problems and movement of the Kingdom along its path to a knowledge-based economy is truly remarkable.

From an idea in the mind … a concept for a new business, products and innovative improvements in process technologies or composite material … to design research, prototype production, first-phase manufacturing, full-scale production, and global commercialization, KACST has a direct and facilitating hand in all of it. Some of the most advanced research in the Middle East and the world is occurring inside the Kingdom at KACST and its affiliated program and project sites throughout the country. Usually, when one engages in a discussion about recent developments or news concerning science and technology in Saudi Arabia, KACST invariably surfaces somewhere in the conversation. There are few public or private entities within the Kingdom, perhaps with the exception of Saudi Aramco, which skillfully manages as diverse a mandate.

There are two important overarching functions of KACST and the offices of the vice president that go far in defining the impact the organization is having on the advancement of STI and the path the Kingdom is following toward a knowledge-based economy. The first is the office of the vice president for research institutes that manages KACST's innovation and commercialization sector, which in turn manages the national center for technology development (TDC), the technology innovation centers program (TIC), the national technology incubator program (BADIR) initiative, and the national program for technology parks. Second is the office of the vice president for scientific research support, which manages, among a host of other responsible functions, the Saudi patent office (SPO). A brief discussion of the TDC and its TIC, BADIR programs, and addressing the importance of the SPO is warranted in presenting the fullest view of the public sector's contributions to raising the levels of STI in Saudi Arabia.

KACST conducts extensive scientific research and engages in an array of developmental activity in the discovery and creation of new technologies, especially those that may have industrial and commercial applications. The TDCs are one of the primary tools KACST has at its disposal to bring industry, academia, and government together in the advancement of the Kingdom's interests in STI. Projects proposed and approved under Saudi Arabia's NSTP and NSTIP are focused within those sectors the Kingdom views as having the optimal probabilities of success, given its existing natural resources, home-grown talent, and standing and national competitive advantages. KACST and its TDCs promotes the R&D and commercialization of five sector focus areas: water, oil and energy technology; environment and biology; advanced materials and nanotechnology; information technology (it) and electronics, communications, and photonics (ECP); and technology, space, and aeronautics technology.

The vision of the TDC is to serve as a significant resource of KACST in its support of the development of the Kingdom's national innovative ecosystem (NIE) and to act as a catalyst in the country's transition to a knowledge-based society. The TDC states its mission as:

Initiating plans and implementing programs that facilitate the development of Saudi Arabia's NIE through:

- Facilitating the acquisition and adaption and/or improvement of existing technologies that show promise of successful commercialization in KSA markets.
- Encouraging networks among major parties involved with the development of technology.
- Brokering common research projects with beneficiaries.
- Suggesting research programs to KACST research institutes, according to national need.
- Assisting in the creation and support of technology parks and incubators.
- Helping create technology development projects in industry.
- Supporting technology transfer operations throughout the innovation process, as well as developing and spreading technology.
- Participating in setting standards and specifications and negotiating methods for technology transfer.[18]

The TDC's primary strategic planning program areas are: the program for technology incubators (BADIR), which is the chief operator or national incubators specializing in the development and commercialization of innovative technologies in the five strategic areas; the Saudi business innovation research program (SBIR), which supports Saudi businesses through funding innovative research and technologies; intellectual property management program (IPM), which manages the process of intellectual property (IP) development by working with inventors to establish processes, policy, and activities that move IP from conceptualization to commercialization; the technology innovation centers program (TIC), which promotes the creation of research centers within the industrial sector, hosted by Saudi academic institutions that serve the interests of addressing and solving vexing problems of the Kingdom by emphasizing the three major goals of education and training, excellence in research, and knowledge transfer to industry; and the national innovation ecosystem (NIE), which is a collaborative effort between KACST and the Al-Aghar group, a renowned Saudi think tank promoting a knowledge-based society in the Kingdom by engaging all stakeholders in the discovery of creative and strategic options. The NIE is the main framework through which the task of advancing STI in Saudi Arabia is focused on the six pillars of infrastructure, human capital, governance, innovative capacity, networks and attitudes, and finance and capital.

The TDCs and all of their component divisions have produced truly impressive results since beginning its work. Every year, KACST holds various conferences and meetings to introduce the fruits of its research. The products and services that are unveiled at these gatherings further enhance what has already become a much anticipated showing of the Kingdom's growing STI arsenal. Although too numerous to list in this book, a brief listing of a small portion of some of the new products, services, and accomplishments produced by KACST over the years within its five main areas of focus include the following (shown in Table 2.1).

This listing is by no means exhaustive. An examination of press releases, media coverage, and public announcements of new products, services, and accomplishments of KACST over the years is an exercise many Saudis should undertake. Many Saudis, and certainly even non-Saudis familiar with the Kingdom, are unaware of the STI gains in proficiency Saudi public institutions achieve every year. One would expect a considerable level of technological achievement in the downstream petrochemical industry given the prominence oil and gas occupy in the nation's economy. In July 2014, KACST announced that an R&D team at the National Petrochemical Technology Center, an affiliated entity to the Materials Research Institute of KACST, in collaboration with IBM Global, the University of California at Berkeley and the Eindhoven University of Technology in the Netherlands discovered a new class of industrial polymers that could deliver cheaper, lighter, stronger, and recyclable materials, particularly suitable for the electronics, aerospace, airline, and automotive industries.[19] Also in the petrochemicals sector, in August 2013, KACST announced its researchers developed a new foam concrete containing microcarbon materials that

Table 2.1   KACST TDC's Products, Services, and Areas of Accomplishments

Water, Oil, and Energy Technology

Products

Advanced Nanofiltration control technologies
Concrete developed from local white sand used as
  radioactive shields
Heat- and fire-resistant polymeric mixtures for cable
  insulation
Sewage water recycling and reuse
Geophysical technologies to locate environmental pollution
Various types of fuel cell poles
Photovoltaic solar cell panels

Services

Advanced reservoir engineering tests
Wells measurement using geophysical techniques
Wind energy data monitoring
Near surface velocity estimation
Assessment of resistance to environmental factors (UVA
  rays)
Solar resources data and assessment

Environment and Biotechnology

Products

Cloning and production of camel insulin hormone
Acoustic detection of red Palm Weevil
Development of DNA-based tool to detect genetically
  modified foods
Spatial database for Khoraim meadow
Erythropoietin drug cloning and production via bioreactors
Herbarium with more than 20,000 plant species
Production of Artemia eggs for fish food

Services

Remote sensing and GIS in biosurveys
Deciphering genetic codes and genes
Utilization of ionized rays to remove pesticides
Measurement of radiation doses in Earth's crust
Identification of microorganisms in oil fields
Detection of genes causing hereditary and infectious diseases
Pharmaceutical production using thermal extrusion

Advanced Materials and Nanotechnology

Products

Advanced Materials: Supported transition metal oxide
  catalysts for clean fuel production; Metal molybdate
  catalysts for propylene production; Catalyst materials for
  conversion of benzene into phenol; Distilled hydrocarbons
  for clean fuel; Carbon nanotubes materials; Humic and
  fulvic acids; High molecular weight polyethylene
Nanotechnology: Nickel nanoparticles; Chrome and
  aluminum nanoparticles; Silicon layers for solar cells;
  Supported metal nanocatalyst; Nanostructure nickel
  composite used as protective membranes

Services

Advanced Materials: Sample analysis of catalysts, petroleum
  derivatives, metal alloys and polymers; Toxic and
  hazardous chemicals use awareness; Training courses in
  oil, petrochemical, and polymer fields

Nanotechnology: Scanning electron microscope;
  Transmission electron microscope; Atomic force
  microscope; Clean rooms for nanomaterials production

IT and ECP Technology

Products

Automatic Arabic speech recognition
Data transmitter
Laser Radars (LIDARs) for aircraft crews
Fourth linear accelerator
Tandem electrostatic accelerators
Arabic Parser
Optical Recognition of Arabic Braille

Services

Pipe burst testing
Monitoring of oil pipes and data reading and transmission
  to control centers
Digital file encryption and transmission to computers
Circuit design and electronic panels manufacturing
Pull test measurements
Data transmission to remote areas
Fluid flow calibration

Space and Aeronautics Technology

Products

Satellite images of various types and resolution
Geometrically corrected satellite imagery
Digital maps of cities and urban areas
Navigational maps of cities
3D images

Services

Remote sensing and GIS
Ground Control Points Acquisition (GCP)
Design and implementation of training programs for experts
Agrarian survey applications in contractual projects, project
  implementation, and technical support and assistance[20]

increase its resistance to breakage and reduces its thermal conductivity.[21] There have been many other discoveries and innovations in the petrochemical industry. In fact, SABIC is believed to be the single largest corporate holder of intellectual patents in the Middle East.

Interestingly though, a bit afield from petrochemicals, KACST developers have produced three types of drones made of carbon and fiberglass with increased capabilities to evade radar and reconnaissance equipment. Furthermore, KACST studies continue to augment the Kingdom's knowledge in the area of animal husbandry and infectious diseases. A study released by KACST in July 2014 identified previously undiscovered fever symptoms of unknown origins in a number of domesticated animals inside the country. This study has been of critical importance since one method of human infection is thought to come through contact with infected animals. The deadly contagion of the Middle East Respiratory Syndrome coronavirus (MERS-CoV) has caused the deaths of 298 people since its initial detection in September 2012. Although publicly unstated, many attribute the April 2014 replacement of former Minister of Health Abdullah Al-Rabiah with Saudi minister of labor, His Excellency Adel Faqih, as the health ministry's acting minister to the dramatic and unabated rise in infectious MERS-CoV cases in 2013 and 2014. As the world witnessed the beginning of what the World Health Organization (WHO) called an "international health emergency" in August 2014, the spread of the EBOLA virus in West Africa, and cases spread to other countries, including the United States, continuing research in the area of infectious diseases being conducted in Saudi Arabia is of growing importance to that country and the world.

As the NSTP made KACST primarily responsible for programs that promote education and training R&D, technology transfer, indigenization and development of technology, the spread of technology and the optimization of its use including social benefits, KACST in turn has made the TDC's trade innovation centers program (TIC) the prime dispersal agent for harmonizing the drive to a knowledge-based society between academia and industry. Once fully implemented after phased-in initiation, developmental, and operational periods, TICs are designed to be financially self-sustaining collaborations between Saudi universities and the industrial sector. They will undertake research projects that address problems identified by teams composed of faculty and students within selected universities and engineers from participating companies. TICs will emphasize three major goals: education and training, excellence in research, and knowledge transfer to industry.

As envisioned by KACST, after a period of maturation, the TICs will be expected to: demonstrate that teams of university faculty and students can collaborate effectively with industry on industry-identified problems; increase the level of mutual trust and respect between university faculty and industry; demonstrate actual solutions to selected industry problems; and develop competence in the management of technology, research, and collaborative projects among center faculty, students, and technical staff.[22] Under the TIC program, the selection of the academic institutional and industrial participants are through a competitive process with winners and adopted research proposals occurring in the initial five-year period. With this program, KACST's goal is to have created three to five TICs that have produced actual solutions to problems, cultivated competent and experienced individual teams members sought for their unique abilities and successes, and TICs that have contributed to an increased level of trust and mutual respect between university faculty and industry.

Government's role in assisting the commercialization of technology by nurturing start-ups promising new technology and the creation of spinoffs has been done through incubating such activities at least since the early 1950s. Saudi Arabia's most forceful, full-scale, and dedicated entry into the incubation business began with KACST's national technology incubator program (BADIR) initiative. BADIR's vision is: "to encourage, facilitate, and support the establishment and development of a sustainable technology incubator industry in the Kingdom."[23] Its mission is: "to support organization[s] [sic] that assists individual incubators to foster technology entrepreneurship and the commercialization of technology business opportunities. Those individual incubators will assist entrepreneurs with the transfer of technology created in laboratories and in converting market-driven ideas into business opportunities to exploit local and international markets."[24]

The origin of the BADIR program can be traced back to the vision and recognition of His Highness, Prince Dr. Turki Bin Saud Mohammed Al-Saud, vice president of KACST, that the stakeholders of a more technologically advanced and innovative Saudi Arabia should be brought together to discuss and debate what the Kingdom needed to do to strengthen its entrepreneurial ecosystem. Beginning with the first incubator and continuing until today, KACST and the BADIR initiative have evolved by honing its approach to developing an effective and productive technological and entrepreneurial ecosystem. A national technology incubation policy has been established to ensure consistency across all incubators and that the goals of the NSTP and NSTIP are served through the provision of staff training, marketing, shared establishment, and management services.

BADIR focuses on priority technology areas that include ICT, biotechnology, nanotechnology, advanced manufacturing, and energy. The BADIR initiative was launched in January 2008 with the ICT incubator, the first of what is to be five national technology incubators. The ICT incubator became operational in July 2008 and has fostered new developments in computer technology, communications, and software and multimedia architecture. ICT was followed by the biotech incubator in November 2009. This incubator works to develop biological technology through the adoption and development of strategic projects of researchers and doctors that aim to provide advanced medical services supporting the transfer of technology and contributes to the improvement of the Kingdom's health sector. These projects are contributing to advancements in the health care, pharmaceutical, environmental, and agricultural sectors. The third incubator in the advanced manufacturing sector was established in May 2010 and is involved in supporting new discoveries and innovations in advanced industrial materials and their manufacturing.

The BADIR initiative is one of the best-managed and productive public-sector funded programs aimed at supporting entrepreneurship, a knowledge-based society and greater Saudi-led global innovation through the establishment, cultivation, and commercialization of incubators. It is governed by a supervisory board chaired by the KACST vice president for research institutes with representatives from the private sector, technology industries, financial institutions, and government, selected on the basis of their expertise and ability to support the BADIR initiative. Each incubator operates autonomously and is supported by local experts as well as international consultants who provide the day-to-day guidance required to maintain the focus on generating results. Since its creation in 2008, BADIR's results have been quite impressive. It has incubated more than 100 technology projects, created 200 jobs, and trained close to 800 Saudis. The program has created over $150 million of economic activity. A few well-publicized success stories have emerged over the last few years of BADIR-incubated projects that have made it big.

Ms. Latifah Al-Waalan, a Saudi woman and master's degree holder in management of technology from the University of Washington in the United States, presented a proposal to KACST and its BADIR program to develop an automatic Arabic coffee maker and to commercialize the invention. BADIR accepted the application and Ms. Al-Waalan, using BADIR's engineering and manufacturing expertise support system, was able to perfect her specific blend of Arabic coffee and have a coffee machine with an electronic processor designed and made called "Yatooq." The machine is sold around the world.

Another BADIR success story is that of Mr. Abdullah Al-Zamil and his commercial technology project "Ismi," which won the 2012 World Bank Award for Business Incubators. Mr. Al-Zamil joined BADIR's ICT incubator in 2008 and began developing Ismi, a technology that provides communications services utilizing the Short Message System (SMS) and other data packaging systems, as well as interactive interchange and mobile applications. The World Bank Award selects the top 50 emerging commercial technologies worldwide. The year Mr. Al-Zamil won the award, his Ismi technology place fourth among more than 750 technology projects that were reviewed from more than 65 countries.

Dr. John Mercer, executive consultant to Mr. Nawaf A. Al-Sahhaf, chief executive officer of the BADIR program, and Ms. Sultana M. Bin Saleh Bin Sultan, project management office director, helped me gain insight into the successes and challenges BADIR faces. These BADIR officials underscored the premise of what constitutes a successful incubator program, namely that the foundation of a good incubator program is one that accepts of the notion that incubator programs are a long-term economic development strategy. The validity of a sustainable program is one that has historical data to demonstrate that it works. To put it simply, Dr. Mercer explains, "It is only when you have lots of graduates is when you have measured economic benefit."

The first U.S. business incubator is commonly thought to be the Batavia Industrial Center in Batavia, New York, 43.5 miles west of the City of Buffalo. The Batavia Industrial Center was started in 1959 in a warehouse. Since then, there have been thousands of incubators established in the United States and more than 7,000 created worldwide. Most share common characteristics such as offering business that successfully apply to enter an incubator shared support services such as utilities, management, mentoring and coaching consultations, technology commercialization assistance, and testing equipment and facilities.

In Saudi Arabia, many believe that the first real incubator was Saudi Aramco. As we will observe later in this book, many of the Kingdom's most accomplished companies got their start with Saudi Aramco as fairly inexperienced start-ups engaged in a number of oil and gas operations related activities such as the provision of foodstuffs and catering, piping, and air conditioning equipment and services. Saudi Aramco offered these companies advice and support on how to run their businesses in exchange for reliable and consistently delivered vendor and supplier and subcontractor services. Many accept this period during the reign of King Faisal and the start of the Kingdom's Five-Year Development Plans as the humble beginnings of the country's nascent industrial ranks. As recognized by Saudi Aramco:

> [T]he government also encouraged the development of the non-oil sector in agriculture and industry by providing low-cost industrial sites and special tax and customs incentives. The Kingdom's entrepreneurs began to branch out into plastics, steel, cement, tiles, and other services to the construction and automobile trades.[25]

According to Dr. Mercer at BADIR, the key difference that set BADIR apart from most so-called incubator programs in the Kingdom is that

BADIR's program has a narrow focus in respect to the types of technologies it seeks to incubate and goes deep when it comes to the scope of assistance it provides accepted applicants. "BADIR only takes a small amount of clients—64 in BADIR currently—they are divided up into separate industry categories and receive intense support in bringing their technologies and ideas forward," says Dr. Mercer. Distinguished from BADIR, according to Dr. Mercer, are other incubator and start-up support programs in the Kingdom that are broad in terms of the type of applicants they accept and shallow in terms of the comparative support offered those accepted. These programs, by seeking to reach as many deserving entrepreneurs as possible, are perceived to be reactive in their support of start-ups. This "narrow and deep" approach taken by BADIR versus what is perceived as a "broad and shallow" method has allowed BADIR to post some impressive economic impact statistics within the short time they have been in business.

BADIR has also taken a strong lead in promoting cross-collaboration and networking among all incubators in Saudi Arabia. In 2009, BADIR established the Saudi business incubator network (SBIN). Its motto: "Working together to develop a world class incubation industry in Saudi Arabia" understates its influence among the country's incubators and the work it does in providing a "nurturing, instructive, and supportive environment for entrepreneurs during the critical stages of starting up a new business."[26] The SBIN stresses the importance of enhancing the knowledge base and connections between and among professionals and organizations engaged in the work on incubation. Incubator developers, managers and staff, consultants, academics, and those within the public and private sectors are all constituents. The question as to whether there is enough coordination among the Kingdom's institutions that facilitate entrepreneurship and startups is a reoccurring one in this book. The SBIN seems to be one of the few publicly funded coordinating entities in existence.

KING ABDULLAH UNIVERSITY FOR SCIENCE AND TECHNOLOGY (KAUST)

First-time initiatives emanating from Saudi Arabia's kings that tend to draw national and international attention are rarely described as bold, given their conservative approach to governance and the senior citizen status that virtually all of them have shared. In the fall 2007, however, when ground was broken for the construction of the 25-year-old dream of the late Saudi King Abdullah Bin Abdulaziz Al-Saud, a world-class graduate research university located on 9,000 acres in Thuwal, Saudi Arabia, the consensus at the time viewed the development as a resolutely courageous move toward a knowledge-based society. Five years after its inauguration, King Abdullah University of Science and Technology (KAUST) is already approaching fulfillment of King Abdullah's dream of having KAUST become one of the world's leading scientific research universities contributing to the furtherance of discoveries and advancement of technologies that facilitate resolution of problems and challenges obstructing full economic development and social prosperity for Saudi Arabia and the world.

The multifaceted purpose of KAUST is embodied in its stated mission: "KAUST integrates research and education, leveraging the interconnectedness of science and engineering, and works to catalyze the diversification of the Saudi economy through economic and technology development.[27] KAUST centers itself on the pursuit of academic excellence, scholarship, diversity in faculty, staff and student body, and sustained relevance of its research to the challenges faced by the Kingdom and the world. The university has attracted some of the most accomplished faculty members from around the world and graduate degree candidates from equally diverse parts of the globe. KAUST offers graduate degrees through its three academic divisions: chemical and life sciences and engineering (CLSE); mathematical and computer sciences and engineering (MCSE); and physical sciences and engineering (PSE).

KAUST conferred its inaugural PhD degrees on December 14, 2012. Among those graduates receiving degrees were engaged in research areas of computational modeling of materials systems, Red Sea research, plant stress genomics, and mathematical techniques for geophysical subsurface imaging. In addition to doctoral degrees, nearly 200 master's degrees were conferred in 2012. These graduates as well as students and subsequent graduates have benefited from the many collaborations and cooperative initiatives KAUST has entered into since its creation. The institution has initiated research partnerships with institutions such as Woods Hole Oceanographic Institution, Institut Francais du Petrole, National University of Singapore, American University of Cairo, Hong Kong University of Science and Technology, Technische Universitat Munchen, University of California at San Diego, IBM, GE Global Research Center, King Abdulaziz City for Science and Technology, King Fahd University of Petroleum and Minerals, and Saudi Aramco.

KAUST has amassed equipment and built laboratories that represent the highest levels of technological capability and quality to be found in any academic or research institution in the world. State-of-the-art research equipment and provisioned laboratories operational within KAUST's walls are permitting expert staff scientists, faculty, and graduate students to pursue some of the world's most advanced research. The core labs and major facilities in KAUST operate six core labs and several workshops

containing advanced analytical, computational, and other research platforms in the areas of laboratory analytics; biosciences and bioengineering;
coastal and marine resources; imaging and characterization; nanofabri-
cation and thin film; supercomputing; visualization; and advanced design
and manufacturing.

KAUST is home to the Middle East's largest and most powerful supercomputer, the Shaheen (Peregrine Falcon) II supercomputer, an IBM System
Blue Gene supercomputer capable of analytical computations at a theoretical peak of 5.536 petaflops. A petaflop is equal to about one quadrillion
calculations per second. One estimate suggests it would take a human about
32,000,000 years to complete the same task. And, much to the academic provisioning prowess and vision of KAUST, in 2015, for the first time in history,
the TOP500 project, which was launched in 1993 and biannually lists the
most powerful supercomputers, ranked a supercomputer based in the Middle East (KAUST's Shaheen II Peregrine Falcon) on the list of the world's top
10 most powerful computers.[28] The British Broadcasting Corporation (BBC)
reported that "Kaust has spent about $80m (£51m) buying, installing, and
operating the Cray machine, which is about 25 times more powerful than
the machine it is replacing."[29]

Besides the matriculation of graduate students and their provisioning
with the very best academic environment, laboratories, equipment, and faculty available, KAUST's accomplishments are also viewed through the prism
of economic development. KAUST states its mission as:

[T]o contribute to the transformation of Saudi Arabia to a knowledge-
based economy.

- Be a model—prove that university research can deliver new products
  and be the basis for forming new companies in the Kingdom.
- Be a catalyst—share the approach with others and validate the model
  with many technologies and companies.
- Focus on what people can do now—find ways to help start and grow
  technology-based businesses in the Kingdom today.
- Be a technology magnet—attract major corporations and entrepreneurs
  to locate their R&D facilities and businesses at KAUST.[30]

KAUST has been especially forceful in promoting entrepreneurship and
the pursuit of innovative technologies that serve the development goals of
Saudi Arabia and aid the world in the resolution of its problems. It has
joined hands with the Saudi private sector and with companies from around
the world to greatly explore the possibilities for research and development
being realized from KAUST and its programs and curriculum. The university's economic development role is fulfilled through its five units: (1) the

KAUST industry collaboration program (KICP); (2) research park and innovation cluster (RPIC); (3) technology transfer and innovation (TTI); (4) new ventures and entrepreneurship (NVE); and (5) the technology application and advancement group (TAAG). From these economic development operating units, KAUST addresses the needs of individuals and businesses requiring assistance, collaboration, and support in transforming new ideas for products, services, and technologies into new businesses that in turn create new markets and jobs for the Kingdom.

The KICP has attracted broad interest from Saudi Arabia's private sector and international companies operating in the Kingdom. KICP states its value proposition as:

- Builds, nurtures, and manages industry relationships with KAUST and maximizing the value of industry-KAUST partnerships.
- Acts as the interface between industry and KAUST and helps align industry partners' R&D needs with the needs and capabilities of KAUST.
- Serves as a link between industry and economic development programs that include the technology transfer and innovation, research park and innovation cluster, seed fund program, new ventures, and the entrepreneurship center.
- Serves as an interface between industry and KAUST's research enterprise including faculty, research centers, and KAUST's academic partners.
- Facilitate partners' sponsored research agreements with the office of research services (ORS).
- Provides an ideal platform for recruitment of KAUST students and graduates for internships and job placements, respectively
- Links industry with the KAUST's university development for donations and sponsorships.

Along with KICP, the center industry affiliates program (CIAP) sits at the forefront of leveraging KAUST's R&D program and the university's technological resources and human talent base to serve the interests of companies seeking to optimize their commercialization output. The CIAP is a membership-based program whereby industry partners select a specifically designated research theme and contribute their knowledge of regional and global markets, thereby helping to set the center's direction and strategy.[31]

Offering three levels of industry partner memberships from its elite strategic partner status, down through its associate and honorary levels, these programs offer virtually unlimited access to on-campus engagement with the university's staff, physical resources such as laboratories, testing and verification facilities, and interface with KAUST's international network of research institutions. Businesses immediately recognizable on the global corporate stage have become a part of the KICP program. They include the following corporations:

Mars, GE, Total, Boeing, Saudi Aramco, Veolia, Lockheed Martin, Sumitomo Chemical, IBM, Saudi Bin Laden Group, Dow, Rolls-Royce, Halliburton, Siemens, BAE Systems, Alstom, Xenel, Shell, and SABIC.

In September 2014, Boeing opened the Boeing research and technology (BR&T) office in partnership with KAUST to develop aerospace technologies and to support the Kingdom's efforts to establish knowledge-based programs and expertise.[32] For more than 68 years, Boeing has enjoyed almost iconic American brand status within Saudi Arabia and has built upon its commitment to the Kingdom through various partnering efforts in a wide range of projects benefiting the Kingdom such as in the areas of human resources and capital building, transportation, energy and technology knowledge transfer.

The Dow Chemical Company (Dow), a founding member of KICP, has a comprehensive cooperative agreement with KAUST and KICP that established Dow's Middle East and Africa R&D center on the KAUST university campus. The agreement enhances Dow's offering of academic and professional opportunities within Saudi Arabia. Under the terms of the agreement, Dow and KAUST collaborate on a range of academic research programs suited to KAUST's areas of excellence in research and education.[33]

Another founding member of KICP is SABIC, one of the world's largest producers of petrochemicals. There is no company having a greater impact on the future of the petrochemical industry worldwide than SABIC. SABIC's size, international investments, state-of-the-art research capabilities, and its focus on the evolution of consumer products development have placed the company at the pinnacle of the international petrochemical industry. It has a formidable global manufacturing presence. In Asia alone, SABIC has nine manufacturing centers in China, Japan, South Korea, and Southeast Asia. SABIC Innovative Plastics has grown operations to include facilities in 35 countries and six global technology centers that are yielding some of the most advanced production technologies and consumer products in the world.

SABIC has also made a considerable investment in its presence at KAUST. In 2013, SABIC launched one of four new technology and innovation centers designed to upgrade its global technology, applications, and solutions. SABIC's corporate research and innovation center (CRI) at KAUST is using SABIC's existing innovation systems to develop new technologies, improve its manufacturing processes, and contribute to a sustainable environment with Saudi communities and world communities. The collaboration between SABIC's corporate research and innovation center (CRI) and KAUST has already yielded scientific breakthrough technologies and discoveries. One example of such successes has been SABIC's work with KAUST's functional nanomaterials and devices group in the discoveries of new innovations in flexible electronics.

Led by Dr. Husam Alshareef, professor of materials science and engineering at KAUST, the collaboration with SABIC has produced five international patent filings and a number of high-impact journal papers. Published research from their collaborative efforts has revealed developments related to polymeric electronic memory, useful in printed and flexible electronic applications such as radio-frequency identification (RFID) tags, storage capacitors, and sensors. The all-polymer memory devices are attractive to the flexible printed electronics community, as they are low cost, solution processed, scalable, highly transparent, flexible, and fabricated at very low temperatures.

Further examples of innovative technologies, new products, and scientific discoveries resulting from KAUST teaming up with Saudi private industry are growing annually. These examples include a 2012 KAUST signed memorandum of understanding (MOU) with the National Prawn Company (NPC), a Saudi company founded in 1982 and based in Al-Lith, Saudi Arabia. The 2012 MOU was signed following a visit by a senior delegation of KAUST faculty members including those from KAUST Chemical and Life Sciences and Engineering; Red Sea Science & Engineering; Computational Biosciences; and the Water Desalination and Reuse Centre. The largest producer of shrimp in the Middle East, NPC offers a wide variety of fish, seafood, and marine by products as chemical and pharmaceutical ingredients to countries around the world. The MOU has led to a variety of aquaculture research projects in the areas of shrimp genome research, shrimp disease research, and research on the impacts of aquaculture and agriculture on the Red Sea. After an outbreak of white spot syndrome virus (WSSV) in 2011, causing diseased shrimp resulting in severe damage to shrimp aquaculture worldwide, including Saudi Arabia, on May 18–19, 2013, KAUST's Center for Desert Agriculture (CDA), together with the National Prawn Company (NPC) and the Saudi Aquaculture Society (SAS), convened a workshop on the control of the WSSV of shrimp. The purpose of the workshop was to bring together leading scientists engaged in WSSV research and other relevant fields to assess the current state of knowledge about the virus, identify limitations of current control strategies, and devise new biological approaches to eradicating the disease.[34]

New discoveries at KAUST extend beyond plastics and animals to even encompass plant research. In 2011, the university announced its team of researchers developed new genomics molecular scissors. In a paper published in the "Proceedings of National Academy of Sciences, USA" (PNAS) on January 24, 2011, Dr. Magdy Mahfouz and a research team articulated a new way of genetically engineering plants to tolerate aggressive environments and improve their quality, yield, and resistance to diseases. The development of this "repair tool" or "molecular scissors," composed of protein, precisely locates on the genome where it is to be cut using a genetic "postcode" and subsequently deletes, adds, or edits the gene for the desired outcome. It has profound implications not only for plant biology but for human DNA testing and genetic correction therapy.[35]

INDUSTRIAL CLUSTERS PROGRAM (IC), SABIC, AND SAUDI INTELLECTUAL PROPERTY

The strategy in Saudi Arabia of having academia hold hands with the private sector to produce positive economic development gains is becoming firmly embedded in the Kingdom's macro and microeconomic approach guiding itself to a knowledge-based economy. Plant biology may not be a priority for the country, but the same collaborative approach that brought on the SABIC and NCP innovations is helping the Kingdom steer toward a more efficient and rational economic use of its resources by concentrating government, industry, and its well-established and growing regional and global academic excellence in resources in a unified direction. This is embodied in the Kingdom's national industrial strategy (NIS) and its sister program, the national industrial cluster development program, now commonly known as the industrial clusters program (IC).

The promulgation of the NIS was made official by the Saudi Council of Ministers' adoption of its Resolution Number Thirty-Five, dated June 25, 2009 (7/2/1430 AH). The aim of the NIS has been to achieve measurable levels of diversification of the Saudi economy away from being powered by the inherited wealth of the country's natural resources toward a much enlarged capacity for economic growth driven by expanded production of goods and products from select key industries. Through a set of carefully defined objectives and outcomes, the NIS ambitiously set specific rates of achievement to be realized by the end of the year 2020. The NIS strategy set out to accomplish the following:

- Increase industry's contribution to the gross domestic product to 20 percent.
- Increase industrial value-added activity to three time the current level.
- Increase industrial exports share from the current rate of 18 percent to 35 percent.
- Increase technology-based exports from the current rate of 30 percent to 60 percent.

- Increase Saudi industrial labor force from the current rate of 15 percent to 30 percent.
- Upgrade the Kingdom's status to rank at least among the best-performing 30 industrial countries by 2020, improving its annual ranking by two places.

The NIS was one of a number of planning initiatives governing the focus and direction the Kingdom wanted its government-supported economic, academic, and research organizations to embrace and maintain. In Saudi Arabia, when the government decrees policies that establish the direction its economy will take, it not only sets the rules everyone is expected to follow, it also sets a tone. This tone is picked up by the Kingdom's citizenry ... individual and corporate. In the case of government directives affecting the private sector, it is most often adopted by corporate leaders and incorporated into their own development strategies when done so profitably. There is no doubt that the compelling rationale for this self-alignment to government policy by the nation's private sector is that, on the whole, Saudis are very patriotic and its business people want to see the nation not only prosper but take the right directions when it comes to its development. The IC is a big part of integrating the private sector into laying the groundwork for establishing and expanding innovative production and manufacturing industries within Saudi Arabia by optimizing the country's use of its strategic resources and competitive positions.

The IC is supervised by two government agencies, the ministry of commerce and industry and the ministry of petroleum and mineral resources. Its main objectives are to act as a catalyst for the development of five targeted industrial sectors:

1. Automotive
2. Minerals and metal processing
3. Solar energy
4. Plastics and packaging
5. Home appliances

Acting as an economic development expert with sector focus, the IC facilitates potential investor expansion into the targeted industries and constantly seeks out ways to maximize the investor's environment to foster successful market ventures. The main IC partners are Saudi Aramco and SABIC. They are the lead players, along with a host of Saudi and foreign industry sector investors operating in the Kingdom's industrial petrochemical plant complexes such as Jubail and Yanbu, Rabigh, and other locations in the country. World powerhouses in the petrochemical and refining business such as SABIC, Al-Kayan, Chevron-Phillips, Dow Chemical, Saudi Aramco, Sumitomo Chemical, ExxonMobil, National Industrialisation Company (Tasnee), Saudi International Petrochemical Company (Sipchem), and Shell Oil Company are just a sampling of private-sector investors contributing to the growing diversification of Saudi Arabia's industrial strength.

In December 2013, in Boston, Massachusetts, Saudi Aramco opened the first of three planned U.S.-based research and development centers intended to enlarge its global research capabilities. The Aramco Research Center, the named new center, will develop new technologies that meet the challenges of the upstream and downstream industries. The Boston research center, along with the other two centers to be established in the United States in Detroit and Houston, will join Saudi Aramco's other research centers in Saudi Arabia, the Netherlands, France, Korea, and China.[36]

SABIC began to take its own path toward establishing research and development centers well before Saudi Aramco. There are very few companies these days having greater impact on the future of the petrochemical industry worldwide than SABIC. Its size, international investments, state-of-the-art research capabilities, and its focus on the evolution of consumer product development have placed it at the pinnacle of the international petrochemical industry. SABIC's rise to global prominence has been recognized as much for its skillful selection of its joint venture partners as for the expansion of its formidable worldwide manufacturing presence. The company's subsidiary in Asia, SABIC Asia, includes nine manufacturing centers in China, Japan, Korea, and Southeast Asia. SABIC Innovative Plastics, the subsidiary most responsible for new technologies and products in plastics, has grown its operations to a presence in 35 countries and six global technology centers that continue to yield some of the most advanced production technologies and consumer products in the world. Recent SABIC investments in cracking and upstream operations around the world have afforded SABIC, and, in turn, the Kingdom of Saudi Arabia, an uncommon diversification throughout the entire hydrocarbon production chain and the ability to offer increasingly revolutionary downstream products.

SABIC's relentless pursuit of excellence in the discoveries of innovative technologies and products is often done with academic institutions such as KAUST and King Saud University (KSU), giving tens of millions of dollars in various projects that link SABIC and its corporate partners with academia. SABIC established the SABIC polymers chair, local scholarship programs for post-graduate students (both master's and doctoral), and the innovation center, which conducts advanced research and application production activities in plastics and petrochemicals.

In closing this chapter on innovation in the Kingdom, a discussion on Saudi technological discovery and invention would not be complete without looking in on the patent environment. As mentioned earlier, the Saudi patent office (SPO), housed within KACST, is the receiving agent and caretaker for the Saudi storehouse of Patents, Layout Designs of Integrated Circuits, Plant, Varieties and Industrial Designs from the instance of application filing to grant. The SPO is an office run by its director general, Mr. Sami Alsodais. He is supported by 123 highly trained, experienced, and hard-working executive and support staff members. In my interview with Mr. Alsodais for this book, the director general stressed the importance of several aspects of the work of SPO according to its strategy which aims to improve the office's services, the efficiency of its operations and skills, the capabilities of SPO's personnel, and raising IP awareness of all national institutions and individuals engaged in inventing tomorrow's technologies and products. SPO personnel include 50 examiners, and a number of legal advisors, patent informational specialists, and administrative workers. They receive periodic and programmed training by the World Intellectual Property Organization (WIPO), the European Patent Office (EPO), the United States Patent and Trademark Office (USPTO), the Korean Intellectual Property Office (KIPO), the State Intellectual Property Office of the P.R.C. (SIPO), and other institutions concerned with patents.

In 1982, KACST was notified of Saudi Arabia's accession to membership in WIPO by royal decree. SPO began operations in 1989 and the first Law of Patents was issued by the royal decree No. (M/38) dated January 18, 1989, and was modified in 2004 in compliance with the terms of the Kingdom's accession to membership in the WTO. In the early years of the SPO, it was heavily criticized for its slowness in processing patent applications. At the time the patent laws were modified in 2004, the SPO had granted only 615 patents since the year of its creation. Much to the credit of His Highness Prince Dr. Turki Bin Saud Mohammed Al-Saud, and Dr. Abdulaziz M. Alswailem, the SPO has revamped and greatly increased its efficiency. The streamlining of the patent application and review process has been occurring since 2010. Today, the SPO has granted more than 4843 patents since its establishment and received 2406 patent applications in 2015.

In regard to the average time a patent application takes from its filing to its final decision, the streamlining of the SPO and its administrative processes has paid dividends. Historically, this time length has been as much as five years or longer. The average time now in the Kingdom is between one and two years. This is well in line within modern economies such as the United States, the United Kingdom, and South Korea, where the time length averages 18 to 36 months.

Since the SPO began operations, the majority of patent applications filed with SPO, 85 percent have been by foreign companies. In 2015, patent filings by Saudis have increased dramatically to increase to 30 percent of all patent applications filed by Saudis nationals. Director General Alsodais credits this increase to raising IP awareness among the public and the enhancement of filing procedures and developing an e-filing system. According to Mr. AlSodais, the SPO's usage of other communications mediums, including social media, has bolstered its efforts to educate the public concerning patent registration and respecting IP rights. A SPO short film on the importance of patent registration and how to commercialize inventions has been seen by 285,000 viewers. SPO organized workshops are also now delivered via videoconferencing as well.

The SPO has also advanced its client services system to include an e-filing system, live chat and callback customer service, and has offered an Internet patent application fee payment option.

The world is taking note of the advancements in innovation in the Kingdom through the SPO. The 2012 Nature Publishing Index (NPI), a global catalog of the world's research output through following published primary research articles, noted Saudi Arabia's ascension among the ranks of innovating nations. The NPI, begun in 2009, tracks research accomplished within a multitude of sources, including government research institutes, universities, and private sector companies. Saudi Arabia's performance in the NPI registered a 140 percent annual average increase between 2008 and 2012 moving the Kingdom seven places up in the ranking to forty-first place on the NPI 2012 index.[37]

In 2013, the Kingdom strengthened its bona fides within the world intellectual property rights community by joining another international cooperative patent organization. In an article appearing in *WIPO* magazine, Director General Al-Sodais stated:

> *In May 2013, Saudi Arabia joined the Patent Cooperation Treaty (PCT). This important development promises to further boost the country's innovation landscape and to put us squarely on the global patenting map. While there is still much to accomplish, Saudi Arabia's strong commitment to innovation and technology development is catalyzing efforts for the country to become a fully fledged knowledge economy in the coming years.*[38]

With a world-class patent protection system in place, innovators and inventors in Saudi Arabia have the regulatory environment, comparable with any of the world's modern economies, to have their inventions and discovered technologies benefit the Kingdom for years to come.

It is to Saudi Arabia's family-owned businesses and the role they play in the Kingdom's developing economy that we now turn in Chapter 3.

NOTES

1. Kingdom of Saudi Arabia, Ministry of Economy and Planning, Riyadh, Ninth Development Plan for the Kingdom of Saudi Arabia, *General Framework of the Directions of the Plan, 2.4, Toward a Knowledge-Based Economy, 2.4.4*, 2005–2010 (1431–1436 AH), 34.
2. Cornell University, INSEAD, and WIPO (2013): "The Global Innovation Index 2013: The Local Dynamics of Innovation," Geneva, Ithaca, and Fontainebleau, 37.
3. Cornell University, INSEAD, and WIPO (2013): "The Global Innovation Index 2013: The Local Dynamics of Innovation," Country/Economy Profiles, Geneva, Ithaca, and Fontainebleau, 127.
4. The Saudi Fund for Development, "Making a Difference, the Saudi Fund for Development Annual Report 2004," www.maxhill.co.uk/pdfs/SAUDI%20 FUND%20BOOK.pdf, 35.
5. Ibid. 27.
6. Peter F. Drucker, *Innovation and Entrepreneurship: Practice and Principles* (HarperCollins e-books-Kindle edition), Reprint edition, March 17, 2009.
7. Ibid. 2, "Purposeful Innovation and the Seven Sources for Innovative Opportunity."
8. Ibid.
9. KACST, www.kacst.edu.sa/en/about/stnp/pages/principles.aspx (Accessed July 19, 2014).
10. Ibid.
11. Ibid.
12. The Kingdom of Saudi Arabia, Ministry of Economy and Planning, King Abdulaziz City for Science and Technology, "Strategic Technology Program Summary Document," Doc. No. 04P0001-PLN-0001-ER01, 6.
13. Ibid. 7.
14. King Abdulaziz City for Science and Technology, www.kacst.edu.sa/en/about/Pages/default.aspx (Accessed July 28, 2014).
15. Muslim Science, http://muslim-science.com/profiles-in-leadership-1-dr-mohammed-ibn-ibrahim-al-suwaiyel-kacst-nstp-measuring-benefits-of-science (Accessed July 29, 2014).
16. The White House, www.whitehouse.gov/administration/eop/ostp/about (Accessed July 29, 2014).
17. Ibid.
18. King Abdulaziz City for Science and Technology, "The National Center for Technology Development, Doc. No. 10P0013-BKT-0001-ER01, Overview.
19. *Arab News*, "KACST Research Discovers New Class of Industrial Polymers," July 7, 2014, www.arabnews.com/news/597701.
20. King Abdulaziz City for Science and Technology, Technology Development Center, "Products and Services," Doc. No. 10P0005-BKT-0001-ER01, 5.
21. *Arab News*, "KACST Researchers Develop New Foam Concrete," August 23, 2013, www.arabnews.com/news/462203.

22. King Abdulaziz City for Science and Technology, "The National Center for Technology Development, Doc. No. 10P0013-BKT-0001-ER01, Technology Innovation Centers Program.

23. King Abdulaziz City for Science and Technology, "The National Center for Technology Development, Doc. No. 10P0013-BKT-0001-ER01, BADIR.

24. Ibid.

25. Saudi Aramco, *A Land Transformed: The Arabian Peninsula, Saudi Arabia and Saudi Aramco* (Aramco Services Company), Reprint edition, 2006.

26. The Saudi Business Incubation Network, www.sbin.org.sa/en/about/overview (Accessed August 18, 2014).

27. King Abdullah University for Science and Technology, "Our Vision at KAUST— Mission," www.kaust.edu.sa/vision.html (Accessed August 19, 2014).

28. The Top500 Project, "TOP500 List of the World's Most Powerful Supercomputers, June 2015," www.top500.org/lists/2015/06/.

29. The BBC News Online, "Saudi Supercomputer Enters Top Ten List," July 13, 2015, http://www.bbc.com/news/technology-33506479.

30. King Abdullah University for Science and Technology, "About Economic Development," http://www.kaust.edu.sa/economic-development-entrepreneurship.html (Accessed August 20, 2014).

31. King Abdullah University for Science and Technology, "KAUST Industry Collaboration Program (KICP)," *Through Inspiration, Discover, an Economic Development Publication,* www.kaust.edu.sa/assets/downloads/kicp/kaust%20 kicp_reduced%20size.pdf (Accessed August 20, 2014).

32. *Saudi Gazette,* "Boeing R&D Office at KAUST to Boost Local Talent Development," September 15, 2014, www.saudigazette.com.sa/index.cfm? method=home.regcon&contentid=20140915218177.

33. Dow in the Middle East, "DOW Launches Innovation and Sustainability Agendas at KAUST," March 14, 2011, www.dow.com/middleeast/news/ releases/2011/20110314a.htm.

34. King Abdullah University for Science and Technology, http://cda.kaust.edu .sa/Pages/Event-May.aspx (Accessed August 26, 2014); See also The Fish Site (www.thefishsite.com), "OIE: White Spot Disease Reported in Saudi Arabia," October 5, 2011, www.thefishsite.com/fishnews/15692/oie-white-spot-disease-reported-in-saudi-arabia.

35. Seedquest.com (www.seedquest.com), "King Abdullah University of Science and Technology Develops Plant Genomics 'Molecular Scissors'," February 23, 2011, www.seedquest.com/news.php?type=news&id_article=15028&id_ region=&id_category=2161&id_crop=.

36. *Offshore* magazine, "Aramco Opens R&D Center in Boston Area," December 10, 2013, www.offshore-mag.com/articles/2013/12/aramco-opens-r-d-center-in-boston-area.html.

37. *Nature* Publishing Index 2012/Global, Macmillan Publisher Ltd., 2013, 30, 42.

38. Sami al-Sodais, *WIPO* magazine, No. 5, October 2013, "Science, Technology and Innovation in Saudi Arabia," 25.

CHAPTER 3

The Development of Family-Owned Businesses in Saudi Arabia

DEFINING THE FAMILY-OWNED BUSINESS (FOB)

Before the specifics concerning family-owned businesses (FOBs) in Saudi Arabia, a definition of this form of doing business and some key concepts are in order.

There are many definitions of FOBs that pare down its few but essential operating parts into concise descriptions. One of the most simple yet useful definitions of an FOB that I have found, however, is by the International Finance Corporation, which in its *IFC Family Business Governance Handbook 2008* says, "A family business refers to a company where the voting majority is in the hands of the controlling family; including the founder(s) who intend to pass the business on to their descendants."[1] The IFC continues with its definition to deem the terms "family business," "family firm," "family company," "family-owned business," "family-owned company," and "family-controlled company" as interchangeable in usage in its publication. We shall do the same in this book.

The *IFC Family Business Governance Handbook* also offers what it views as several insightful attributes of the FOB as it defines some of their distinguishing characteristics. In citing the inherent strength of the family's commitment to the firm's longevity, the IFC states:

> *The family—as the business owner shows the highest dedication in seeing its business grow, prosper, and get passed on to the next generations. As a result, many family members identify with the company and are usually willing to work harder and reinvest part of their profits into the business to allow it to grow in the long term.*[2]

I like this description because it describes very well many of the family-owned businesses with which I am familiar. These are companies in which their founders, through sheer personality and drive, have created enterprises that long retained those virtues and have in turn inspired successive generations to the cause of enterprise preservation, longevity, and growth for their offspring's future. The strength of family companies in Saudi Arabia, and for that matter worldwide, is as the IFC identified as the family enterprise's inherent ability to pass on "accumulated knowledge, experience, and skills" to succeeding generations of family members. Because the family name is the most visible identity of a family-run enterprise, the pride and effort that family members engaged in the business exert in growing it and maintaining its reputation are enduring strengths.[3]

In 2013, there were a reported 1.8 million commercial establishments in Saudi Arabia. This statistical reference from the Ministry of Labor included all commercial registrations of companies active and inactive.[4] Although no hard figures are available in terms of commercial registrations categorized by establishments run as family owned businesses, the Jeddah Chamber of Commerce and Industry estimates there are approximately 5,000 family-owned businesses in the Kingdom, 156 of them are trading on the Tadawul, the local Saudi bourse. The Chamber estimates that the activities of these businesses contribute 25 percent to the Kingdom's GDP.[5] There is no doubt that the government of the Kingdom of Saudi Arabia recognizes the importance and contributions of Saudi family-owned businesses to its vitality and economic future.

A viewing of the growth of Saudi Arabia's family-owned businesses, and in some particular cases their notable decline, has been a kind of time lapse photographic depiction of the challenges, struggles, triumphs, and growing pains of the Kingdom itself and its changing economy. Some of today's most recognized Saudi family business names, such as the Al-Quraishi, trace their lineage as merchants and powerful actors from the time when the Prophet Mohammad, Peace Be Upon Him (PBUH), walked the thoroughfares of the Islamic holy cities of Mecca and Medina. In his germinal book on the big businesses of Saudi Arabia and the Gulf States, Michael Field, noted one senior member of the Alireza family during his interview for Mr. Field's book traced the hereditary path of his family to commercial prominence in the Kingdom to "Amr ibn al Aasi, one of the lieutenants of the Prophet Mohammad (PBUH) and the man who had won Egypt for Islam in 640 A.D."[6]

Another important book on Saudi businesses, J. R. L. Carter's *Merchant Families of Saudi Arabia,* is replete with notable business families that trace their lineage and success in business to their fighting alongside King Abdulaziz during his struggles to unite the country, the two world wars, the arrival of the Islamic faith to the Arabian peninsula and even as far back to the days of the ancient spice trade of the region. Many of Saudi Arabia's business families have seen their fortunes rise and fall in spite of, and often coinciding with, the political intrigues, military conquests, and economic developments that have occurred within the Kingdom. The history of family-owned businesses in Saudi Arabia is a fascinating one whose story, if told in the historical context, would engage the reader in dramas, tragedies, comedies, and suspenseful episodes ranging the full spectrum of the human experience. It would occupy volumes of literary work. Although such a chronicling of the subject would be a worthy and noble undertaking, my ambitions with this chapter are necessarily more modest.

The global activities of many of the Kingdom's family-owned businesses in the technology-hyped and globally linked world of today belies the humble beginnings many of them experienced in their rise to notoriety. In olden times, families engaged in mercantile and agricultural pursuits constituted the bulk of the commercial class in Saudi Arabia, well before the industrial age or the creation of the modern Saudi state. As alluded to at the beginning of Chapter 1, dating from eighteenth, nineteenth, and much of the twentieth centuries back to the dawn of Islamic society (and even the pre-Islamic period) the main engines of the Saudi economy have been agriculture, the activities of the durable merchandise and commodity trade routes that trekked across the Arabian peninsula, and the enduring pilgrimages to Mecca and Medina. The chief money earner for nations in the region in the pre-oil period, however, has far and away been the trade in goods and commodities.

In this regard, a common reference used by those familiar with Saudi and Arabian Gulf businesses is to broadly describe them as a commercial class with a "trader's mentality." The pith of the reference and those of their kind is to describe the Saudi businessman as one accustomed to building prosperity and the growth of their businesses under the protected cover of a kind of mercantile environment within which they have operated. Until very recently in the Kingdom's history, leading up to its succession to WTO membership in 2005, this was an environment in which goods and commodities were available to them for purchase at the lowest prices allowing them to sell at the highest prices, sheltered by a government that protected their market interests by limiting foreign competition in a great deal of commercial areas within the Kingdom's borders. The stereotypical image of the meticulously appareled Arab negotiating trades in his equally regaled desert tent is a visual ingrained in most Western minds thanks to cinematic portrayals handed down since the early days of film. We humans are often creatures in search of simplistic ways of explaining the phenomena and environments we experience. It is true that the overwhelming majority of "merchant families" described in J. R. L. Carter's *Merchant Families of Saudi Arabia* and many of the progenitors of Saudi Arabia's largest and best-known family-owned businesses came from simple trading backgrounds. To describe today's Saudi business community as a nation of traders, however, is an oversimplification that begs the question and prevents a true understanding of the Saudi businessman. It is tantamount to referencing eighteenth-century America and describing the United States today as a nation of wealthy landowners.

The names of Saudi family businesses that have come from humble beginnings and the nation's trading ranks are seemingly endless. The Alireza family, a business clan with worldwide holdings whose founder, Zainal Bin Alireza, emigrated to Jeddah, Saudi Arabia, from Iran in the 1840s while a boy, is one of the iconic business families in the Kingdom. The son of a camel caravan owner, Zainal and his sons and heirs all went on to contribute mightily to the development of the city of Jeddah and indeed the Kingdom in many areas beyond trade such as infrastructure, education, and politics.

The Al Gosaibi family, a family begun in the late nineteenth century by two brothers, Abdullah and Hamad Gosaibi, left behind a couple of mud villages to become traders in pearls, gold, foodstuffs, and contractors of oilfield services. It would be difficult to talk about family-owned businesses in the Kingdom's Eastern Province without the Al Gosaibi name coming into the conversation. Yet, as an illustration of the perils facing family-run businesses, perhaps more than any other, this business family has had its internal family dissension and strife dragged through the local, national, Gulf regional, and international press for all to view. As *The National,* a daily news journal out of Abu Dhabi, reported in 2010:

> *Gulf financial circles were shocked to hear of the default of two Bahraini banks, The International Banking Corporation (TIBC) and Awal Bank. Their financial problems quickly spread to their owners, Ahmad Hamad Al Gosaibi and Brothers of Saudi Arabia (Pepsi bottlers, builders, and paint makers) and the Saad Group (property, import-export, and fancy financial transactions), respectively. Saad is owned by Mr. Al Sanea, a Kuwaiti-born entrepreneur who gained the trust of the Al Gosaibi family through his marriage to Sana, the sister of Saud Al Gosaibi, who is the managing director of the family's master company. Investigation by the Bahraini authorities and the Al Gosaibis found serious financial problems in their own businesses and in the Saad Group, which led to allegations—well-documented in New York and London courts— that Mr. Al Sanea had perpetrated a huge fraud on the family.[7]*

The Al Gosaibi embroilment and its very public nature have unsettled even the most jaded and experienced first-generation Saudi family business owners. Family matters, whether of the domestic or business variety, are always a matter of privacy in Saudi Arabia. The Al Gosaibi case has given many family business owners pause and led them to take stock of their own situations. As will be discussed later, having one's siblings as business partners proves challenging enough in the managed growth of a business. There is an added element of complexity, however, when partners and business participants enter the family business through marriage.

In selecting the few Saudi-owned businesses for highlighted discussion in this book, I received a good deal of advice on which family businesses to include. Some with whom I spoke thought it best to select businesses based on industry sectors. Others opined that it would be advisable to choose my subjects based on the length of time they could trace their lineage to doing business in the Kingdom. Still others, prominent business owners in their own right, advised me to select from only the largest of family-owned businesses. Choosing from within any of these categories would have yielded many interesting companies. As with Al Gosaibi and the Alireza, so it is with Al Olayan, Al Jumaih, Al Hokair, Al Othaim, Al Juffali, Binladen, Al Kanoo, Al Turki, and Al Rajhi. All are able to lay claim to deep and long-aged roots in the Kingdom with virtual mastery over everything in business from automobiles, food, banking, and chemicals to steel pipes, construction, and consumer retail. A discussion of all or most would have been impractical. What I aim to accomplish in this chapter, however, is to feature a few of the better-known family-owned businesses in Saudi Arabia that stand out in their rise from humble beginnings, the vision for growth of their businesses, and their concern for and service to the larger Saudi business community.

The Al Quraishi, Al Zamil, and Al Jeraisy are Saudi families whose businesses I have known since my diplomatic service in Saudi Arabia. I am acquainted with their owners and my admiration and respect for their hard work, attention to corporate governance, concern for their nation and business peers, and their successful global ventures have grown over the last dozen or so years. They have welcomed this book and graciously agreed to have some of their key family members interviewed for its content. I am deeply grateful to them and hope the presentation of their thoughts and views on the subject of family-owned businesses in the Kingdom will give the reader a greater appreciation for this important aspect of business in Saudi Arabia. Any company seeking to do business in the Kingdom must possess a good understanding of the dynamic environment within which these businesses operate, the unique challenges they face concerning corporate succession and the need for them to remain relevant in a rapidly changing and incessantly competitive world.

Before presenting the three highlighted Saudi family businesses, a review of a few overarching themes of critical importance to family-owned businesses in Saudi Arabia will serve to bring greater clarity to the subject matter. These themes and related issues are not exhaustive of all relevant questions facing these businesses in regard to their nature or future. I have selected, however, a few focus areas of discussion concerning Saudi family-owned businesses that I believe best facilitate an applied understanding of these businesses and the dynamics germane to their development within the Kingdom and the global business community. From the perspective of any prospective FOB partner or co-investor, or anyone looking to do business with these companies, an understanding of key elements of the family-owned business in Saudi Arabia is crucial to conducting business with them.

Let us examine: (1) the *corporate* versus *social* nature of the Saudi family-owned company or group of companies that is of fundamental importance when managing a relationship with such businesses; (2) the issue of corporate succession within Saudi family-owned businesses and the process of integrating second- and third-generation family members in to the businesses; and (3) the management of the strategic focus of generations-old family businesses and the importance of corporate governance to their future.

THE CORPORATE VERSUS SOCIAL NATURE OF THE SAUDI FAMILY-OWNED BUSINESS

One of the chief distinguishing characteristics of any family-owned business is that the energy that propels it both emanates from and is dispersed into its two fundamental defining states of existence, its corporate and social natural states. The rigors of running a family-owned business in adherence to an ever-changing national and international regulatory and competitive environment present pressures that are managed to varying degrees and influenced greatly by the personalities of its owners and those family members engaged in its operations. In the case of most Saudi family-owned businesses, a single founder, or two or more siblings or other close family members started the business. As is the case with Western corporations, building a profitable business in chosen business sectors and managing it to ensure its longevity have been of primary importance to Saudi family-owned businesses. However, unlike Western non-family corporate concerns, social considerations such as using a successful business to assure the welfare of immediate and extended family members, assimilating the input of key family members in the strategic direction of the business, and their integration into its operations are often all of equal import.

Many of today's powerhouse family-owned businesses of influence and prominence in the Kingdom were started by their founders in the 1940s,

1950s, and 1960s. It was their determination, vision, and vigor that acted as the initial catalyst and subsequent power source for the early successes of their businesses. By virtue of them literally being "one-man shows," these businesses were often run dictatorially or were authoritarian in manner of operation. Whatever the boss said is what most often happened. These pioneers knew of the Kingdom's aspirations to become a modern state and were well aware of the action it planned to take for it to fulfill its ambitions. In surveying the Saudi landscape in those days while assessing various ways to make money in a burgeoning economy, during a time when change was a slower-moving phenomenon, the opportunities must have appeared endless to these Saudi mavericks.

In these early days, FOBs were usually not governed by boards of directors. Certainly no one outside the family had any definitive say in the actions of the business or its strategic development decisions. Among its founding first generation and key family members, decisions were most often made through consensus after considerable debate. New commercial directions for an established and successful FOB were often taken slowly and frequently after the collection of facts and opinions concerning the overall prospect for success offered by a number of peers during informal gatherings or private conversations. Even in the modern era, when Saudi family-owned businesses assumed more formal corporate operating structures, including those with boards of directors, people outside of the family rarely exercised effective influence over the strategic directions of Saudi FOBs.

Today, a noted exception to the general absence of non-family-exercised influence in the operations of Saudi FOBs is most often found in the distinction between Saudi FOBs primarily engaged in industrial businesses as opposed to those with traditionally trading company platforms. Increasingly in the Kingdom, Saudi FOBs are forming joint ventures, strategic alliances, and other equity and business ventures whose governance is overseen by boards composed of family and non-family members. As Saudi FOBs begin to form more international partnerships to gain greater market, industrial, and capital access opportunities, their non-Saudi equity partners are requiring their participation on the governing boards of Saudi partnership entities and in some cases the board of the Saudi parent itself.

As any Western executive of a company participating with a Saudi FOB will attest, close proximity to daily operations of their Saudi partner in the Kingdom can yield a treasure trove of how business is done in Saudi Arabia. This is particularly the case if the Saudi FOB partner suspends the usual off-limits boundaries that normally separate Saudis from non-Saudis, and those separating Saudi FOB family members from non-family-member Westerners with whom they do business. The growing trend away from American and other Western companies stationing their executives in neighboring countries to Saudi Arabia such as the United Arab Emirates (U.A.E.), Bahrain, Kuwait, and Qatar in favor of a full-time presence in the Kingdom speaks to the wisdom in knowing more and becoming more fully engaged in not only the corporate realities of the Saudi FOB, but the social corporeality of the Saudi entity. If the foreign executive representing the Western partner of the Saudi FOB is attuned to and learns from the social perspectives and responsibilities all Saudi companies share, all aspects of the partnership are likely to be strengthened because of it.

As most often is the case in Saudi Arabia, new opportunities for business are discovered in conversation … casual conversation in social settings or in business meetings among peers. Anyone (exclusively males for purposes of this illustration) who has had the privilege to have been invited to a Saudi wedding and attended in the circle of prominent businessmen is familiar with the sense of community these gatherings connote. Serving as family gatherings, these occasions also bring together social peers and acquaintances that evoke tempered and considered ideas that may bring forth discussions on a wide range of the day's relevant matters, including potential areas of new business.

It has been suggested by many, and generally accepted by most, that the cultural and social attributes of life in the Arab world have guided the development of family-owned businesses toward a predilection for privacy in all matters and a penchant for using government and political power structures as a means of gaining new business and preserving its stature.[8] When we discuss "social" considerations pertaining to Saudi family-owned businesses, one should not only consider issues affecting individual family members in the business, but reflections on the societal norms governing how these companies interact with governmental agencies and political power structures that must go into the calculus as well.

There is a level of support expected by the nation's leaders of all Saudi commercial enterprises in the Kingdom. Call it a type of responsible corporate nationalism or a kind of Saudi corporate patriotism. However one chooses to reference it, the act by the majority of the nation's businesses in publicly supporting accepted policy exists. Business communities in any country are usually expected, sometimes unreasonably, to get behind economic policies envisioned by their nation's leaders as engendering and fostering the improvement of the lot of its citizens. Even in a country as industrially advanced and globally linked as the United States, American business is expected to adopt governing policies and operating procedures in line with official U.S. government regulations and economic policies that are not detrimental to the nation's interests. This can most recently be seen in the United States between the U.S. President Barack Obama's administration and corporate America over the issue of tax inversion, the action taken by a company through which it becomes a subsidiary of a new, foreign, parent company for the purpose of falling under the beneficial tax laws of that newly acquired corporate domicile.[9]

On September 22, 2014, the Obama administration announced new rules it said would discourage U.S. corporations from engaging in tax inversion through moving their corporate headquarters from the United States to a foreign tax jurisdiction, thereby avoiding U.S. corporate tax rates. While recognizing the economic benefit to the United States of having U.S. corporate investment capital find its way to overseas markets, U.S. Treasury Secretary Jacob J. Lew in effect took corporate America to task for putting their interests before, in their view, what are in the best economic public interests of the nation by engaging in tax inversion transactions. In its September 22, 2014, press release on the subject, the U.S. Treasury Department said:

> *Genuine cross-border mergers make the U.S. economy stronger by enabling U.S. companies to invest overseas and encouraging foreign investment to flow into the United States. But these transactions should be driven by genuine business strategies and economic efficiencies, not a desire to shift the tax residence of the parent entity to a low-tax jurisdiction simply to avoid U.S. taxes.*[10]

Furthermore, U.S. Treasury Secretary Lew said of the new proposed rules targeting tax inversion:

> *This action will significantly diminish the ability of inverted companies to escape U.S. taxation. For some companies considering deals, today's action will mean that inversions no longer make economic sense. These transactions may be legal, but they're wrong. And the law should change.*[11]

Similar to the quandary faced by American companies when considering the usefulness of tax inversion, businesses around the world often confront like predicaments when having to choose between the competing forces of profit and operational behavior that champions the greater economic good. Sometimes the way government wants the private sector to act is both good for the company and good for the nation. However, as is the case with the tax inversion issue with American companies, legal actions in the pursuit of profits taken by private sector entities in other countries ultimately may prove detrimental to the economic interests of those countries as well. Saudi FOBs are no different. In the end, it is the law, promulgated by those in national leadership positions, that defines what is good for the country. Businesses, like individual citizens, follow the law.

Saudi FOBs, particularly those that have reached a size whereby they have taken on strategic foreign partners and acquired global market presence, in many instances, have had to yield the promise of expanded profits to political and economic expediency. There is a type of corporate allegiance, a patriotism, if you will, owed and shown by Saudi companies to the greater good of the Kingdom of Saudi Arabia. Although the voice of the Saudi corporate sector is always heard when it objects to government-imposed policies that adversely affect their interests, as is the case with the earlier-discussed labor policy initiative Nitiqat, there is most often a widespread "implied buy-in" by business when it comes to government policies it recognizes as having been formulated, promulgated, and implemented with true and valid national interests at their core. Once again, the Nitiqat labor initiative and its stated goal of making more jobs available to Saudi citizens proves a suitable example of how Saudi FOBs have reacted with corporate social responsibility to government policy for the greater good.

The private sector's contentious opposition to the adverse effects Nitiqat and the shift toward more aggressive government policy to force increased employment of Saudi workers on the backs of expelled foreign workers from the Kingdom was mentioned in Chapter 1. This government policy represents an example of how previously legal business practices of relatively unrestrained private sector hiring of foreign workers ran contrary to the generally accepted goal of a much higher labor participation rate by Saudi citizens. I argue that although owners of Saudi businesses genuinely accept the need for much higher employment levels of Saudis, the perennial source of cut-rate labor from foreign worker pools and the dip in profits partly caused by their expulsion tended to trump the social conscience of many companies in this regard. For foreign companies partnered with Saudi companies and FOBs, the reluctance of some Saudi firms to hire Saudis over foreign workers went beyond the mere fact that Saudi workers came with a higher wage bill than their foreign counterparts.

During my time serving as U.S. commercial attaché in Riyadh, I often found it mystifying when some Saudi business owners would admit in private their reluctance to hire Saudis because of a seemingly stereotypical perception of them as unreliable and relatively unproductive in comparison to their foreign counterparts. I do not believe this is a widely held belief, however. It appears to be an all too familiar sentiment within the Kingdom. Some in the business community view Saudi workers as not as productive as foreign workers and are not disposed to take the kind of blue-collar, menial jobs expatriates readily fill. Compounding the problem, business owners relate experiences with Saudi hires, especially those filling office positions, of these new employees reporting for work for only a few hours after which extended coffee breaks are taken followed by "optional early dismissals" well before the workday ends.

The cliché of the irresponsible and undependable Saudi worker has not yet become trite in over-usage. As the ranks of employable Saudis are more fully engaged in hireable positions, however, these workers are gradually beginning to dispel the notion of the spoiled and capricious hireling.

Saudi government officials have consistently encouraged the Kingdom's businesses to assume more of the critically important role of making more jobs available to Saudis and reducing foreign employment. Both local and central government officials have articulated their view that offering more jobs to Saudis ensures that the mutual national interests of employer and employee are safeguarded as the Saudi government continues its decades-old effort of "Saudization" through the current iteration of Nitiqat. As if to underscore the nexus between the imperative of more jobs for Saudis and the inferred perils of a restless youthful unemployed en masse population, on November 25, 2013, the director of police for the city of Jeddah, Major General Abdullah Mohammed Qaitani and the director of the labor office, Abdul Monem Shahri, implored the business community at a Jeddah chamber of conference and industry (JCCI) organized conference to adhere to the rules of employment and participate in nation building through increased employment of young Saudis. The officials further urged the business community to search for Saudis with relevant skill sets and replace expelled foreign workers by employing them.[12]

Acting in fulfillment of their social responsibility, often contrary to what are perceived as their best economic interests, Saudi companies and FOBs are stepping up to the challenge to train and hire greater numbers of the Kingdom's citizens. The foreign partners of Saudi companies and FOBs are also realizing the need to hire more Saudis and to adhere to enforced Ministry of Labor regulations requiring them. They are also receiving help from business and trade associations within the Kingdom eager to show that the private sector is doing its part in assisting more Saudis join the ranks of the employed.

The Riyadh Chamber of Commerce and Industry (RCCI) established a center for employment and training, and has issued periodic reports on its progress in efforts to assist Saudi workers. In a report covering the first half of 2014, the RCCI reported that only 1,760 young Saudi men and women applied for 11,751 job vacancies made available by 70 private-sector firms in the capital city of Riyadh.[13] The report stated that vacancies open to Saudis were offered by some of the Kingdom's largest companies engaged in the food, technology services, contracting, tourism, and retail industries, among other sectors.

As of the end of October 2014, 86 percent of companies and establishments in the Kingdom are compliant with the classification requirements for them to be in the green and platinum Nitiqat zones. Only 14 percent of firms in Saudi Arabia are classified in the unsafe yellow and red zones.

A new enforcement regime was implemented in December 2012 targeting companies with 1,000 to 3,000 employees. The next phase of aggressive enforcement will cover companies with 500 to 1,000 employees. Deputy Minister of Labor for Inspection and Development, Mr. Abdullah Abu Thunain, reported that as a result of the ministry's enforcement program, more than 1.9 million workers, including 400,000 Saudis employed at a total of 731 firms have benefited.[14]

The Al Zamil Group, of which we will learn more in this chapter, has been among a group of Saudi companies that have determinedly pushed forward with collaborations and partnerships with the aim of increasing Saudi employment within their own companies and within the private sector at large. Various aspects of the Al Zamil Group's dedication to corporate responsibility as it pertains to employment and training can be viewed on their website from the "Overview" tab. This section of their website includes information on the company's "Abdullah Hamad Al Zamil—AHZ Community Service Center." The mission of the AHZ Community Service Center states:

> *Our mission is to help create a productive and efficient society that contributes toward the development of the Kingdom. We make training opportunities available to our youth to help them achieve self-dependency so that they can fulfill their economic ambitions and meet their social obligations.*

The company further states the goals of the Center as:

1. *To serve our Kingdom and citizens as part of our compelling duty toward the nation and society*
2. *To extend all efforts to create employment opportunities for those in need*
3. *To make available administrative and technical training in accordance with scientific and technical norms*

The AHZ Community Service Center encourages young Saudi men and women to pursue their areas of interest into full employment and funds small projects in which these trainees can go beyond their training to further distinguish themselves in their chosen areas of expertise. The center, and the Al Zamil Group's commitment to this area of corporate and social responsibility has an end goal of finding "real and renewed employment opportunities for Saudi youth."[15] The Al Zamil Group also runs a jointly administered program with the Saudi government's human resources development fund (HRDF) and the national system for joint training.[16] On April

28, 2013, Zamil Industrial Investment Company, a Zamil Group's building materials–owned company, entered into a cooperation agreement with Dammam College of Technology to support the recruitment of Saudi graduates for employment placement.[17]

The sense of social responsibility felt by the founders of Saudi FOBs has been passed on to successive generations of those firms. Even as younger Saudis of prominence within these establishments begin to take on ever increasing areas of responsibilities, the awareness of a duty owed to society higher than the business itself endures within these circles. To be sure, the fervency with which this sense of duty owed is felt varies, depending on the individual. This is the case with opinion held by incoming generations concerning any aspect of the business. The methods and skills by which Saudi FOBs employ to coalesce the entry and effective deployment new family members into the business are a fascinating and critical aspect of these entities and the subject of the next section.

CORPORATE SUCCESSION WITHIN SAUDI FAMILY-OWNED BUSINESS AND NEW GENERATION INTEGRATION

Corporate successions as they occur in Saudi Arabia are distinct phenomena that are fascinating and instructive from a business perspective for anyone interested in the Kingdom commercial environment. As mentioned, Saudi FOBs are such an important part of not only the Saudi economy but are equally an integral part of the social fabric of society. Major shifts and well-publicized occurrences within well-known Saudi FOBs are readily discussed, content for featured newspaper stories, and easily become identifiable seams in the milieu of Saudi life. The passing of the founders of distinguished FOBs in the Kingdom are notable events. Depending on how well the transition from founder to second generation or second generation to third may proceed, these events also provide lessons for the wary FOB owner. When considering that 90 percent of all companies in the Kingdom are FOBs, this has serious consequences for the future prosperity and health of such firms in Saudi Arabia.

The subject of corporate succession has been studied and written about extensively around the world. There are industry organizations, global study groups, private sector associations, and whole sections within universities dedicated to the study of family-owned businesses, and in particular, the succession of generational owners into corporate management authority. One of the most interesting studies done on Saudi FOBs has been the study "Family Businesses and Succession in Saudi Arabian Culture and

Traditions" by Abdulrahman Dahlan, MSA, and Dr. Leslie Klieb, published by the publication *Business Leadership Review.*[18]

The Dahlan-Klieb study provided a framework for examining Saudi FOBs in the context of their surrounding culture and traditions. They studied six factors of culture and traditions influencing the "sustainability and performance" of Saudi FOBs: "cultural attributes, family goals and values, founder's personality attributes, theory of planned behavior and the founder, successor attributes, and religious and legal attributes."[19] An impressive undertaking, the study managed to examine a variety of influence factors on FOBs in the Kingdom with a high degree of thoroughness and insight. In discussing the core nature of the Saudi FOB, Mr. Dahlan and Dr. Klieb state:

> *In many SA [Saudi Arabian] family businesses, relationship is a principal factor determining management succession. The institutional values of family firms in general are determined by the family. When key managers are from the same family, their traditions, values, and both verbal and non-verbal communications are established from a common source. Family relationships among the owners and key employees impact the business as a whole. The entire family is affected by what happens in the business, and vice versa. The business system is mostly impersonal with profit maximization as the primary driving force, while the family system is mostly personal with maintaining harmony and good family relationships as fundamental goals. Striking a balance between the objectives of family and business systems is key to the success of family businesses.*[20]

The Dahlan-Klieb study centered its examination on the nature of an FOB and how its operations are either "family" or "business" focused. The study sought to show how the "family" or "business" nature of an FOB influences its succession. Of course, as the study points out, it has been surmised that most Saudi FOBs experience difficulties in resolving internal issues. Founding members of most of today's largest FOBs are shrewd, astute, and business savvy enough to have not only considered corporate succession planning at length, but have acted on their concerns on the subject in consultation with their lawyers. Although not pervasive, many Saudi corporate leaders run global conglomerates with disparate interests in many world markets, so it stands to reason that the most capable among this commercial class would not leave a matter as important as the survivability of their firms to chance. Nevertheless, it is widely thought that widespread acceptance of the need for careful succession planning among the vast majority of Saudi FOBs has yet to be realized.

As the Kahlan-Klieb study suggests, an FOB's successful handling of internal disputes or generational succession often depends on whether its natural "default mode" is a "business" or "family" model. The drive toward "profit maximization" in a "business-natured" FOB may influence first-generation owners or FOB founders to more amicably face succession issues with one or two second-generation family members. When there are disputes containing the potent mixture of the competing personalities of family members and their emotional and financial interests with those pure business interests of the firm, however, you can end up with a lethal concoction that may sound the death knell of the company. This may be particularly true for companies that are trading companies or "establishments." Such entities are essentially similar to sole proprietorships in common law jurisdictions. In regard to which family members take possession of family business assets or assume management control when multiple family members are involved, the absence of a succession plan can translate into uncertainty over an extended transition period. Such situations have resulted in operational paralysis for some companies and have had long-term deleterious effects for the survivability of those businesses.

For many of the Kingdom's well-established FOBs, the strong personalities of their founders have been the defining features of the stamina and growth of those firms. The imprints of their personalities and character speak volumes as to how they have managed to surmount untold challenges to their development and very existence. For those that have passed and whose generational family members have assumed ownership and management of their businesses, the influence of these leaders can still be felt. Besides the durable personalities of these business owners, another distinguishing feature of the Saudi FOB is the fact that their owners often die while still firmly at the helm of their companies. It is not uncommon in Saudi Arabia to see an original founding member of an FOB and his siblings or other family members, well into the eighth decade of living, running day-to-day operations despite the obvious advancement of old age. It is well-known in Saudi Arabia, and is often the subject of humor, that second- or third-generation members of Saudi FOBs who work within the family business for many years patiently waiting for their opportunity to take over and run the company watch the months on the calendar roll off without ever seeing their day of ascension arrive.

When the death of a founder of a Saudi FOB that is a joint venture partner with a foreign firm occurs, there are a number of issues and potential consequences befalling the joint venture, which should be considered.

An instructive piece prepared by the law firm of Crowell and Moring, and authorized for reprint in this book, examines these considerations in the box that follows:

JOINT VENTURES AND THE DEATH OF THE SAUDI PRINCIPAL

There are sound business reasons, and sometimes valid legal reasons, for foreign businesses that want to carry out business in Saudi Arabia to do so through a Saudi legal entity established in cooperation with a Saudi partner (a JV). But what happens when an individual Saudi joint venture partner (the SJVP), or the principal of a corporate SJVP, dies? What are the consequences for the JV and for the foreign joint venture partner (the FJVP) and how might such consequences be mitigated?

1. ASSUMPTIONS

This note assumes that:

(a) The JV will be established as a Saudi limited liability company (an LLC). Depending on the type of activity that the JV will undertake, Saudi law might mandate a specific form for the JV: Saudi banks and insurance companies, for example, must be established as joint stock companies.[21] However, beyond those limited instances where Saudi law mandates the form of the JV, the LLC is the quickest and cheapest—and therefore the most popular—form for a JV between a foreign entity and a Saudi partner; and

(b) The SJVP is not a public joint stock company whose shares are traded on the Saudi Arabian Stock Exchange. The corporate governance rules applicable to public joint stock companies are such that the death of a founder or other principal of the public joint stock company is unlikely to prejudice the management continuity of the company.

2. A NATURAL PERSON

Where the SJVP is a natural person,[22] then upon the death of the SJVP, the ownership of the SJVP's shares in the JV will be transferred[23–25] to the SJVP's heir(s)[26] in accordance with the terms of Islamic law as enforced in Saudi Arabia. It is important to note that the distribution of a Saudi national's estate in Saudi Arabia must be undertaken in compliance with Islamic law as enforced in Saudi Arabia; a Saudi national cannot—by a will or other document—exercise any control over the distribution of his estate after his death. As a result, neither the SJVP, the FJVP, nor the JV itself can influence who shall inherit the SJVP's shares in the JV after the death of the SJVP.

Although there is no scope to influence who shall inherit the SJVP's shares in the JV after the death of the SJVP, there are steps that can be taken by the FJVP when the JV is incorporated in order to mitigate the consequences to the JV and the FJVP of the death of the SJVP.

(a) Management Control

The companies' regulations[27] do not mandate any particular management structure for an LLC. Accordingly, the shareholders in an LLC enjoy wide latitude to structure the management of the LLC as they see fit. In this context, where a FJVP wishes to mitigate the consequences to the JV and itself of the death of the SJVP, the FJVP should take care to structure the management of the JV so as to ensure that it—the FJVP—controls the management of the JV.

Ensuring the control of the JV's management by the FJVP can be achieved in a number of ways, depending on how the JV's management is structured:

(i) If the JV is to be managed by a board of managers, the membership of the board can be structured to ensure that the FJVP appoints a sufficient majority of the board members to ensure that such members will carry any vote;

(ii) If the JV is to be managed by a single general manager, that manager can be appointed in all circumstances by the FJVP; and

(iii) If the JV is to be managed by a combination of a board of managers and a general manager, both approaches (i) and (ii) can be adopted.

The management of the JV must be structured when the JV is incorporated, although it can be amended subsequently with the unanimous approval of the JV's shareholders.[28]

(b) Majority Shareholding

The companies' regulations mandate that certain activities can only be undertaken by an LLC with the approval of a majority, supermajority, or all of the LLC's shareholders. For example:

(i) An ordinary resolution of the LLC's general meeting of shareholders can be adopted by shareholders representing at least

50 percent of the LLC's capital or such higher percentage as the LLC's articles of association may specify;[29]

(ii) A resolution of the LLC's general meeting of shareholders to amend the LLC's articles of association can be adopted by shareholders representing at least 75 percent of the LLC's capital or such higher percentage as the LLC's articles of association may specify;[30] and

(iii) A resolution of the LLC's general meeting of shareholders to change the nationality of the LLC or to increase the shareholders' financial liability must be adopted by all of the LLC's shareholders.[31]

In this context, an FJVP that holds more than 50 percent of the capital of the LLC (or such other minimum as is required by the JV's articles of association) can control most internal matters of the JV (e.g., the approval of the JV's annual balance sheet, profit-and-loss statement, management report, and the declaration of dividends) through its majority shareholding.

The amendment of the JV's articles of association can, in practice, never be controlled by a single shareholder regardless of the size of its majority shareholding. Although the companies' regulations state that shareholders representing at least 75 percent of an LLC's capital can approve an amendment to the LLC's articles of association, in practice the shareholders' resolution to amend the LLC's articles of association must (among other things) be:

(iv) Approved by the Ministry of Commerce and Industry; and

(v) Notarized by a notary public in Saudi Arabia.

As the notary will not notarize the shareholders' resolution amending the LLC's articles of association unless representatives of all of the LLC's shareholders appear before the notary to sign the shareholders' resolution, amending an LLC's articles of association in practice requires the active cooperation of all of the LLC's shareholders.

(c) Multiple Shareholders

The companies' regulations require an LLC to have at least two shareholders at all times.[32] In this context, an FJVP should consider dividing its investment into the JV between two separate shareholders, such as (for example) a foreign business and the foreign business's affiliate or subsidiary. Such an approach would (assuming a willing seller) permit the FJVP to purchase—through its two shareholders in the JV—the shares in the JV of the SJVP subsequent to the SJVP's death.

3. A BUSINESS ENTITY

Where the SJVP is a business entity, the death of a principal of such business entity can again have implications for the SJVP and for the JV.

Much depends on the type of business organization of the SJVP. If the SJVP is a business entity with an existence separate and distinct from its shareholders (a corporate entity) (e.g., an LLC or a joint stock company), then the death of the principal of the SJVP will likely have no direct legal impact on the JV itself because there is no change in the JV's shareholders. Alternatively, if the SJVP is a form of business entity that can dissolve upon the death of one of its principals (a partnership) (e.g., a general partnership[33] or a partnership limited by shares[34]), then the death of a principal of the SJVP can result in a change in the JV's shareholders.

Fortunately, there are measures that an FJVP can take when the JV is incorporated in order to mitigate the consequences for the JV and the FJVP of the death of the principal of the SJVP.

(a) Management Control and Majority Shareholding

As with the situation where the SJVP is a natural person, maintaining management control of, and a majority shareholding in, the JV will help the FJVP mitigate the effects of the death of the principal of the SJVP where the SJVP is a business entity.

(b) Multiple Shareholders

Again, as with the situation where the SJVP is a natural person, making its investment in the JV through two or more entities will help the FJVP and the JV survive the death of the principal of the SJVP.

(i) Existence Separate and Distinct from Its Shareholders

Where the SJVP is a corporate entity, distributing the FJVP's investment in the JV amongst two or more shareholders controlled by the FJVP will (assuming a willing seller) allow the FJVP to purchase the SJVP's shares in the JV if the death of the SJVP's principal results in a change of management in the SJVP that is not acceptable to the FJVP.

(ii) Dissolution Upon the Death of One of Its Principals

Where a JV has a single FJVP and a single SJVP and the SJVP is a partnership, then if the SJVP is dissolved upon the death of one of its principals, the investment by the FJVP in the JV through two or more shareholders controlled by the FJVP should enable the FJVP—acting through its two share-holders in the JV—to exercise a pre-emptive right to compel its purchase of all of the SJVP's shares in the JV pursuant to Article 165 of the companies' regulations.

(c) The Joint Venture Agreement

Where the SJVP or a principal of the SJVP is an important consideration for the FJVP in entering into the JV with the SJVP, the shareholders in the JV can agree in the joint venture agreement to dissolve the JV in the event of a change of control in any share-holder. As a mere contract, the joint venture agreement can only be enforced through the courts or arbitration. However, if properly structured, a contractual provision calling for the dissolution of the JV upon a change in control of the SJVP should be enforceable.

Shareholders might be tempted to provide in the joint venture agreement that a change in control of any shareholder would give the remaining shareholder(s) or its/their nominee the right (but not the obligation) to purchase all of the shares in the JV owned by the shareholder that has experienced the change of control. However, such a provision would almost certainly be unenforceable in Saudi Arabia as most types of options—including call options—are unenforceable under Islamic law as enforced in Saudi Arabia.

4. CONCLUSION

For foreign businesses thinking of establishing a JV in Saudi Arabia with a SJVP, the good news is that many Saudi businesses—particularly member companies of large, family-owned conglomerates—have typi-cally structured their affairs in advance of the principal's death in order to mitigate the implications for the business of the principal's death. But not all Saudi businesses are so proactive and, depending on the nature of SJVP (e.g., a natural person or corporate entity), the option to act in anticipation of the principal's death might not be available.

Accordingly, when a foreign business is considering entering into a JV with a potential SJVP, inquiries into the implications of the death of the potential SJVP, or a principal of the potential SJVP, should form part of the due diligence review of the potential SJVP and should con-sider (among other things) the business form of the SJVP:

(a) If the SJVP is a corporate entity, then the death of the SJVP's principal will not definitely lead to a change in the shareholding in the JV;

(b) If the SJVP is a partnership and the death of a principal of the SJVP leads to the dissolution of the SJVP, then the death of a principal of the SJVP will definitely lead to a change in the shareholding in the JV but (if the necessary measures have been taken by the FJVP in advance) might give the FJVP the opportunity to compel its purchase of all of the partnership's shares in the JV; and

(c) If the SJVP is a natural person, then the death of the SJVP will definitely lead to a change in the shareholding in the JV that the FJVP cannot control or influence.

Once the due diligence review of the potential SJVP is completed and the risks associated with the death of the SJVP or a principal of the SJVP have been assessed, the FJVP can decide whether it would be in its interests to mitigate such risks by maintaining management control of the JV, maintaining a majority shareholding in the JV, investing in the JV through more than one shareholder, including appropriate provisions in the joint venture agreement, and/or other measures.

The death of a SJVP or a principal of a SJVP can have implications for the FJVP and the JV. But the extent of those implications will vary with the form of business organization of the SJVP and the steps taken in advance of such death to mitigate the implications of the death of a SJVP or a principal of a SJVP.

Although formal succession planning has only recently been adopted as a required part of corporate operations within Saudi FOBs, the method of integrating new family members into the business has been well-established in most businesses. From the early days of the Kingdom's well-established FOBs, founding owners would send their sons, brothers, and nephews off to work in various parts of an FOB conglomerate. The relocation of young family members to FOB overseas subsidiaries, offices of foreign partners, and other extraterritorial locations was intended to give the young aspirant as much exposure to real-world operational and management experiences as possible. The grooming of next generation FOB owners and managers is a task that has always been tended to as much out of fulfillment of family obligations as it has been out of good management practices. And, for some FOBs, the task of selecting family members for placement within the firm's operations can be a daunting task.

It has been the integration of the next generation of Saudi FOB members to the businesses of the Kingdom that has given new vitality and direction to these decades-old firms. Some of these young mavericks have contributed to new directions for Saudi FOBs and in some instances changed the core businesses of these companies. They are also influencing the embrace of best practices in corporate governance with their family's businesses.

MANAGEMENT OF STRATEGIC FOCUS AND THE IMPORTANCE OF CORPORATE GOVERNANCE

Saudi FOBs have come a very long way since the 1930s, 1940s, and 1950s, when many of Saudi Arabia's well-established firms were created. There have always been pronounced distinctions between Saudi FOBs that have been predominantly trading establishments and those that have early on developed into industrial production, construction, and development companies. A significant number of Saudi FOBs that originally began as agents representing foreign manufacturers of goods sold in the Kingdom have evolved to integrate some areas of their business to exploit the rapid and diverse changes in the Saudi industrial landscape.

Some Saudi FOBs were service contractor start-ups in the 1950s and 1960s working for Saudi Aramco, but later diversified into other businesses not directly tied to the nation's oil and gas industry. Well-established and easily recognizable Saudi FOBs achieved their starts through the provisioning of goods and services to Saudi Aramco. Sheikh Ali Tamimi founded his company in 1953 supplying parts to Saudi Aramco. Today, it is a global company known as the Tamimi Group (a member of the USSABC), and engaged in a diverse range of activities such as food, construction, manufacturing, tourism, intermodal transport, and information technology. The Tamimi Group has foreign joint venture partners and agency relationships with such companies as GE, Safeway, Firestone, Halliburton, and Red Wing. Previously mentioned Ahmad Al Gosaibi had its start supplying goods and services to Saudi Aramco.

Other well-known enterprises counted among the Kingdom's original start-ups were those formed by Sheikh Sulaiman Olayan and Khalid Ali Al-Turki. Sheikh Sulaiman Olayan, orphaned in childhood, leveraged his early adulthood experience of working in various positions with CASCO, the precursor of Saudi Aramco, into what is today among Saudi Arabia's most internationally invested and diversified companies. The Olayan Group (a member of the USSABC) has a dazzling array of stellar joint venture partners such as HSBC, JPMorgan, Chase Manhattan, Coca-Cola, Colgate-Palmolive, Credit Suisse, Kraft Foods, Kimberly-Clark, Xerox, and Toshiba, to mention only a few of them.

Sheikh Khalid Ali Alturki, another eminent progenitor of Saudi start-ups who ascended the ranks of current-day Saudi corporate elites through original work done for CASCO, now sits atop a global company with a diversity of businesses owned and managed by Khalid Ali Alturki and Sons (Alturki). Alturki is a leading investment and development company that has been operating in Saudi Arabia since 1975. Its subsidiaries and joint venture companies are focused on construction and infrastructure, building materials, real estate, oil field services and renewable energy, information and communication technologies, and general industrial sectors in Saudi Arabia and neighboring Arab countries. Companies like Alturki have installed good corporate governance practices. Second-generation leadership by family members engaged in Saudi FOBs such as Alturki have been change agents for accelerating the adoption of progressive corporate governance in established and new companies within the Kingdom. Rami Alturki, president of Alturki and the son of Sheikh Khalid Ali Alturki, is an example of one of these change agents and is making a positive difference in his own family's business as well as influencing other Saudi firms. Rami's thoughts on Saudi FOBs and SMEs in Saudi Arabia appear later in this book.

As mentioned earlier, in those days, the idea of having major decisions such as opening new areas of business, disposition or acquisition of significant corporate assets, or changing the structure of the firm taken by a board composed of non-family members was an alien concept. With the complexities of today's Saudi FOB and the myriad challenges faced by these firms, corporate governance is increasingly viewed as the best way to bring regularity and conformance of a firm's management, activities, and investment decisions with globally accepted business practices.

The financial growth of family companies managed by first-generation founders and owners was in many instances self-funded. The accumulated wealth of these businesses was reinvested to sustain the growth of their companies and to meet the challenges of an ever-evolving domestic market in the 1960s, 1970s, and 1980s. As the industrial expansion priorities of the Kingdom created ever-larger projects, with mega-projects in the country becoming more commonplace, securing the capital needed by Saudi FOBs to pursue these large contracts, bid successfully, and ultimately execute them efficiently was of paramount importance. By the 1980s, the demand for more and more growth and operational capital by the Kingdom's largest and industrially engaged Saudi FOBs began to outgrow their own internal finance capabilities. Greater access to commercial bank and public funding was sought.

By the 1980s, there were 12 private commercial banks operating in the Kingdom. Most of these banks were owned by Saudi investors with a portion of public-sector ownership. For example, National Commercial Bank (NCB), also known as Al-Ahli bank (Arabic: البنك الأهلي التجاري), the first Saudi bank to be chartered by royal decree, in December 1953, is the largest bank in the Kingdom and the biggest bank in the Arab world by assets.

In 1999, the Saudi ministry of finance's public investment fund (PIF) became the bank's majority shareholder, greatly expanding its lending capabilities and investment banking through its subsidiary, NCB Capital (US$12 billion in assets under management (AUM)). NCB went public in October 2014 and within 15 days of its debut on the Tadawul, 1.16 million investors were reported to have bought shares of the partially privatized bank, totaling a record value of US$59 billion.[35]

Banks such as NCB have led the way to unprecedented bank lending to the Saudi private sector. Bank lending for megaprojects have been beyond the capacity of Saudi private banks. Saudi public-sector lending institutions such as the PIF have provided added lending volume to satisfy the demand for capital project financing. In terms of private bank financing to the Saudi private sector, however, it has historically been the Saudi private bank sector that the Kingdom's FOBs have relied upon most to fill its funding need for growth. It has been the private banking community's historical willingness to lend to these companies based on their family names and stature within the close-knit national business community that has driven FOB growth financing. In fact, it is has been generally accepted that the tight lending practices of Saudi banks, with the exception of loans to the largest of Saudi FOBs engaged in government-funded projects, caused consternation among smaller Saudi businesses and some government officials.[36]

With the Al Gosaibi debacle of 2009–2010 and the public spectacle made of easy lending practices gone awry, the light shed on corporate governance and transparency within the Saudi business community was never brighter. As foreign banks have become more numerous in the Kingdom, the capital they have to lend Saudi enterprises usually comes with the kind of scrutiny into a borrower's corporate affairs to a degree that most Saudi companies are unaccustomed. Of the 23 institutions that are licensed to carry out banking operations in the Kingdom, 12 are classified as Saudi institutions, while the remainder are branches of foreign banks.

These notes on corporate governance in the Saudi context of the financial strategic direction and growth of FOBs is indicative of the type of modern challenges facing Saudi FOBs as they seek to advance the pecuniary interests of their enterprises. As the Saudi corporate community pursues closer proximity and access to global funding sources, the struggle between observing deeply engrained cultural mores in running one's business and rendering the kind of full disclosure required by international commercial and investment banks have caused weaknesses in corporate governance practices in the Kingdom to visibly surface. In many ways, the strident outside calls for increased corporate transparency and the cultural rules enforcing privacy in business and social matters have always been viewed as conceptually inimical by many Saudi business people.

Despite the historical predisposition of Saudi FOBs against a robust disclosure of sensitive management and financial information about their companies, many are embracing accepted standards of good corporate governance. A growing number of Saudi companies are realizing the advantage of creating established principles of corporate governance that aids the business in conducting its affairs more efficiently, responsibly, and ultimately, more profitably. The added advantage of adopting internationally accepted principles of governance positions the enterprise well in accessing external funding sources from internationally accredited investors.

However, the adoption of globally accepted standards of corporate governance in Saudi Arabia, or in non-Western countries for that matter, has proven to be problematic because of the historical and cultural differences in how enterprises have been managed and operated around the world. For this reason, simple definitions of minimally acceptable corporate governance standards, as the one offered by the Organisation for Economic Co-operation and Development (OECD) are not wholly instructive in the Saudi context. The OECD defines corporate governance as:

> *Procedures and processes according to which an organization is directed and controlled. The corporate governance structure specifies the distribution of rights and responsibilities among the different participants in the organization such as the board, managers, shareholders, and other stakeholders—and lays down the rules and procedures for decision-making.*[37]

Therefore, acceptable definitions of corporate governance as a starting point for most Saudi businesses beginning to contemplate establishing standards will vary, depending on the unique ownership, managerial, and core businesses of the enterprise. One definition of corporate governance quoted with no small amount of credibility is one posited by Sir Adrian Cadbury, chair of the corporate governance committee. One of the greatest impetuses in the creation of this committee, which was constituted in May 1991 by the Financial Reporting Council, the London Stock Exchange, and the accountancy profession in the United Kingdom, was the global financial contagion to the banking community following the 1991 seizure and liquidation of the Bank of Credit and Commerce International (BCCI). This was a financial debacle of global proportions and threatened a huge swath of the world's banking community. In its 1992 report, the Cadbury Committee generally defined "corporate governance" as:

> *Corporate governance is the system by which companies are directed and controlled. Boards of directors are responsible for the governance of their companies. The shareholders' role in governance is to*

appoint the directors and the auditors and to satisfy themselves that an appropriate governance structure is in place. The responsibilities of the board include setting the company's strategic aims, providing the leadership to put them into effect, supervising the management of the business and reporting to shareholders on their stewardship. The board's actions are subject to laws, regulations, and the shareholders in general meeting.[38]

This definition focuses on the operational dynamics of all involved with running the corporation. Other definitions address the mechanics of governance from a regulatory perspective. In particular, some definitions of corporate governance deal directly with the duties, obligations, and expectations of owners and management in regard to the financial aspects of running a business. Actionaries, that is to say, stakeholders in joint stock companies, are recognized under most definitions as owing fiduciary duties to ensure adherence to operational procedures that satisfy the need for openness, transparency, and accuracy in financial reporting as well as disclosure to governmental regulatory authorities required of the jurisdictions within which they operate. As more and more Saudi businesses seek international investor funding, creating good corporate governance structures within their companies is increasingly becoming a competitive imperative for those firms seeking to remain relevant in the global economy.

An often-quoted pair of authorities on corporate governance, renowned economists and academicians, Andrei Shleifer and Robert Vishny, in their 1997 publication "A Survey of Corporate Governance," defined corporate governance as dealing with: "...the ways in which suppliers of finance to corporations assure themselves of getting a return on their investment."[39] The authors further stated: "Most advanced market economies have solved the problem of corporate governance at least reasonably well, in that they have assured the inflows of enormous amounts of capital to firms, and actual repatriation of profits to the providers of finance."[40]

Most of the hundreds of joint ventures between Saudi and American firms operating in Saudi Arabia are composed of U.S. partner corporations containing top management structures controlled by well-entrenched corporate governance bureaucracies that act as bulwarks in protecting these entities against both external and internal threats. More importantly, at least from the U.S. partner side, their established and well-articulated corporate governance practices provide public and private funding sources relatively clear views of their current financial positions and reasonable assurances of returns on capital by way of full financial disclosure. The corporate governance area, and in particular how those practices in the Kingdom are developing, is a subject wherein U.S. and Western firms are having a significant impact. Most Saudi companies have yet to adopt a full range of corporate governance principles that would replicate those found among the foreign joint venture partners with whom they are invested.

The differences in corporate governance principles adopted by Saudi FOBs and well-established corporations from advanced economies may be viewed as a consequence of the differences in their development culturally within their respective countries. For U.S. companies, particularly those whose shares are publicly traded, transparency and financial disclosure are legally mandated and governmentally regulated. For Saudi FOBs, SMEs, or other Saudi corporate entities, there is a tension between meeting the calls for strong corporate governance principles by Western joint venture entities and the need to follow cultural, social, and family accepted norms of conducting business.

The Capital Markets Authority (CMA) of the Kingdom of Saudi Arabia, the nation's regulator and developer of its capital market, was established on July 31, 2003, by royal decree No. (M/30). It is the government agency that regulates and monitors the issuance of securities and is charged with fostering a transparent and trusted investment environment. Those Saudi businesses that become public companies on the "Tadawul," the Kingdom's exchange for trading, clearing, and settling transacted securities, are required to follow increasingly strict regulations concerning how public companies adhere to corporate governance practices.

The Tadawul went into operation in October 2001. On November 12, 2006, the CMA issued regulations governing the corporate governance of Saudi public companies.[41] These regulations, and subsequent amendments aimed at strengthening this law, have brought well-accepted seriousness to the Kingdom's efforts to protect the investing public, resonate its message of transparency to global investors, and follow through with its intentions to improve its competitive position among the world's capital market venues.

In a February 2009 appraisal of Saudi Arabia's financial market regulatory environment, the World Bank praised the Kingdom for improvements it made to the regulatory regime of its securities market. In benchmarking CMA corporate governance regulations against those of OECD nations, the World Bank stated: "The corporate governance laws, regulations, and institutions that have been put in place generally reflect international good practice."[42] The institution also noted some concerns, however. In the "Principle Review of Corporate Governance" section, the World Bank stated:

The operation of the capital market is moderately transparent. Information is generally available about listed companies, and the Tadawul website aggregates listed companies by industry and discloses monthly, quarterly, and annual financial information.

There are factors which potentially undermine the transparency and efficiency of the KSA market, notably: (1) insufficient disclosure of non-financial information (especially on beneficial ownership); (2) an absence of foreign competition (foreign companies are not allowed to access the Tadawul); and (3) improper conduct and abuse of position by brokers and industry insiders. There is nascent support for developing corporate governance disclosure requirements, which are viewed as an important step to develop a more reliable and transparent capital market.[43]

In demonstrating how important good corporate governance practices are to a nation's ability to attract foreign investors, the World Bank went on to recommend further strengthening in specific areas: "Particular areas of emphasis are the disclosure of ownership information and other non-financial disclosure."[44] The need to secure capital for industrial expansion or technological upgrades by Saudi FOBs through partnerships with foreign firms is often tempered by the reality of having to reveal more of their inner workings and the disclosure of detailed financial information. A preferred method of ensuring a foreign partner's interest in a joint venture's strategic direction and preservation of its invested capital is securing seats on the board of directors of the enterprise.

The appointment of external board directors is still uncommon among the core family operating companies of the largest and best-known Saudi FOBs. Although having foreign executives serve on the board of a Saudi FOB is still rare in the Kingdom, registered joint ventures formed between Saudi and American firms often have external board members. External board directors afford a measure of control to foreign entities doing business with Saudi entities in the Kingdom. However, as mentioned earlier under the Crowell and Moring section on corporate succession, steering decisions by diverse boards toward the foreign JV partner's interests may prove problematic when those decision concern the disposition of JV assets.

Proper due diligence on prospective Saudi partners and the fullest view of their ownership, managerial, and financial health is absolutely essential to American companies considering alliances in the Kingdom. But, it is not only Western industry partners that constitute sources of additional expansion capital and management expertise. Saudi companies are turning to other suppliers of investment capital such as investment banks and private equity to serve their plans for growth. These establishments, however, require the same level of corporate governance from target Saudi firms that would provide them reasonable assurances of returns on their investments. There are growing numbers of Saudi FOBs cognizant of the need to bolster their corporate governance bona fides.

In its November 2014 report on the potential of private equity to aid Saudi FOBs and their pursuit for expansion capital, "Saudi Arabia— A Promising Proposition for Private Equity," Alkhabeer Capital, a leading investment and asset management firm in the Kingdom of Saudi Arabia, stated in its report:

Lack of a transparent and reliable legal framework remains an obstacle to the development of the private equity market. Firstly, finding a deal in Saudi Arabia is a difficult task in itself given the poor track record of firms in matters relating to corporate governance. Difficulty in obtaining accurate financial information of companies has often been cited as a key problem faced by potential buyers in the region. Moreover, the influence of family owned businesses usually hinders the process of corporate disclosures, limiting transparency.[45]

Abdulla M. Al-Zamil, chief executive officer of Zamil Industrial Investment Company, and a member of the board of directors of Gulf International Bank, was quoted in the *Saudi Gazette* as recognizing the change in Saudi corporate mentality concerning corporate governance: "Conference and forum, such as this corporate governance in family business forum, is important. It is telling owners of family businesses that it is in their interest to embrace good corporate governance as the way to conduct business."[46]

As Saudi Arabia's FOBs have improved how they run their businesses, they have also grown in the diversity of those businesses. There are hundreds of large family-owned businesses in the Kingdom. There have been several attempts to rank these companies with regard to assets. As discussed, however, due to the lack of transparency, which is so culturally ingrained in the Arab business world as well as in Saudi Arabia, such rankings only afford a slightly luminescent view as to Saudi FOBs' financial stature. It is a widely observed maxim in the business world that good corporate breeding compels one to refrain from inquiring into or discussing one's net worth or company valuations ... that is, of course, unless you happen to be into well-advanced deal terms. There is nowhere in the business world this is more embraced with relish than business in Saudi Arabia. So, as mentioned earlier, I did not select the following three family-owned businesses because they hover at the top of the listings of the largest family-owned businesses in the Kingdom, although all three have been found on several rankings that have been compiled.

To be sure, in today's Saudi business world, your financial strength and size still account for much when you are an owner of a large Saudi FOB and find yourself among one's peers in business or social settings. The measure of the worth of a Saudi FOB today, however, may also be measured by the social and national activities engaged in by its owners and how much they serve the national interests of the Kingdom. By any measure, the founders and following generational leaders of the Al-Jeraisy, Al-Quraishi and Al-Zamil family businesses should be viewed as high contributors in this regard.

ILLUSTRATIONS OF SAUDI FAMILY-OWNED BUSINESSES

The Jeraisy Group

The Jeraisy Group is one of Saudi Arabia's major companies. As we learned earlier, Sheikh Abdulrahman Al-Jeraisy began his journey into Riyadh as a boy. Referring to the Jeraisy family business in Riyadh as one of the Kingdom's first start-ups is no attempt at hyperbole. From the small village of Raghbah, the young Abdulrahman received all the love and care a young boy needed to grasp new horizons in his life from his grandmother. Once in Riyadh, he attended the first public school in the city. After classes, the young boy gained much experience in his job working in his uncle Mohammad's shop doing what helpmates do when so young and inexperienced. The dreams that fueled Abdulrahman's journey beyond Ragbah helped him witness one of his first personal successes when the retail store in which he worked made him a manager. This was just the first stop on the road to a long and tested career in business.

As he transitioned into young adulthood at the age of 17, Sheikh Abdulrahman held on to the dreams of his boyhood and acquired new ones when he started his own independent business. As occurs with many start-ups, then and now, his new business failed within the first six months of operation. That failure, however, did not deter Sheikh Abdulrahman. Soon after that failure, having garnered many hard lessons in the ways to run a business and the ways not to, in 1958 he and a partner established the Riyadh House Establishment (RHE). The Riyadh House Establishment began as a small company selling office furniture and equipment. As with many small businesses after creation, the firm lost money for a time. Through deft management and hard work, however, the establishment shifted to profitability and began to expand. Sheikh Abdulrahman decided to carry the business forward as a sole proprietorship and purchased the interests in the business from his partner. He became the sole owner of the business and the company gradually began to grow and diversify its product and service offerings. As the development of RHE unfolded, it acquired the rights of representing an ever-expanding list of foreign manufacturers of equipment and products that it sold in the Saudi market.

Sheikh Abdulrahman's business has grown into a multi national corporate group of companies. His RHE has changed with the times and commercial landscape of Saudi Arabia. The opportunities in the myriad industry sectors in the Kingdom have undergone many alterations through the decades, but RHE has kept pace. Eventually, to serve the needs of corporate organizational management of the sheikh's businesses, the creation of various subsidiaries was necessary to handle the growing and disparate sectors RHE served. The information technology (IT) area is a prime example for RHE.

When computer technology first began to find interest in Saudi Arabia in the 1970s, Sheikh Abdulrahman embraced the challenge of becoming the first business to lead its commercial introduction to the country. The intention to commercially succeed in the mass introduction of the best of such technologies to the country was coupled with his intense commitment to be most skilled at offering the new tools through after-sales service and a mastery of the technologies by his workforce. Following swiftly his mass commercial introduction of computer technology into the Kingdom, his business successfully managed to collect and offer the most inviting array of products and equipment the Kingdom had seen at that time. The rise in this particular business, owing much to the ferocious domestic demand for the technology, led to the decision to create a subsidiary to manage its growth and operations. Out of RHE, the Jeraisy Computer and Communication Services Company (JCCS) was established in the early 1970s. Today, JCCS is the leading corporation in the Kingdom offering computer, software, and communications products and services and related technologies. JCCS supplies the public and private sector with state-of-the-art technologies, which, in turn, greatly facilitates the efficiencies and expansion of the Kingdom's business and economic development.

The expansions of RHE over the last five decades within various industries and the consequential creation of separate business units eventually led Sheikh Abdulrahman to create a holding company to manage his increasingly disparate interests. The Jeraisy Group Company is a closed joint-stock holding company, owned by Sheikh Abdulrahman, that controls 10 companies. These 10 companies have agency and distribution arrangements with some of the world's largest and best-known global companies in the areas of office automation, equipment and furniture, IT, technical skills training, electronics, paper, and a host of other industries. The 10 companies of the Jeraisy Group are: Riyadh House Company (RHC); Jeraisy Computer and Communications Services Company (JCCS); Jeraisy Internet Services Company (LTD); Electronic Services Center; Al-Areeba for Ladies Skills Center; Jeraisy Computer Paper Products Company; Jeraisy Group Card Tech Factory; Jeraisy Furniture Factory (JFF); Steelcase Jeraisy Ltd; and Al-Jeraisy Group.

It is somewhat axiomatic to suggest that every founder of a family-owned business imparts his or her own belief systems, convictions, and aspirations in an immersive process that may last the life of the business. Although as successive generations become involved in the FOB and they certainly press their own imprint on the business, the lasting philosophy of founders in their core approach to business is rarely disturbed. This is the case with Sheikh Abdulrahman and the Jeraisy Group. The hallmark of the Al-Jeraisy FOB has always been the importance Sheikh Abdulrahman, as its patriarch, has attached to one's faithfulness and service to Allah, one's family, and the Kingdom of Saudi Arabia and its citizenry.

Visiting Sheikh Abdulrahman's offices in Riyadh was always something I looked forward to when I met with him in my capacity as the American embassy's commercial attaché during my time in diplomatic service in Riyadh. In addition to his other businesses, Sheikh Abdulrahman also produces delicious dates, which he always has in delectable supply for guests visiting him. One has only to visit the sheikh's office in Riyadh to view the many plaques and awards that line its interior memorializing the many contributions and benefactions his service to the family businesses, various Saudi business communities, individual Saudi citizens, and the Saudi nation has produced.

For many years, Sheikh Abdulrahman served as the chairman of the Riyadh Chamber of Commerce and Industry (RCCI) and chairman of the Council of Saudi Chambers of Commerce and Industry (CSCCI). His contributions to the business communities of Riyadh and those of the Kingdom's during his years as chairman of the RCCI and CSCCI are well known. Over his years of service as the head of the Al-Jeraisy FOB and during his leadership at the RCCI and CSCCI, there have been many causes for which Sheikh Abdulrahman has given his fervent attention and care that are critically important to Saudi Arabia. There have been innumerable conferences, special committees, roundtable discussions, ceremonies for awards and recognition, and his personal engagement with groups and individuals aimed at the advancement of the interests of SMEs, women-owned businesses, Saudi FOBs, and the Kingdom's most important trade and investment relationships that have occurred under his tutelage. Sheikh Abdulrahman has also viewed his commitment to charitable organizations as inseparable from his obligations to the Kingdom's business communities.

Among Sheikh Abdulrahman Al-Jeraisy's charitable affiliations, positions held include service as the chairman of the Ragbah Charity Society; member of the High Consultative Commission of Prince Sultan Bin Abdul Aziz Al Saud Charity Foundation; member of the Riyadh Philanthropic

Foundation for Sciences and of its founding committee; board trustee of Prince Sultan Bin Abdul Aziz Private University; board of trustees of King Abdulaziz and His Companions Foundation for the Gifted; board trustee of Bin BAZ Charity Foundation; board director for ALBER Charity Foundation; and board director and executive committee member of the Philanthropic for Youth Marriage Support.

Identifying the two most important lessons he learned during his journey in starting and running his businesses, Sheikh Abdulrahman Al-Jeraisy has said:

> *As time passed by, my dream started to turn into a reality formulating in front of my eyes. Since then, I have learned my first lesson: 'Nothing is impossible for the will of God' with good intentions, hard work, and persistence. As a young businessman, my plans faced many obstacles. While I was busy trying to solve them, I discovered that most of these were either caused by me or my colleagues. So, I learned the second lesson: 'It is crucial to have proper studies and planning before going into implementation.'*[47]

The Jeraisy Group is still run by Sheikh Abdulrahman, and he has left his indelible mark on its operations and those of its subsidiaries. Sheikh Abdulrahman's progeny have become actively involved with the running of the Jeraisy Group. Sheikh Abdulrahman's daughter, Huda bint Abdulrahman Al-Jeraisy, has been engaged in the family business and has had high honors in the business world, particularly concerning her work within the Riyadh Chamber of Commerce and Industry. However, none of the sheikh's children have been more actively engaged than his son Ali Bin Abdulrahman Al-Jeraisy.

Following in his father's path in business, Ali Al-Jeraisy, the oldest son of Sheikh Abdulrahman Al-Jeraisy, is the president of the Jeraisy Group. In this capacity, he plays a critical role in the growth and strategic development of the company. In my interview with Ali Al-Jeraisy for this book, we discussed Saudi FOBs and their significance for the future of the Kingdom. It was quite a fortunate conversation for me and this book, particularly in light of the fact that Ali studied family-owned businesses for 10 years during the education he received in Switzerland and afterward. Ali received his degree from the American College of Switzerland and did work on studying FOBs at the renowned International Institute for Management Development in Lausanne, Switzerland. During my conversation with Ali, he emphasized not only the importance of FOBs to the Saudi economy but also their value in safeguarding what he viewed as one of the most worthy competitive advantages Saudi and Arab FOBs have over their Western counterparts—the cultural and religious influences of Islam on how businesses in these FOBs is conducted.

In guiding the growth of the Al-Jeraisy family business, its owners and top management have always sought to look at new ways of managing its interests in the development of the Jeraisy Group and its subsidiaries. Ali acknowledged there have been aspects of corporate governance practiced by companies from Western nations that deserve consideration and even adoption. However, he strongly cautioned against the wholesale adoption and incorporation of such Western standards by Saudi business. The thoughts recorded in my conversation with Ali underscored the recognition of Saudi business, especially FOBs, that their path to a prosperous and sustainable future lies in the successfully marriage of the past with the future. One of the examples cited by Ali was a subject discussed earlier in this chapter, corporate succession, and the inherency of business assets upon the death of an FOB founder and first-generation owner.

In the Islamic world, when a business owner dies, there are clear and unambiguous rules to be followed governing the distribution of assets to inheritable heirs. There are fixed portions of the deceased's estate that must go to his heirs upon his death. This is seen as an advantage over Western jurisprudence when the death of a business owner occurs, particularly when the owner dies intestate. When heirs to a Western business owner who dies with no will scramble to have lawyers line up to protect and champion their interests in probate court, heirs in countries ruled by Islamic jurisprudence would be confident in knowing what their shares would be in their relative's estate. Of course, when the decedent passes away leaving behind extensive and complex global business interests, settling the estate is not always a painless exercise. As Ali suggests, however, it should be viewed as a management technique or tool that can be relied upon as an advantage in unfortunate circumstances.

Ali Al-Jeraisy is like many second-generation FOB leaders who believe that adopting Western standards as a matter of course is not the right approach when it comes to running a modern business. Ali uses the word "localization" to describe the best methodology when it comes to Saudi FOBs examining and adopting Western standards of running a business. The idea is to look at the best of what the West has to offer in regard to business management and processes, and then decide if those practices can be modified to fit within a delivery system that conforms to Islamic teachings and principles. "I am convinced that if the good practices of the West can be modified so that we do not lose our traditions and cultural values, our way of doing things will be recognized as the best."

Ali Al-Jeraisy believes the philosophical approach the government takes toward supporting its FOBs, and for that matter small- and medium-sized enterprises in general, is a direct determinant as to the creation of a robust and supportive environment in which these businesses cannot only survive but thrive. Ali acknowledges the nations that have created exemplary ecosystems for their businesses. Support for business in Germany, the United States, the United Kingdom, and to a lesser extent China were discussed. These are countries that have established government agencies and give support to private sector organizations that nurture these businesses in providing guidance, financial assistance, and management training for such businesses. One prime example we discussed was the U.S. government and its Small Business Administration (SBA). The SBA is discussed further in Chapter 5.

Ali Al-Jeraisy, like many in the second and third generation of Saudi FOB corporate leaders, are carrying on the traditions of the founders and first-generation leaders of these critically important firms. Like his father, Ali is not only engaged with his fellow FOB business leaders and colleagues in the Kingdom, but he is a thought leader. His earnest desire to see that Islamic traditions and social customs remain ingrained in how Saudi businesses run their companies is promoted by the strength of his arguments and interactions with his colleagues.

Ali Zaid Al Quraishi and Brothers (AZAQ)

When one works for the U.S. commercial service in an overseas post, very soon after arriving in a country, you learn to master the list of the most prominent companies the market and the people who own them and those who play a vital role in their management. In 2003, when I assumed the role as commercial attaché, Ali Zaid Al Quraishi and Brothers (AZAQ) was one of those companies and Sheikh Abdulaziz Al-Quraishi was someone I would later come to know, value, and consider as a mentor and supporter.

Sheikh Abdulaziz Al-Quraishi is one of those names in the Kingdom, and internationally for anyone familiar with Saudi business or government matters, immediately recognizable. He is widely respected and quite often venerated for his years of dedicated, unselfish service to the government of the Kingdom of Saudi Arabia and to that of the Saudi business community. The vast and disparate corporate holdings Sheikh Abdulaziz, his brothers, and now second-generation Al Quraishi family members, have amassed over the past half century speak as much to the fidelity and vision of this admirable family as to the skills, abilities, and leadership individual family members have brought to bear in the management and stewardship of AZAQ and its various operating units.

AZAQ was formed in 1958 as a partnership among the Al-Quraishi brothers, Ali, Abdulaziz, Khalid, Salih, Abdalkarim, and Abdalrazzaq.

From the time it was founded until present day, AZAQ has been a diversified company engaged in numerous businesses. AZAQ has well over 1,000 employees and has established market dominance in the Kingdom with some of the most recognized brands in the world. The Al-Quraishi holding company, AZAQ, has its core business operations in finance and information technology, investments, real estate development, and corporate and business development. From within these core operations, AZAQ engages in marketing and distributing top brands in leisure goods, household products, timepieces, office furniture, telecommunications, electronics, electrical equipment, and motor vehicles. In recent years, AZAQ has expanded its field of operations to include the supply, manufacture, installation, and servicing of heavy electrical products, including motors, transformers and switchgears. Representing historical and global leaders in the electrical industry such as WESCO in the Kingdom, a company created in 1922 by the Westinghouse Electric Corporation to sell and distribute its manufactured products, AZAQ has become a leader in supplying infrastructure products and equipment to heavy industry.

The Al-Quraishi are descendants from the Bani Khalid of Hail, one of the oldest and best-known tribes of the Arabian peninsula. The Bani Khalid was one of the most populous with many clans that held sway over Saudi Arabia and the Gulf region.

One has only to imagine the benefit of such accumulated knowledge held by a family over centuries on how to run and maintain a business. The experience of being one of the accepted and respected repositories of the dos and don'ts of local etiquette on Saudi business culture, incorporating all relevant knowledge and applied awareness of changing political landscapes must have been something many Saudi FOBs aspired to know. To have the blessing and privilege of applying such knowledge, while steeped in the traditions and cultural anchors of a society solid and confident in the understandings of itself and in the business world of today must truly be counted as a paramount competitive advantage.

I believe this is what many Western companies, especially those from America, tend to underestimate or outright miss about doing business in Saudi Arabia. There is a profound cultural aspect of doing business in the Kingdom unlike many other places in the world. I have had the privilege during my years in promoting U.S. business around the world to have engaged commercial communities within a variety of cultural settings. I have found it true that Americans tend to want to get down to business with the least amount of social pleasantries extended. For some business owners and executives from the West, the concept of getting to know your foreign customers and partners on a first-name, family, or social basis even today presents an uncomfortable proposition and one viewed as unnecessary to a profitable relationship.

Luckily, this approach to courting and securing business by American firms to doing business has experienced significant erosion in recent times. To know someone as sagacious and experienced in government, business, and life in general as Sheikh Abdulaziz Al-Quraish, and even to want to do business with him and a company like AZAQ, one would be well advised to learn of their family and appreciate its cultural and social influences before the nitty-gritty of business terms come up in conversation.

If you ask Sheikh Abdulaziz about being recognized as one of the Kingdom's most important business personages, he would remind you that many of his more notable professional accomplishments have occurred while serving government in various public administrative and institutional leadership positions. As with a surprising number of Saudis who graduated from U.S. universities in the late 1950s and the decade following, Sheikh Abdulaziz graduated from the University of Southern California with a master's degree in business administration. Even today, the U.S. state of California is a popular destination for Saudis seeking graduate and post-graduate educations.

After graduation, Sheikh Abdulaziz's professional life began in 1961 when he worked for the government railroad in the Eastern Province. From 1968 to 1974, he served as president of the Civil Service Bureau in Riyadh. He served as minister of state as a member of the Council of Ministers. In 1974, Sheikh Abdulaziz became the first Saudi to be appointed to run the Saudi Arabian Monetary Agency (SAMA) as governor. He served as governor of SAMA from 1974 to 1983, and was retired by royal decree. He still serves SAMA as a member of its board of directors. After two decades of service in the public sector, Sheikh Abdulaziz became managing director of the family business, Ali Zaid Al-Quraishi and Brothers Co. Ltd. He later became vice chairman of the owners' council. Faisal Al-Quraishi serves as AZAQ's chairman of the board of directors of the second generation. Shaikh Ali Al-Quraishi is the chairman of the owners' council.

Like many senior Saudi public and private-sector renowned personalities such as Sheikh Abdulrahman Al-Jeraisy who have reached ages well into their seventies and mid-eighties, Sheikh Abdulaziz has maintained an often bewildering active professional life since retiring from government service in 1983. He was chairman of the Industrial Group in Riyadh and the Saudi Chevron Petrochemical Company in Jubail, Saudi Arabia. He was a member of the Gulf Cooperation Council (GCC) High Consultative Council, which serves as an advisory board for the heads of the GCC. He was a member of the international board of Security Pacific Bank in Los Angeles, California, from 1984 to 1991. He was chairman of the National Company for Cooperative Insurance in Riyadh and the Saudi International Bank in London, United Kingdom, from 1986 to 1994 and 1987 to 1996, respectively.

From 1997 to 2000, Sheikh Abdulaziz served as chairman of the Royal and Sun Alliance Insurance (Middle East) Ltd. in Jeddah, Saudi Arabia.

In addition to his service and accomplishments in business and government, Sheikh Abdulaziz has had a profound impact through his service to the Saudi-U.S. bilateral commercial relationship. Twenty years ago, he became a founding co-chairman, along with Mr. Hugh L. McColl Jr., former chairman of NationsBank, of the U.S.-Saudi Arabian Business Council. As the Saudi co-chairman of the USSABC who recruited me as president of the USSABC in 2006, along with then-USSABC American co-chairman, Alfred DeCrane, I became closely aware of Sheikh Abdulaziz's service to the business communities of the Kingdom and the United States and the importance attached by him to the unique historical relationship both communities share. Even after relinquishing the USSABC co-chairmanship, Sheikh Abdulaziz has worked to continue to strengthen U.S.-Saudi business linkages.

As one of the Kingdom's well-known Saudi FOBs, AZAQ is undergoing its own transition from first to second generation leadership. The progeny of Sheikh Abdulaziz and his brothers have been moving into management and leadership positions within AZAQ and its subsidiaries for a number of years now. One of the Al-Quraishi second-generation family members who has assumed a heightened profile of responsibility in AZAQ's leadership and management is Sheikh Abdulaziz's son, Adel. During my diplomatic posting in Saudi Arabia, I met Adel. Much like his father, I have always found Adel to be a man who always considers carefully what he contemplates saying before words ever begin to form. This is an often-rare commodity indeed these days. Adel currently serves the family business as a member of the board of directors of AZAQ and Brothers, chairman of the board of directors of United Motors Corporation (dealers of Chrysler, Dodge, Jeep, Fiat, and Alfa Romeo vehicles in the Kingdom), and director of National Advanced Systems Co. Ltd. as well as a director of Credit Suisse Saudi Arabia. Adel graciously consented to an interview for this book and I sat down with him to note his thoughts on the topics covered in this book.

After graduating from university, Adel took the path that many second-generation youth take who are bound for the corporate suites of their FOBs. Like his cousins, Yousef, Ahmed, Sulaiman, Faisal, and Majed, Adel began the acquisition of real-world business experience by working within private-sector companies in areas targeted to enhance the skill sets needed once they joined the business full-time. For three years, Adel worked for Samba Bank, one of the region's largest banks and once linked to Citibank through its equity shares held in the institution. By 2004, Citibank fully divested its shareholding in Samba. Adel gained valuable on-the-job experience, however, during the few years spent at the bank, working half of that time in its treasury unit and the other half in its corporate banking section. Adel says he did not become an expert in these areas of financial services. He says, however, that he gained enough proficiency in executing credit analyses, evaluating funding proposals, and performing other critical credit examinations to carry those valuable experiences into the family business.

Adel believes that the typical large Saudi FOB is undergoing a fundamental shift in regard to how they perceive their own unique paths toward the future. While acknowledging that all Saudi FOBs view the safeguarding and chosen methods of growing their business interests as ultimately a family matter of great import, like second-generation Saudi FOB leader Ali Al-Jeraisy, Adel believes there are some aspects of how Western businesses are run that hold some value for Saudi FOBs in terms of mapping the way forward. In my conversation with him, he pointed out that it is seldom productive to draw comparisons between managing companies in the Kingdom and those in the United States or the United Kingdom. The often-dizzying array of regulations faced by Western firms such as those in the areas of securities, taxation, product efficacy and safety, worker and factory safety compliance, and observance of shareholder rights and activism in public companies make comparisons of management models with Saudi firms exercises in near futility. One area Adel believes this holds true in is corporate succession.

Adel agrees that corporate succession is one of the most challenging issues facing many Saudi FOBs of size. One of the most troublesome issues for Saudi FOB founders or first-generation owners and managers is that they find it very difficult to let go. Most of these first-generation business founders and leaders have a kind of passion for what they started that has in no way dissipated or diminished over the decades that have passed since they first began to accumulate and grow their business assets. Often, when impassioned first-generation founders and owners reach an age when practicality should dictate a lessening of day-to-day engagement in the management of their businesses and transfer to younger generation family members, Adel has observed in other family businesses that the founders and first-generation owners view any suggestion of change affecting business assets as a personal affront and an insult in extreme cases.

In the case of AZAQ, Sheikh Abdulaziz's eldest brother, Ali, started the family business in the 1950s. As Sheikh Abdulaziz's other brothers, Khalid, Salih, Abdalkarim, and Abdelrazzaq grew older, they began to engage in the running of the business and assume ever-increasing roles in its direction and management. Brother Ali had a vision, shared by his brothers, that when the time arrived for second-generation Al-Quraishi family members to take up their respective roles in the business, they would do so while he and his first-generation brothers were still on the scene, counseling and guiding them in their labor. To this end, an "Owners Council" was created that was superimposed on top of the existing board. The existing board's members had been composed of the original Al-Quraishi brothers. As the younger sons of the original brothers desired a seat on the board, a mechanism, the Owners Council, was created to allow the second generation to exercise near full authority in taking decisions affecting the management, strategic direction, and productivity of the company while the original brothers retained veto power over spending and the disposition of assets.

Adel sees the solution of the Owners Council as just one approach one Saudi FOB has taken to ensure a meaningful and effective transition in ownership and management from first to second generation business family members. Beyond that, Adel sees the younger generations of Saudi FOB owners as being more open to bringing external board directors and senior managers to their family businesses. Among second and third generation FOB members active in companies, there is a belief that you should hire the best for key positions within the company whether they are from the family or from outside. There is a growing consensus that not to do so contributes to the FOB's failure rate of transition from one generation to the next. It is thought of FOBs around the world that family politics and pride often blind those in control of FOBs to their detriment.

The renowned author and professor of business economics and management, Alfred DuPont Chandler, was among the first to delineate the shift within businesses from irregular and makeshift management methods to more efficient, systematized processes. These led Chandler to invent a new vocabulary concerning transitioning from outdated approaches to management by entrenched business owners to more modern systems executed by outside recruited managers.[48] More and more Saudi FOBs are considering the advantages and business judgment of incorporating external senior managers into the family business. How widespread this becomes among Saudi FOBs in the years to come will remain to be seen.

What is certain in the changing and insular world of FOBs in the Kingdom, as these businesses transition from one generation to the next, is that change will be talked about and contemplated by Saudi FOB owners among themselves at formal and informal gatherings. Even among the younger generation, business leaders speak among themselves concerning a range of business issues. Adel Al-Quraishi noted that he and a number of fellow second-generation Saudi FOB family members engaged in business solicit and offer advice to one another from time to time. He characterizes it as a kind of fraternity of personal relationships that have benefits beyond the social side of life. When they gather, conversations often turn to the issues of the day for Saudi FOBs as conversations among these unique individuals have for many decades in the Kingdom.

Zamil Group

During the 1950s and 1960s, which is what I refer to as the "incubation decades," or in Islamic terms a time of the "Salaat-ul-Istikhaarah," an Islamic prayer with the intention of searching for guidance, many of today's best-known and potent Saudi FOBs were formed by men of great vision, determination, and aspiration. A number of these firms arose from relative commercial anonymity from their respective regions within the Kingdom. Few Saudi FOBs have ascended, however, to become one of the Kingdom's most industrially diverse and globally engaged family businesses as the Zamil Group. The rise of the Al-Zamil is instructive in understanding many critical aspects of the Saudi FOB today and how a skilled set of family members might optimize talent within the family, spanning several generations, to advance the firm's interests to reach global proportions.

Like most large FOBs, the Al-Zamil is a family not originally from the three main cities of the Kingdom, Riyadh, Jeddah, and Dammam. The Al-Zamil are known to have descended from the Bani Thawr of Sbiya and from the Qasim area and Anaiza. Other places of historical significance for the family's sojourn were Basra, Iraq, where the family still holds family and tribal ties, and Bahrain, where the family business experienced some of its beginning through the sale of food and textiles.

The Al-Zamil come from a long line of merchants and businessmen. The pinnacle of the Al-Zamil FOB is the Zamil Group, legally registered as the Zamil Group Holding Company, formerly known as A. H. Al-Zamil Group of Companies and H. A. Al-Zamil and Brothers Company. It is an 85-year-old company that was originally founded by Sheikh Abdullah Al-Hamad Al-Zamil in the 1920s as a small business engaged in trading and real estate. Sheikh Abdullah had 12 sons, Mohammad, Abdulrahman, Hamad, Abdulaziz, Zamil, Ahmad, Sulaiman, Khalid, Fahd, Adib, Waleed, and Taufik. As the brothers received their education, graduated, and began to acquire their own professional training and experience, they joined the family business over the 1960s and 1970s. Working together as a family unit, these brothers transformed the family business from one concentrated on a few narrowly defined commercial sectors into one of the Gulf region's most industrially diverse and globally extended conglomerates.

The growth of the company that Sheikh Abdullah began in the 1920s to gather steam when the industrial growth policies started to take hold during the reign of King Faisal during the latter half of the 1960s. During the 1970s, the Al-Zamil FOB capitalized on the Saudi government's initiatives to grow the non-oil sector of the economy and used the incentives for production and manufacturing within the area of the economy to develop businesses in air conditioning, construction materials, and steel and steel-alloyed products.

Each of the Al-Zamil brothers carved out their individual contributions for the Al-Zamil FOB. Early on, Mohammad, the oldest brother, grew the business in Bahrain. Dr. Abdulrahman Al-Zamil, the current chairman of the Zamil Group family board of directors and current chairman of the Council of Saudi Chambers of Commerce and Industry was once the deputy governor of the Riyadh Electrical Corporation. Brother Hamad, graduating with a master's degree in business administration and hospital administration, ran the family business in the Eastern Province as its president. Abdulaziz serves as chairman of the board of directors of the Zamil Group Holding Company, chairman of Saudi International Petrochemical Company (Sipchem), the Sahara Petrochemical Company, and is also the chairman of Alinma Bank, one of Saudi Arabia's most recently established banks. Brother Zamil served as president of Zamil Marine. Khalid, who sits on the board of directors of the USSABC and with whom I am privileged to have a working relationship with through the business council, sits on the board of directors of the Zamil Group family board and serves as president and managing director for strategy of the Zamil Group Holding Company. The list goes on. A more lengthy enumeration of impressive professional, academic, and public service achievement many families in business in the Kingdom would be hard pressed to match. All of the remaining 11 brothers (Mohammad is deceased), sit on the Zamil Group family board of directors.

The Al-Zamil family business empire stretches across borders through 60 countries and employs over 12,000 people worldwide. The Al-Zamil strongly believe that the cultural and ethnic diversity that characterizes its workforce is one of the elements of their FOB that affords it a significant competitive advantage. The family business operates on the philosophy that recognizes having the best talent throughout its operations at all levels of its activity, especially Saudis, optimizes its potential for success and longevity.

The Al-Zamil Group has seven main areas of operations within which more than 50 companies, divisions, and operating units run the Al-Zamil FOB. The seven main areas of operations are: building materials (Zamil Industrial Investment Company—"Zamil Industrial"), and Zamil Architectural Holding Company); chemicals and plastics (Zamil Chemical and Plastic Holding Company); petrochemicals; marine and offshore; trade and services; and real estate. All of these companies have been built over time. Passing into this millennium, the Al-Zamil FOB entered a period of great expansion, which has not yet abated.

In 1998, when discussions had been well under way within the family business to project the FOB well beyond their stature at the time, the decision was made to form Zamil Industrial Investment Company as a closed joint stock company. Then, over the next couple of years, the company began to expand through international acquisitions in a number of countries including Austria and Italy. In 2002, Zamil Industrial underwent an initial public offering on the Tadawul and began trading under the Tadawul symbol 2240, ISIN CODE: SA0007879410. Capital and industrial expansion continued after going public with the construction of numerous production and manufacturing facilities in the Kingdom and other countries such as the United Arab Emirates, as well as the formation of joint ventures with partners from Germany, Canada, and India. In 2008, the following joint ventures were formed:

- Zamil New Delhi Infrastructure Private Ltd.: A joint venture with New Delhi Tele-Towers Private Ltd., to supply passive telecom infrastructure—galvanized telecom towers, shelters with sandwich panels, air conditioning equipment, and power interface units
- Zamil Hudson Company: A joint venture with Hudson Products Corporation of the United States that focuses on the manufacture, assembly, and maintenance of air cooled heat exchangers serving utility, petroleum, chemical, oil and gas processing, and industrial customers in the Middle East, Africa, and Central Asia
- Armacell Zamil Middle East Co. Ltd.: A joint venture with Armacell of Germany, a global leader in the manufacture of engineered foams and flexible technical insulation materials
- Rabiah and Nassar and Al-Zamil Concrete Industries Company Limited: A joint venture with RANCO Precast, a subsidiary of Rabiah and Nassar Group
- Zamil Advantec Coils: A joint venture with Advantec Coils Private Limited, India, a growing air conditioning manufacturer and operator of a completely integrated manufacturing facility[49]

Today, Zamil Industrial continues to be the high-flying unit upon which the Al-Zamil FOB has come to rely. Zamil Industrial describes itself and updates the public on its condition this way:

Founded in 1998 and headquartered in Dammam, Saudi Arabia, Zamil Industrial Investment Company (Zamil Industrial) is a premier business group engaged in the development of innovative design and engineering solutions for use in the construction industry. Also a leading manufacturer and fabricator of construction materials, Zamil Industrial implements its engineering excellence through a wide range of products: pre-engineered steel buildings, steel structures, air conditioning and climate control systems designed for a wide range of commercial, industrial, and residential applications, telecom and transmission towers, process equipment, precast concrete building products, fiberglass, rockwool, and engineered plastic foam insulations, and solar power projects. The company also offers award-winning installation and erection services. Through its various industrial sectors, Zamil Industrial provides a broad range of products and solutions that meet the increasing needs and requirements of the global building and construction industry.

Zamil Industrial employs more than 10,000 people in 55 countries and derives 30 percent of its revenues from outside Saudi Arabia. Zamil Industrial products are sold in more than 90 countries around the globe, and the company operates manufacturing facilities in Saudi Arabia, United Arab Emirates, Egypt, India, Vietnam, and Italy. For the year ended December 31, 2013, Zamil Industrial posted a turnover of USD $1.44 billion, with net profit, after Zakat contribution, of USD $62.8 million, an increase of 16.8 percent over 2012. Post-Zakat earnings per share during 2013 was USD $1.1. Stockholders' equity grew by 10.1 percent to USD $501 million.[50]

The Zamil Group's operational and growth strategies are best summed up in its own words:

Zamil Group Holding Company continues to invest in new technologies and in new and increasingly efficient production facilities to create a strong core industry and a highly trusted brand in regional and international markets. We are highly involved in the markets we serve: we enhance our client relationships through unparalleled aftermarket services—which through direct involvement with our clients—refines our ability to anticipate and meet their evolving needs and expectations. This differentiates us, our brand, and our products and services. Our entrepreneurial strategy also focuses on the diversification of our traditional industrial base into the more capital-intensive petrochemical and chemical sectors. We are developing and growing a wider portfolio of activities in promising businesses and continue our involvement in major projects. Over the past few years we have invested immensely in capital projects and regularly take a leading role in forming successful joint ventures with major regional groups and global technology and market leaders. The impact and contribution of Zamil Group Holding Company is critical to the success of new ventures. The value we bring includes management expertise, accumulated operational competence and added resources such as capital, corporate staff services, and local market intelligence and knowledge.

The Zamil Group is distinguishing itself among Saudi FOBs in crafting exemplary corporate governance policies. To run a global conglomerate as large as the Group is and with as many disparate operating units, requires a certain singularity of organizational focus. The approach to effective and productive management of such a business compels all involved in running it to be fully aware of the mission, goals, and values of the entity. And, most importantly, to individually exert one's best efforts in fulfilling the mission and observing those corporate virtues. The Zamil Group commemorated its policies in this regard when it launched its "Core Values Pocketbook" (CVP) on February 19, 2014, during a ceremony officiated by Mr. Hamad Al-Zamil at the holding company's headquarters, Zamil House, in Riyadh.

The Zamil Group's CVP is a printed guide made available to all Zamil managers and team members that offers a comprehensive reference to the core values to which the Zamil Group gives great import and requires its employees, especially those entrusted with managing people and projects, to observe in the daily performance of their duties and responsibilities to the company, its subsidiaries, divisions, and operating units. The CVP, the size of a small booklet that scales the size of an average full hand, is designed as an easily accessible, on-the-go orientation tool offering tips and techniques to address common issues that arise among members of the Zamil Group in daily operations, and that arise between its members and its customers, stakeholders, vendors, and suppliers and other parties of importance to the business.

As Khalid Al-Zamil states in the CVPs welcome to the guide:

The core values exist for all members of the Zamil Group—business leaders, executives, middle-level managers, front line supervisors or workers. They are for all of us to read, to understand, and to live by. The core values are much more than minimum standards. They remind us what it takes to get the mission done. They inspire us to do our very best at all times. They are the common bond among all employees, and they are the unifying force that guides us to achieve our vision. Study them…understand them…follow them…and encourage others to do the same.[51]

The core values of the Zamil Group are:

- *Honesty and integrity*
- *Customer and excellence*
- *Innovation and change*
- *Leadership and prudence*
- *Community and prosperity*

The CVP offers tips and techniques to improve one's self within the organization, guidelines on how to deal with specific workplace situations that might pose ethical or moral dilemmas, and suggests self-examination practices to increase one's self-awareness of the core values and how to apply them in daily work life.

One of the enlightening core values enunciated in the Zamil CVP is the "Community and Prosperity" section. As with the Jeraisy Group and AZAQ, there is a genuine and serious commitment from the founders throughout the leadership of these businesses to ensure that a significant portion of their time and resources are spent for the betterment of the Kingdom and its various communities. The CVP introduces the core value of "community and prosperity" as:

> *We believe in mutual prosperity. We aspire to thrive in business while bringing progress and prosperity to our own people and communities where we operate. Our culture, our ideas, our practices, our environmental concern, and our teamwork lead us to creating superior values for people and communities around us.[52]*

This commitment to serving community and the prosperity of society is exemplified by the years of service in government and areas of the non-governmental sectors by many of these business founders and original owners. It is demonstrated most clearly by the contributions of their time and money to the individuals, organizations, and charities that are uplifted by their generosity and sense of obligation to the Kingdom and its people. It is most telling that these men and their businesses often go to great lengths to ensure the anonymity of their philanthropic works.

It is not just the founders and original owners of the companies that labor diligently to uphold these corporate virtues of public service and societal commitments. Second- and third-generation family members of these Saudi FOBs are standing out in this regard as well.

Citations of this kind on the part of Al-Zamil family members are too numerous to mention; however, I mention just a brief few:

> *Abdulrahman Khalid Al-Zamil, serves on the Youth Council of the Eastern Province, an entity that addresses issues of concern to Saudi youth as well as promoting young Saudi talent in various fields; Yasser Hamad Al-Zamil received an award on behalf of the Zamil Group for the support and contributions it has made to the rehabilitation of drug addicts; Abdulaziz Al-Zamil, on behalf of the family business, donated USD $800,000 to Al-Yamamah University in Riyadh for the Ghazi Al Gosaibi chair for cultural*

studies; Costing over USD $13,000,000, the family established "The Zamil Institute," a training facility with a capacity to serve 300 Saudi youth to improve their professional careers and vocational skill sets; Abdulla Mohammed Al-Zamil, CEO of Zamil Industrial Investment, serves as a member of the founding board of directors of "Endeavor Saudi Arabia," an affiliate organization of "Endeavor Global," whose principal mission is to select and service high-impact entrepreneurs in the Middle East; and Mrs. Lulua Abdullah Al-Zamil, the eldest sister in the family, has been recognized for her 44-year period of service to the less fortunate and needy within the Kingdom and was honored by the HRH Prince Mohammed Bin Fahad Award for Charity Contributions for her outstanding work.

This list of activities does not do justice to all of the generations of Al-Zamil family members, individually and through the family businesses, that work to support, improve, and enrich the lives of their fellow Saudi citizens. For the business community of the nation, this is no more conspicuous in scale of contribution than by Dr. Abdulrahman Al-Zamil, the current chairman of the Zamil Group family board of directors and current chairman of the council of Saudi Chambers of Commerce and Industry.

Dr. Abdulrahman exemplifies the energy, drive, determination, and commitment of the Al-Zamil family to the Kingdom's business communities, national culture, and civil society. He is known to possess quite an irrepressible and ebullient personality. I have often considered Dr. Abdulrahman's occasionally mischievous demeanor, quick wit, and playful manner to belie his obvious keen intellect and considerable powers of discernment and judgment. I have observed these qualities in the brothers I have had interactions with: Khalid, Abdulaziz, and Hamad. As mentioned, Khalid sits on the board of the USSABC, and Abdulaziz and Hamad have attended numerous events and activities of the USSABC and those of the U.S. embassy during my diplomatic service. Dr. Abdulrahman met with and hosted a number of mission delegations of American companies visiting the Kingdom that were organized by the USSABC during his tenure as chairman of the Riyadh Chamber of Commerce and Industry. I can say without reservation that these gentlemen and their companies understand and appreciate the importance of the Saudi-U.S. bilateral commercial relationship, and also avidly support the engagement of Saudi firms in international markets around the world.

The three Saudi FOBs portrayed in this section, as well as many other firms in the Kingdom, encourage and support Saudi SMEs and the programs that assist them. Many third-generation and younger members of these family businesses are entrepreneurs themselves and interact and often partner with other young Saudi entrepreneurs in their commercial pursuits. The definition of "entrepreneurship," a sphere of commerce from which all Saudi FOBs have ascended at some point or another, is one that is frequently debated within the Kingdom. We turn now to the subject of entrepreneurship in Saudi Arabia, how the term is defined among Saudis, and what it means to do business successfully as an entrepreneur in that country.

NOTES

1. International Finance Corporation (IFC), *IFC Family Business Governance Handbook*, 2008, 14, www.ifc.org/wps/wcm/connect/159c9c0048582f6883f9 ebfc046daa89/FB_English_final_2008.pdf?MOD=AJPERES.
2. Ibid. 15.
3. Ibid.
4. Kingdom of Saudi Arabia, Ministry of Labor, Riyadh, *Annual Statistics Report*, 1434–1435   AH,   http://portal.mol.gov.sa/ar/Statistics/Documents/%D8%A7 %D9%84%D9%83%D8%AA%D8%A7%D8%A8%20%D8%A7%D9%84 %D8%A7%D8%AD%D8%B5%D8%A7%D8%A6%D9%8A%202013.pdf (Accessed September 29, 2014).
5. *Arab News*, "Family Businesses Contribute 25% of GDP," July 25, 2012, www .arabnews.com/family-businesses-contribute-25-gdp.
6. Michael Field, *The Merchants: The Big Business Families of Saudi Arabia and the Gulf States* (Woodstock, New York: Overlook Press, 1984), 3.
7. *The National*, "Al Gosaibi Drama Forgotten ... But Not for Very Long," March 16, 2010, www.thenational.ae/business/al-gosaibi-drama-forgotten-but-not-for-very-long.
8. Al-Mashah Capital Limited, "MENA Family Businesses: The Real Power Brokers?" http://almasahcapital.com/uploads/report/pdf/report_25.pdf (Accessed October 7, 2014).
9. *Financial Times* ft.com/lexicon, definition of "tax inversion," http://lexicon.ft .com/Term?term=tax-inversion (Accessed October 21, 2014).
10. U.S. Department of the Treasury, Press Center, Press Release: "Treasury Announces First Steps to Reduce Tax Benefits of Corporate Inversions—Unfair Practice Erodes the U.S. Tax Base," September 22, 2014, www.treasury.gov/ press-center/press-releases/Pages/jl2647.aspx.
11. *The Washington Post*, "Obama Hits at Companies Moving Overseas to Avoid Taxes," September 22, 2014, www.washingtonpost.com/business/economy/ 2014/09/22/e5294e0a-429d-11e4-b437-1a7368204804_story.html.
12. *Arab News*, "Business Community Must Strictly Abide by the Rules of Employment," November 27, 2013, www.arabnews.com/news/483746.
13. *Saudi Gazette*, "Few Takers for 10,000 Jobs Offered by Riyadh Firms," June 14, 2014, www.saudigazette.com.sa/index.cfm?method=home.regcon& contentid=2014061620859.

14. *Saudi Gazette,* "86% of Companies in Nitiqat Safe Zone," October 28, 2014, www.saudigazette.com.sa/index.cfm?method=home.regcon&contentid= 20141029222697.
15. Al Zamil Group, "AHZ Community Service Center." Retrieved from www.zamil .com/ahz_community.php?lang=en (2014).
16. Ibid.
17. *Saudi Gazette,* "Zamil to Hire Saudi Fresh Graduates," May 1, 2013.
18. Business Leadership Review VIII: DBA www.mbaworld.com/blr, September 2011, 2011 Association of MBAs.
19. Ibid. 1 of 17.
20. Ibid. 4 of 17.
21. See Article 3 of the Banking Control Regulations, as enacted by Royal Decree No. M/5 dated 22/2/1386 AH/June 11, 1966, as amended, and Article 3 of the Cooperative Insurance Companies Control Regulations, as enacted by Royal Decree No. M/32 dated 2/6/1424 AH/July 31, 2003.
22. When entering into a joint venture with a Saudi joint venture party, a foreign joint venture party should be aware that the form of Saudi business organization known as an "establishment" is similar to a common law sole proprietorship, in that there is no legal distinction between the business owner and the business itself. Accordingly, where the SJVP is a business in the form of an establishment, the SJVP is in fact a Saudi natural person.
23. Article 165 of the Companies' Regulations establishes a mandatory procedure for the transfer of shares in an LLC, which procedure usually gives the LLCs other existing shareholders a pre-emptive right to purchase any shares that would otherwise be transferred to a third party. However, Article 165 of the Companies' Regulations states expressly that its procedure shall not apply to the transfer of shares by inheritance or bequest.
24. Where the SJVP is a natural person, following the death of the SJVP, the SJVP's heirs will apply to the General Islamic Courts (a) to have the SJVP's assets—including his share(s) in the JV—inventoried and (b) to have the SJVP's assets distributed amongst the SJVP's heirs. When the JV's management is presented with (c) the Court's inventory of the SJVP's assets and the distribution of such assets amongst the SJVP's heirs and (d) a notarized power of attorney signed by all of the SJVP's heirs appointing a representative to be named as the owner of the SJVP's share(s) in the JV, the JV's management (the Representative), the FJVP, the Representative, and the JV's management can proceed to amend the JV's foreign investment license, Articles of Association, and share register to reflect the transfer of the SJVP's share(s) in the JV to the Representative.
25. Because the JV can only be incorporated after securing a foreign investment license for the JV from the Saudi Arabian General Investment Authority (SAGIA), it will be necessary to amend the JV's foreign investment license to reflect the change in the ownership of shares in the JV resulting from the death of the SJVP. It will also be necessary to amend the JV's Articles of Association and share register. It should be noted, however, that the ownership of the deceased SJVP's shares in the JV by the Representative will not be effective as against the

JV or any third parties until the heir's ownership of the shares is recorded in the JV's share register. See Article 166 of the Companies' Regulations as enacted by Royal Decree No. M/6 dated 22/3/1385 AH/July 21, 1965, as amended.

26. A share in an LLC may be jointly owned by more than one person but can only have a single owner registered in the LLC's share register. See Article 158 of the Companies' Regulations, as enacted by Royal Decree No. M/6 dated 22/3/1385 AH/July 21, 1965, as amended.

27. The Companies' Regulations, as enacted by Royal Decree No. M/6 dated 22/3/1385 AH/July 21, 1965, as amended.

28. See section 2(b).

29. See Article 172 of the Companies' Regulations, as enacted by Royal Decree No. M/6 dated 22/3/1385 AH/July 21, 1965, as amended.

30. See Article 173 of the Companies' Regulations, as enacted by Royal Decree No. M/6 dated 22/3/1385 AH/July 21, 1965, as amended.

31. Ibid.

32. See Article 157 of the Companies' Regulations, as enacted by Royal Decree No. M/6 dated 22/3/1385 AH/July 21, 1965, as amended.

33. See Article 35 of the Companies' Regulations, as enacted by Royal Decree No. M/6 dated 22/3/1385 AH/July 21, July 1965, as amended.

34. See Article 156 of the Companies' Regulations, as enacted by Royal Decree No. M/6 dated 22/3/1385 AH/July 21, 1965, as amended.

35. *Arab News,* "NCB Share Sale Raises Record SR215.76bn," November 3, 2014, www.arabnews.com/news/654296.

36. *Financial Times,* "Arab Finance and Banking: Saudi Small Business Remains Reliant on Friends and Family for Funds," May 28, 2014, www.ft.com/intl/cms/s/0/c94ed262-c2b1-11e2-bbbd-00144feab7de.html#axzz3JdQeQLfV.

37. Organisation for Economic Co-operation and Development (OECD), Glossary of Statistical Terms, "European Central Bank, 2004, Annual Report: 2004, ECB, Frankfurt, Germany (Financial Statistics): Sourced: http://stats.oecd.org/glossary/detail.asp?ID=6778.

38. The Committee on the Financial Aspects of Corporate Governance, "Report of the Committee on the Financial Aspects of Corporate Governance," December 1992, Burgess Science Press, United Kingdom, 14.

39. Andrei Shleifer and Robert W. Vishny, "A Survey of Corporate Governance," *Journal of Finance* 52, no. 2 (1997): 737–783.

40. Andrei Shleifer and Robert W. Vishny, "A Survey of Corporate Governance" (April 1996). NBER Working Paper No. w5554. Available at SSRN: http://ssrn.com/abstract=10182, 2.

41. Kingdom of Saudi Arabia Capital Market Authority, Board of Capital Market Authority, "Corporate Governance Regulations in the Kingdom of Saudi Arabia, Pursuant to Resolution No. 1/212/2006 dated November 12, 2006, based on the Capital Market Law issued by Royal Decree No. M/30 (Official CMA English Translation.

42. The World Bank, "Report on the Observance of Standards and Codes (ROSC) Corporate Governance Country Assessment," February 2009, 3, www.worldbank.org/ifa/rosc_cg_saudia_arabia.pdf.

43. Ibid. 23.
44. Ibid. 3.
45. Alkhabeer Capital, "Saudi Arabia—A Promising Proposition for Private Equity," November 2014, www.alkhabeer.com/press-releases/alkhabeer-capital-assesses-opportunities-and-challenges-private-equity-saudi-arabia.
46. *Saudi Gazette,* "Family Businesses Aware of Corporate Governance," May 11, 2011, www.saudigazette.com.sa/index.cfm?method=home.regcon&contentID=20110511100394.
47. Jeraisy Riyadh House, www.rhc.com.sa/index.php/pages/renderPage/12 (Accessed December 14, 2014).
48. Alfred D. Chandler Jr., *The Visible Hand: The Managerial Revolution in American Business* (Cambridge, MA: Belknap Press, 1980).
49. Zamil Industrial, "Key Milestones," www.zamilindustrial.com/index.php?r=ourCompany/index&id=6&lang=en (Accessed December 30, 14).
50. Zamil Industrial, www.zamilindustrial.com/index.php?r=ourCompany/index&id=5&lang=en (Accessed December 30, 2014).
51. The Zamil Group, Zamil Group Corporate Human Resources, "Core Value Pocketbook," Welcome note, 2014 1st Edition, 1.
52. Ibid. 45.

CHAPTER **4**

Entrepreneurship in Saudi Arabia Today

DEFINING "ENTREPRENEUR" IN SAUDI ARABIA

Early in preparation for this book as I began to conceptualize the archetypal Saudi entrepreneur, I found myself thinking of him or her foremost as possessing the drive, luster, and promise of youth. In the United States, entrepreneurs are of all ages and come from a diversity of life's situations and backgrounds. When most Americans think of entrepreneurial pursuits, they think of them as primarily being started by people from different age groups including middle-aged career veterans as well as the recently unemployed. In Silicon Valley, however, the bastion of the U.S. high tech industry, the needle on the entrepreneurial age meter turns hard toward the identity of the "young entrepreneur."

There is a growing tendency in the United States to think of startups and entrepreneurial ventures, particularly in the high-tech industry, as those begun by those aged 30 years or younger. If you ever visit Silicon Valley, you will be undoubtedly struck by the scarcity of people aged 40 years or older. As Noam Scheiber, political and economic writer and commentator, wrote in an article on age and Silicon Valley in *The New Republic* magazine: "Silicon Valley has become one of the most ageist places in America. Tech luminaries who otherwise pride themselves on their dedication to meritocracy don't think twice about deriding the not-actually-old."[1] In the article, Scheiber went on to refer to a 2007 comment attributed to Facebook CEO, Mark Zuckerberg, who said: "Young people are just smarter." Scheiber writes: "As I write, the website of ServiceNow, a large Santa Clara [California U.S.]–based IT services company, features the following advisory in large letters atop its "Careers" page: 'We Want People Who Have Their Best Work Ahead of Them, Not Behind Them.'"[2]

In Saudi Arabia, the country's demographics force the age composition of its entrepreneurial class. Fifty percent of the Saudi population is below

120

the age of 25. Although no accurate statistics are kept concerning the ages of those registering businesses in the Kingdom, most startups are believed to be launched by Saudis under 40 years of age, a relatively safe presumption given the youthful demographics of the country. So at least in that sense, Saudis are well aware of Silicon Valley given its global brand and the notoriety of some of its corporate residents, but they can also relate to the youthful character-istics of its populace as well. In fact, there has been a growing realization by Saudi public- and private-sector leadership that the growth of Saudi Arabia's entrepreneurial class should be an integral part of any meaningful economic growth plan for the Kingdom.

There continue to be volumes of research and literary works produced on the subject of entrepreneurship and the business of startups worldwide. There is no lack of opinion as to how "entrepreneur" should be defined by experts and many of the world's best-known and celebrated entrepreneurs. Some of these entrepreneurs have parlayed startups into commercial entities valued in the billions of dollars. The subject of the entrepreneur has been studied, dissected, and reconstituted from virtually every angle locally, nationally, and internationally. However, for as many scholarly works, research pieces, and serial entrepreneur biographies that have been written on the subject of the entrepreneur, the number of definitions of "entrepreneur" have also grown. I believe this is because there are so many facets, beyond those most generally accepted, to what it takes to be a successful entrepreneur in our hypervelocity world. An accurate definition of "entrepreneur" may be all but impractical except for those most general in nature. Nonetheless, in this book, an examination of some definitions of "entrepreneur" will be valuable not only for a basic conceptual understand-ing, but as an aid to understanding the approaches taken in Saudi Arabia to support this commercial breed.

Most scholars point to medieval Germany as the first reference to a conceptual and applied understanding of an "entrepreneurial class" of business people who were licensed to offer crafted products and services for sale to the public through guilds. Not until the Irish-French economist, Richard Cantillon, however, articulated his definition in his "Essay on the Nature of Trade in General," referred to in short as his *Essai,* that a modern and institutional study of the entrepreneur took flight. A youthful banker and merchant in the eighteenth-century "age of reason," Cantillon made arguably the first major contribution to the formal literary body and study of political economics with *Essai*. The writing of *Essai* and Cantillon's views were later to influence other easily recognizable world literary figures of the eighteenth century such as the legendary Scottish economist and moral theorist, Adam Smith, and French economist and businessman Jean-Baptist (J. B.) Say. These were men greatly influenced by the great swirl of political, social, and economic change occurring in eighteenth-century Europe and the shifting sands repositioning the class barriers separating people.

A comprehensive discussion of the various definitions of "entrepreneur" from eighteenth- and nineteenth-century economists and authors, the fountain of classical economics, would be excessive here in this section of the book. I might also unnecessarily extenuate a review of the main distinctions among them and possibly impede a meaningful application of those definitions to today's Saudi entrepreneur. Nevertheless, a brief mention of two of the best-known and most referenced definitions from this cornerstone period of the eighteenth century will be helpful. We turn to the definitions offered by Richard Cantillon and J. B. Say.

Richard Cantillon, born in Ireland and part of the great landed gentry of the seventeenth century, became an émigré to France, where eventually through family connections and his own talent rose to become an owner of a prominent bank in Paris with affluent British, Irish, and French clientele. It was Cantillon's business association with Scottish financier and explorer John Law that catapulted him into great wealth. Law, who introduced the system of public financial management based on unbacked paper money to a nearly bankrupt French government, which was soon to be run by French King Louis XIV's brother, the Duke of Orleans, after the death of the "Sun King" in 1715. John Law persuaded the regent to establish a private bank whose majority capital consisted of bills of exchange and bank notes, all guaranteed by the king's name. In 1716, enthroned King Louis XV ordered the Banque Générale Privée (General Private Bank) to be created and placed John Law at the head of it. In 1718, General Private Bank subsumed a number of other banks and commercial trading houses to become the Banque Royale (Royal Bank) and thereafter maintained a virtual monopoly on the finance of French merchant banking and international commerce.

Under this new system of public finance, debts were taken on and discharged by the French government with a type of coin of the realm unsupported by gold, silver, or any other accepted hard asset of the day. Great wealth accrued to Law and his business partners, including Richard Cantillon, and financial speculator extraordinaire, Joseph Edward "Beau" Gage, as they financed exploration and support of French colonies around the world. John Law was made France's minister of finance, and the money engine kept churning out paper money eventually along with corresponding inflation. Important to this discussion of entrepreneurial pursuit, the vaporous French treasury and its coffers greatly contributed to what is known as the "Mississippi Bubble," a calamitous affair for the French crown, its imperial prestige, and John Law, its greatest contributing architect.

After the creation of the General Private Bank with John Law placed at its head, Law invested his money in various companies including the

Mississippi Company, whose principal activity was to support the trade, investment, and colonization interests of France in the New Orleans and Louisiana settlements in North America. Through the successes of the Mississippi Company in financing the growth of French settlements in New Orleans and Louisiana, John Law's reputation for making the French government and his private clientele rich, albeit in paper profits only, he managed to attract extraordinary public demand for the purchase of shares in the Mississippi Company.

In early 1720, the General Private Bank and the Mississippi Company's assets and interests were merged. The public's perception of the value of investing in the company and its holdings in Louisiana would soon change to a realization as to how far the actual value of those investments outstripped the current inflated valuations. Richard Cantillon was a co-investor with Law in the Mississippi Company and a shrewd evaluator of risk. He had accurately foreseen the market collapse of investor sentiment in Louisiana and in turn the value of Mississippi Company shares. Eventually, the weight of France's accumulated debt and the rampant speculation reached a hysterical state. Having initially shared in the risk in co-investing in the investment vehicle, he quietly sold his shares and related debt holdings in the Mississippi Company when demand was still high. He left France for Italy, a multi millionaire, well before the impending doom became clear.

As the story goes, and as with many over-rated investments then and now, the momentum of investor skepticism overtook skewed investor fervor and the bubble burst in the Mississippi Company in 1720 when all at once investors demanded redemption of the notes issued by the company. Unable to satisfy the run on the General Private Bank and the Mississippi Company, the French government was forced to admit technical insolvency. John Law was dismissed from public service and fled France with the greatest damage done to his personal and professional standing.

When considering the definition of entrepreneur, Richard Cantillon's business life is just as instructive as his commentary on the subject. The whole lugubrious tale of John Law and the Mississippi Company and Cantillon's own role in it is contextually useful when considering his definition of entrepreneur. It provides an interesting prism through which to look at how Saudi entrepreneurs might best be defined.

In the *Essai*, Cantillon's view of the world was shaped by the agrarian and merchant-based economy that prevailed in the seventeenth and eighteenth centuries. For Cantillon, in these predominantly feudal type systems, there were two classes of people, landowners and non-landowners. For Cantillon, land was everything and the source from which all wealth sprang. In the first few pages of *Essai*, he explains: "Land is the source or matter from which all wealth is drawn; man's labor provides the form for its production, and wealth in itself is nothing but the food, conveniences, and pleasures of life."[3] In Cantillon's day, and through his approach to economic theory, wealth not only sprang from landowners, but their selected use of their wealth created entrepreneurial opportunities for business-minded artisans and skilled laborers who started their own enterprises in close proximity to the moneyed landowners. Reaching critical mass, the accumulation of these "entrepreneurs" clustering around the landed gentry eventually gave birth to villages and then whole cities.

Throughout his life, Richard Cantillon's business pursuits involved great risk, of his own money and personal reputation and those of others. To Cantillon, that is what an "entrepreneur" does ... place one's own resources or those borrowed from others at risk in the pursuit of profits that have no certainty of being realized. The risks in Cantillon's time are the same as those existing today. An entrepreneur accumulates or acquires the resources needed to begin his or her business and maps out a plan to deploy those resources in what is hoped will be a money-making and profitable venture. Unless it is a "sure thing" ... as unlikely today as it was then ... usually there are a lot of hopes and wishes tied to the success of the business.

One hopes that the novelty of the product or service will be enough to attract, acquire, and retain the customer's buying interest. One hopes that the enterprise's business plan, marketing and financial prowess, and after-sales customer service is sufficient in surmounting the challenge of one's competitors so as to allow for profit and growing market share. One hopes that over time they have the creativity and stamina to consistently beat the competition through innovations in improved products, services, and pricing so as to retain or increase market share. And lastly, and perhaps most important from an investor's perspective, one hopes that after taking all of those risks and exerting maximum effort and skill, the business is successful enough to return a profit on the investment in the resources expended to make a go of the business. As Cantillon wrote: "These entrepreneurs never know how great the demand will be in their city, nor how long their customers will buy from them since their rivals will try, by all sorts of means, to attract their customers. All this causes so much uncertainty among these entrepreneurs that every day one sees some of them go bankrupt."[4]

Most people readily make a direct correlation between youth and risky behavior. However risky starting a business may be, in the United States Americans do not find the prospect all that alien. Paul Reynolds is a key figure in the founding of the Global Entrepreneurship Monitor, an ongoing academic research study project that examines the behavior of individuals starting and managing a business. It was initiated as a joint venture between Babson College and the London Business School. Mr. Reynolds commented on the predilection in the United States for starting entrepreneurial ventures when he wrote: "By the time they reach their retirement years, half of all working men in the United States probably have a period of self-employment of one or more years; one in four may have engaged in self-employment for six or more years. Participating in a new business creation is a common activity among U.S. workers over the course of their careers."[5]

In Saudi Arabia, in what many perceive as a culturally influenced risk-averse environment, a youthful population struggles to meet one of Richard Cantillon's critical definitional elements of being entrepreneurs ... the willingness to take risks. The possibility of failure of a new business venture in Saudi Arabia is an altogether different proposition from what it is in the United States. In Saudi Arabia, culturally one's failure in starting a business is not only viewed as a personal defeat, but is often viewed as a stain on one's reputation and is thought of by some as an abiding social humiliation. The prospects of ever shedding oneself of such pejorative predations dims significantly when the business failure results in default on the repayment of borrowed monies originally secured to start the business. This is a serious impediment to starting business ventures in the Kingdom. Aspiring Saudi business people and serial entrepreneurs have cited stories of failed ventures and defaults in repaying bank borrowings only followed by denials for credit and further borrowing by lending institutions for anything. This is a formidable deterrent for anyone in Saudi Arabia looking to start a business venture and has limited access to funding.

In Saudi Arabia, the willingness to take on the risk of starting a new business and the ability to secure the financial resources to do so are viewed by many as such significant barriers that the Saudi government has stepped in with public spending in order to address the problem. As one newspaper reported: "The government has found it hard to promote startups in a society that lacks a culture of risk-taking and where financing options for small firms are rare. As a result, it is plowing oil money into small ventures in an unusual combination of state intervention and private entrepreneurship."[6] We will discuss most of the Saudi government's efforts to ameliorate the plight of would-be entrepreneurs in search of startup and growth capital later in the next chapter.

The attendant risks of starting a business, squarely settled upon the entrepreneur's shoulders, are elemental and essential to the definition of "entrepreneur." As the "EY G20 Entrepreneurship Barometer 2013" noted concerning the risk of financial failure, establishing a business is inherently risky. The report recommended that countries learn to refrain from penalizing entrepreneurs for their failure and strike a proper balance between the pecuniary interests of their creditors and the accommodation of entrepreneurs to fail and keep moving toward their goals of creating a successful enterprise.[7] It is important to understand, however, that it is not only the risk of financial failure with which a startup has to contend, there are other risks endemic to new business ventures. To satisfy Richard Cantillon's definition of "entrepreneur," the risk of customer rejection, insufficient market demand, failure in market penetration amongst stiff competition, failure to maintain suitable price points, and the risk of failing to acquire and employ necessary management skills are all hurdles an entrepreneur has to clear before being considered a successful one.

Before expanding on the definition of "entrepreneur" through a look at J. B. Say's perspectives on the term, an important point should be made at this junction on the subject of risk. When applying the word in the Saudi context, there are some popular notions in Saudi Arabia that must be considered before any useful definition is deduced. So, let's ask ourselves: Can the word entrepreneur be applied to a second- or third-generation Saudi FOB member who undertakes a new business venture within the confines of an existing FOB or starts his or her own venture using family money?

Saudi Arabia possesses some of the brightest young business minds in the world. As has already been discussed, some pretty brilliant older ones have proven their worth there, too. They come from all walks of life and areas of business. Their origins mirror the great diversity of economic opportunities that all Saudis see every day in the Kingdom and also view on its future horizons. The traditional idea of an entrepreneur is someone who has a business idea, develops the proper business plan, acquires the requisite knowledge and skills to present that plan to able and willing investors and funding sources, launches, successfully markets the products or services, and then works to make the business grow. However, could not the definition of a Saudi entrepreneur fit the circumstances of a second- or third-generation Saudi working in the family's business while developing his or her own idea for a business venture? Although the financial capital to pursue an idea may come from the FOB, a pool of money the first-generation owners set aside for such entrepreneurial offshoots, it is still "something new." Conceptually at least, and most importantly for this discussion, the goal of this new undertaking is ultimately to add value to the FOB and the resources expended to develop the product or service and execute the plan for the new business.

Any attempt to have the Saudi entrepreneur meet Cantillon's early definition of the word will yield some differences in applying his definition when considering the idea of the traditional single-man startup. This is particularly so in cases of second- or third-generation FOB members who strike out on their own to start new businesses under the watchful eye of the FOB's first-generation founders. As opposed to the traditional single-man startup scenario, the financial capital to start a new venture may be more easily accessed from a Saudi FOB, particularly one that has achieved great success and a formidable capital structure over decades. Also, the risk of financial collapse of the new business may be more deftly absorbed by the financial wherewithal of an established Saudi FOB. And lastly, the prospects for recovering one's good name after it has been tainted from a failed business is much brighter when that good name is attached to a well-known Saudi FOB and the notoriety of such a failure is muted and shielded from public view by other prominent and successful family members.

In researching this book, some Saudis with whom I have spoken told me they do not consider the second- or third-generation Saudi FOB member an entrepreneur in any context. The most common rationale for their position is that these individuals do not risk anything substantial they actually own since they have their family's business standing behind them. For those holding this opinion, risk is the pre eminent feature and inextricable element of becoming and being an entrepreneur. Going back to the early development of the definition of "entrepreneur" and entrepreneurial activity, however, decades after Richard Cantillon's seminal *Essai*, J. B. Say had much to say about the "undertaker of risks" of which Cantillon spoke.

French economist and businessman Jean-Baptiste Say (1767–1832) was an ardent follower of exalted classical free market economist Adam Smith. Smith's impact on economics is rarely overstated and he has been highly venerated from the time he began his literary engagement in the discipline. J. B. Say translated Smith's great work *An Inquiry into the Nature and Causes of the Wealth of Nations,* commonly referred to as *The Wealth of Nations* into French and was heavily influenced by the celebrated and towering Scottish economist and moral philosopher. J. B. Say's thoughts on the "entrepreneur" and its impact on economics, however, had less to do with classical economics or mainstream economic theory than with the perceived real-world impact on the dynamic operation of economies. For Say, the economic point to be made with the "entrepreneur" was not so much the usage of existing resources to maintain equilibrium in an economy as much as the change in the value and character of those resources as a result of their planned use by the entrepreneur.

The renowned modern business management theorist Peter F. Drucker, previously quoted, wrote of J. B. Say: "The entrepreneur," said the French economist J. B. Say around 1800, "shifts economic resources out of an area of lower and into an area of higher productivity and greater yield." But Say's definition does not tell us who this "entrepreneur" is. Since Say coined the term almost two hundred years ago, there has been total confusion over the definitions of "entrepreneur" and "entrepreneurship."[8] This is the change in the value of the resources the entrepreneur presses into service and the resultant assets that forms the core foundation of Say's definition of "entrepreneur."

As Drucker goes on to write: "Admittedly, all new small businesses have many factors in common. But to be entrepreneurial, an enterprise has to have special characteristics over and above being new and small. Indeed, entrepreneurs are a minority among new businesses. They create something new, something different; they change or transmute values."[9] It is in Drucker's interpretation of J. B. Say's definition of "entrepreneur" that we find the concept most expansive and accommodating of the Saudi entrepreneurial context once combined with the essential element of risk. It is when this type of commercial alchemy occurs when Saudi men and women start their own businesses and create new products, goods, and services that the definition of "entrepreneur" takes on life within the Kingdom.

Perhaps the Saudi entrepreneur creates a new industrial process for making an old product. Or, let's say hypothetically a Saudi business woman takes such a ubiquitous item as the *abaya,* a woman's outer robe-like garment (normally black in color) and required public dress for Saudi women inside the Kingdom, and creates a completely new garment with pockets and wiring melded into its fabric, lending the robe groundbreaking functionality in smartphone communication and connectivity to social media. Whatever the new or "next best thing" may be, it is in the utilization of what exists in regard to resources and how they are presently applied to produce a higher yield or market value that best defines what is an entrepreneur ... a Saudi entrepreneur. Again, in applying both Cantillon's definition (risk) and Say's definition (value transmutation) of entrepreneur, the entrepreneur has to have started his or her own business, commercialized a new invention, service, or process while somewhere along the way having assumed certain risks associated with the potential success or failure of the business and loss of value. Whether the money to launch the new business is borrowed or already owned (individually or by family), it is the ingenuity, innovation, and the sweat of the brow of the entrepreneur that drove them to take acquired resources and produce something of elevated value that ultimately found market receptivity.

There is one other economist whose views on entrepreneurship and commercial activity has relevance to the definition of "entrepreneur" in the evolution of entrepreneurship and small businesses in Saudi Arabia.

Joseph Alois Schumpeter, Austrian-American economist and academician, and one of the most influential and quoted authors on the subject of capitalism, is perhaps best known for coining the term "Creative Destruction." In his book *Capitalism, Socialism, and Democracy,* Schumpeter described the process of the evolution of international and domestic economies through the irrepressible and constant agitation of industrial mutation. Schumpeter wrote: "The opening up of new markets, foreign or domestic, and the organizational development from the craft shop and factory to such concerns as U.S. Steel illustrate the same process of industrial mutation—if I may use that biological term—that incessantly revolutionizes the economic structure from within, incessantly destroying the old one, incessantly creating a new one."[10]

Schumpeter developed a theoretical approach to understanding the changing foundations of evolving economies by viewing their super-structures differently from the prevailing economic thought of the time. Schumpeter dismissed the common economic theory of the day, which viewed the behavior of industries as a kind of management of existing and static structures rooted in a terra firma upon which capitalists directed their steady march to higher prices and profits. Schumpeter sought to supplant this textbook analysis with one in which the multi faceted behavior of capitalism's actors results in not only a shifting of the ground upon which these structures reside, but businesses being created and destroyed in an incessant cycle of the demise and rebirth of whole industries and their markets. As Schumpeter further wrote: "The fundamental impulse that sets and keeps the capitalist engine in motion comes from the new consumers' goods, the new methods of production or transportation, the new markets, the new forms of industrial organization that capitalist enterprise creates."[11]

Although in his theoretical musings in *Capitalism, Socialism, and Democracy* Schumpeter pondered the ultimate fate of capitalism and the possibility that the entrepreneur eventually could go the way of the dinosaur, he repeatedly underscored the essential role of entrepreneurism. He stated: "We have seen that the function of entrepreneurs is to reform or revolutionize the pattern of production by exploiting an invention or, more generally, an untried technological possibility for producing a new commodity or producing an old one in a new way, by opening up a new source of supply of materials or a new outlet for products, by reorganizing an industry and so on."[12]

As has been mentioned before, the variety of definitions of the term "entrepreneur" and the opinions on what exactly that word means are seemingly inexhaustible. It is not my purpose in this book to create a new definition of the term "entrepreneur," even in the Saudi context. A useful assemblage of critical elements that would serve to describe the essentials of what it takes to be a Saudi entrepreneur in the Kingdom today, however, can be cobbled up. This conceptual understanding would include familiar and generally accepted ideas of entrepreneurship such as size, risk, novelty in invention, innovation in new product, technology or service development, and the truly maverick nature of commercial individualism. A contextual understanding of the word "entrepreneur" in the Saudi context would require a pooling of the views of Richard Cantillon, J. B. Say, and Joseph Schumpeter on the assumption of risk, transmutation of the value of resources, and creative destruction, respectively, to arrive at a representative portrait of today's Saudi entrepreneur.

So, crafting an amalgam of definitional elements from Cantillon, Say, and Schumpeter, we can say that for one to be considered a Saudi entrepreneur, there is a requirement that there be a securing of resources, through loans or utilization of pre-owned assets, a Saudi business person employs in producing a product or service. Attendant to this requirement is that the value of those resources be at risk and is dependent upon the ultimate profitability of the business. (Cantillon) The second requirement is that the Saudi business person, through his or her actions, ingenuity, and drive has taken the value of those resources and transmuted them into something that is different and of higher value (Say). The third prerequisite, and perhaps the most elusive, is that the Saudi businessperson be engaged in an act of "creative destruction" affecting the industry sector of relevance so as to help set new market realities in terms of price, demand, process, and current product or service innovation (Schumpeter).

As we turn next to look at the Saudi entrepreneur and his or her environment in the Kingdom, let us look at them through these three elemental defining lenses.

Perhaps one of the most uncluttered yet inclusive definitions of "entrepreneur" I have found is one offered by M. J. Gottlieb, author of *How to Ruin a Business Without Really Trying* (Morgan James Publishing, 2014). He is quoted by *Business News Daily* as saying:

> *An entrepreneur is someone who can take any idea, whether it be a product and/or service, and have the skill set, will, and courage to take extreme risk to do whatever it takes to turn that concept into reality and not only bring it to market, but make it a viable product and/or service that people want or need.*[13]

Armed with three main conceptual elements of what defines an entrepreneur, let us now consider the thought processes of Saudis in deciding to become entrepreneurs and specific examples of Saudi entrepreneurship that may help us understand what it means to be an entrepreneur in the Kingdom today.

SAUDI ENTREPRENEURS—THE DECISION TO GO INTO BUSINESS

To be a Saudi embarking upon the start of one's own business venture must seem a daunting proposition. For a culture in which most of life's basic necessities have been provided by either the government, the family extended unit or the family's businesses, and where possessing a strong "work ethic" is only recent gaining momentum in meaningfully defining one's cultural and social identity, becoming an entrepreneur is often perceived in the Kingdom as having mixed rewards. Particularly among young Saudis just starting their own adult lives, the lure of a secure government job has always been the strongest and most attractive option. Although attitudes have been changing, many Saudis still prefer the relative security and stability of employment in the public-sector over private-sector jobs.

Young people seeking employment in Saudi Arabia may commonly be heard deriding menial or tradecraft work. If one is without a university degree, becoming a shop mechanic, taxi driver, tool machinist, hotel desk clerk, or bellhop is still considered to be very much beneath oneself. Even with a degree, most university graduates are widely viewed as preferring to secure jobs in government or senior titled positions in the private sector upon leaving school. As the *Arab News* reported in January 2014, after polling human resource specialists: "Most Saudi graduates still prefer to work for government and would only move to the private sector if offered jobs by large firms in the banking or petrochemical industries ..."[14]

It is a matter of common reporting in the Kingdom that one of the top considerations among Saudi job seekers is job security. In November 2015, *Al Arabiya News* reported on a Boston Consulting Group (BCG) study that surveyed various age groups of Saudis in terms of how they prioritize the importance of their job-related factors. The study, as reported by *Al Arabiya News,* found that for Saudis in their thirties, the most important single job element for Saudi nationals is job security.[15] There are signs, however, that Saudis are warming up to private sector job prospects, and in particular, self-employment through entrepreneurship.

A study published by Bayt.com and YouGov in November 2015 titled "Bayt.com Entrepreneurship in the MENA Survey" has shed keen insight into how individuals in the Middle East–North Africa region view entrepreneurship. The study included more than 8,000 male and female survey respondents 18 years and older from 13 countries, including the Kingdom of Saudi Arabia. Among the Saudi respondents, the study found that while 28 percent stated their preference as seeking a salaried position with a private company, 67 percent would rather be self-employed in their own business.[16] Furthermore, the study showed that though 31 percent of Saudis would prefer to work in a government position, a majority, 69 percent, signaled their preference to work in the private sector.[17]

As the Saudi private sector struggles to comply with ever-more stringent labor laws requiring them to make more of their vacancies exclusively available to Saudi citizens, interest in non-executive titled positions from Saudi job seekers remains apathetic. In a 2014 report by the Riyadh Chamber of Commerce and Industry (RCCI), the *Saudi Gazette* reported that the RCCI found that in the first six months of 2014, the private sector advertised a total of 11,751 job vacancies for positions such as production line employees, accountants, cashiers, engineers, exhibition managers, salesmen and saleswomen, data entry clerks, technical support staff, customer service officials, operations analysts, health supervisors, personnel affairs specialists, marketing employees, mechanics, receptionists, security guards, drivers, electricians, welders, and others. Out of that number, only 1,760 Saudi men and women submitted applications for them.[18] Still, the Saudi government's efforts to change the mind-set of an increasingly expectant youthful population concerning the acceptance of medium- to lower-level skilled and titled jobs are ongoing.

A weekly Saudi television program called "Jobs on Air" televised on the Al-Danah television channel, claims to have provided at least 8,500 jobs for young Saudi males and females since going on the air early in 2015. The program has reinforced the deep cultural influences that guide young Saudi decisions, particularly Saudi males, as to the kind of work they choose when they begin to seek employment. Mr. Mohsin Shaikh Al-Hassan, the program host for "Jobs on Air" was quoted by *Arab News* as saying: "Saudi families did not train their children while small to do chores at home. They provided everything the child needed. That's why children don't want to accept menial jobs when they grow up. Another reason is the fact that 'in our heritage, young Saudi males prefer to work in the government instead of in the private sector.'"[19] Mr. Al-Hassan also suggested that young Saudi males eschew lower-level private-sector jobs from fear of not being considered a suitable marriage partner by Saudi females seeking bona fide spousal prospects.[20]

Increasing employment of Saudis, particularly young Saudis, is a top priority of the government. Publicly announced programs for job creation within the private sector, financed and structured by the Saudi government, have been replete with official exhortations concerning the push to have more Saudis employed at all levels of the economy. In July 2014, the Saudi Ministry of Transportation announced plans to form a joint company with the Saudi Human Resources Development Fund (HRDF) that would provide state of the art taxi service in the Kingdom. The new service would be called "Tahamel Holding Company" and initially be commissioned to operate in Riyadh with a fleet of 500 cars and 600 Saudi-only drivers. Women would not be permitted to be among the 600 drivers since Saudi-observed customs prohibit women to drive.[21]

Government programs to help unemployed Saudis, such as the "Hafiz" program, have helped Saudis find jobs. Introduced in early 2012 by the Saudi Ministry of Labor, "Hafiz," an Arabic word with the double meaning of "incentive" and "motivator," is a program through which unemployed Saudis are paid a monthly stipend of SR2,000 ($553). Recipients must meet a number of conditions to continue receiving the monthly payments. Hafiz applicants are required to continue to actively seek employment and to take advantage of employment opportunities when presented. The program was meant to act as a bridge between job providers and job seekers. The program has a commendable track record of encouraging collaboration with the private sector in the identification and posting of available job vacancies. Much of it is available online to Saudis interested in locating appropriate employment prospects.

While some have criticized the Hafiz program as a form of welfare, others however, have deemed it a necessary financial bridge for Saudis transitioning from a period of post-education and initial unemployment to circumstances of gainful private-sector employment. Still, for many Saudis, the gravitational pull toward government jobs as opposed to private-sector employment is still quite powerful.

On January 3, 2012, the *Arab News* reported on protests by a group of Saudi health care university graduates against a government plan to employ them as doctors and nurses at private hospitals. Large groups of young health care professionals were reported to have protested outside the Ministry of Civil Service offices in Najran, Abha, Taif, and Jeddah, as well as the Saudi Ministry of Health building in Riyadh. The chief complaints against the government's plan voiced by protesters were the comparatively low salaries in the private sector versus those available working for the government and slow, irregular salary increases. The article stated: "The graduates fear working in private clinics and hospitals where they believe salaries and benefits are poorer than those available to government sector employees."[22]

Women, who perennially rank among the most unemployed in the Kingdom and face tremendous, seemingly intractable, structural labor issues, are also rejecting job opportunities in the private sector. Women represent 45 percent of the Saudi population, and routinely average between just 13 to 15 percent of the workforce over the last five years. Recent Ministry of Labor data shows that 85 percent of unemployed Saudi women are university graduates.

One of the intended benefits of the Hafiz program was to aid in correcting the high structural female unemployment problem in the Kingdom. Two years after the implementation of Hafiz, however, it was reported that women were shunning Hafiz-facilitated private-sector jobs, opting instead to work in government positions or jobs in education. It was reported in the media that more than 682,000 females refused to join jobs in the private sector offered by Hafiz. Of this number, 417,000 said they wanted to work in education and 265,000 preferred to work in the government sector.[23]

Moreover, even when Saudi laws and regulations are changed to serve the goal of higher female employment in the Kingdom's private sector, the realization of those admirable objectives are far from certain. Such has been the case in the retail job market and the government's recent approval to mandate Saudi female workers in retail stores.

There was a longstanding ban on women working in retail establishments in the Kingdom. The mixing of Saudi women and men on the sales floors of commercial establishments has been banned in the Kingdom for many decades. This ban has been based on legal regulations as well as religiously, culturally, and societally enforced observances of norms, mores, and customs. In recent years, the Kingdom's leaders have earnestly exerted efforts to change the high tide of female unemployment by opening up jobs in the Saudi retail sector so that women could work in supermarkets, jewelry stores, lingerie shops, and other public commercial places as sales clerks and cashiers. Strong opposition to such moves, including officially sanctioned *fatwas* against such employment liberalization measures, has often stymied progress and seriously affected debate on this critically important topic.[24]

In 2010 and 2011, the Saudi government began to relax restrictions on women working in retail through what many would come to know as the "Feminization Program." After creating a phase-in system of allowing women to assume jobs in a growing list of retail establishments such as jewelry stores, women-only lingerie shops, and supermarkets, the Saudi government used a carrot-and-stick approach to encouraging compliance by the private sector. With the easing of restrictions came also the imposition of fines and penalties against noncompliant owners of stores selling women's consumer goods who failed to employ a female-only floor staff. Faced with fines and restrictions on their ability to recruit foreign workers and renewal of immigrant worker visas, many retailers responded positively by increasing the number of female employees. In 2010, in reaction to the changed regulations, well-known retail supermarkets such as Panda, Marhaba, and Centrepoint began to hire women as cashiers. Centrepoint went further and placed female employees on the sales floor.[25]

Years later, however, despite the failure to achieve satisfactory levels of female participation in the workforce, women appear to be abandoning some of those hard-fought-for retail jobs previously gained in some segments of the market. Furthermore, retailers themselves are complaining about the government's phase-in program to aid women and the drop in revenues they claim they have sustained as a result from their attempts to comply with the new laws.

In March 2014, shortly after implementation of the third phase of the Feminization Program permitting women to sell women's goods such as perfumes, cosmetics, shoes, handbags and accessories, and clothing in shops, Saudi businesses were complaining. The Jeddah Chamber of Commerce and Industry stated that 25 percent of its small and medium-sized retailers incurred costs associated with compliance with the program's requirements that translated into losses of US$160 million.[26] With an estimated 200 malls and 13,000 retail shops in the Kingdom, the Ministry of Labor estimated that going into the third phase of the Feminization Program, which entails the meticulous evaluation and counting of women-only shops in databases, an estimated 65,000 will have been created for women.[27] Among the main reasons cited by women for not choosing retail positions selling female clothing and accessories were long working hours, evening shifts, a lack of transportation to and from work, and low salaries.

Whether male or female, the decision to go into business and become an entrepreneur is a weighty one. For most people, it is a decision that extends beyond thinking about it in purely economic terms. The decision to start one's own business is multifaceted and many considerations such as social, cultural, and those of personal finance all go into the mix. Even if one finds one is without a job and low prospects for gainful employment, thought given to starting one's own business draws in considerations well above purely dollars and cents. This is particularly true in Saudi Arabia.

I have refrained from using the term "ecosystem" in this book. I believe it is an overused and often mis-employed term to describe a set of local, regional, and global realities most new and budding entrepreneurs face when seeking success in starting or growing a business. Descriptions of the most business-friendly self-styled ecosystems commonly highlight certain economic catalysts such as financial incentives (tax credits, soft loans, easy access to capital), proximity to ready customer bases and market channels, nurturing government small business policies, and quick access to intellectual talent pools. To be sure, all of these elements would be useful to any jurisdiction seeking to foster the growth of its entrepreneurial base. Most descriptions of ecosystems, however, often omit the influential role cultural and societal forces play in the inception, growth, and ultimate success of individual business ventures.

In Saudi Arabia, as well as many other Islamic countries, in many instances one's cultural and social orientation will significantly influence one's experience as an entrepreneur. As previously discussed, in Saudi Arabia how your peers, family members, friends, and social acquaintances view your place within the culture and society commands great concern from most Saudis. This certainly applies to the decision to go into business. The power of religion, especially in Saudi Arabia, where those faithful to Islam rely on a high degree of religiosity in setting life's pursuits, is also a determining factor for many embarking upon a path of entrepreneurship.

In the book, *Islamic Entrepreneurship,* authors Rasem N. Kayed and Dr. Mohammed Kabir Hassan, posited that entrepreneurship in the Islamic world has very distinct characteristics and its approach to the phenomena incorporates Islam's inherent values into the totality of related economic activities. The book's research methodology was based in part on surveying and interviewing Saudi entrepreneurs in the Saudi capital of Riyadh. One of the interesting findings of Kayed and Hassan was that their survey results yielded definite opinions concerning how Saudis view the interrelatedness of Islam and entrepreneurship. In Chapter 6 of their book, Kayed and Hassan state: "There was a definite agreement among responding Saudi entrepreneurs in embracing Islamic-based modernization where 99 percent of respondents believe that Saudi Arabia should build upon its Islamic values, not its customs and traditions, in its pursuit of modernization and development. Entrepreneurs have emphasized that Islamic values, not people's traditions, should map their modernization process and guide them toward the state of well-being."[28]

Kayed and Hassan's book also affirmed the view I have found to stand during my research that culture significantly affects a person's business pursuits. The authors state:

> *Data indicates that 44 percent of Saudi entrepreneurs view Saudi culture as placing emphasis on the social status of the individual rather than on his or her own personality and credentials. Furthermore, two in three respondents feel that social capital, such as immediate and extended family members, tribe, friends, and other social associations, play a crucial role in shaping the social and the business status of the individual.*[29]

The views expressed by most of the respondents in *Islamic Entrepreneurship* were also in consonance with the opinions of Ali Al-Jeraisy noted earlier in Chapter 3 in that the belief that the approach to entrepreneurship in the West is not always in the best interests of Saudis to follow. The book stated: "[T]he majority of Saudi entrepreneurs did not agree with the proposition that Western entrepreneurs are 'better' than their counterpart Muslim entrepreneurs regardless of the meaning they attached to the word 'better.'"[30]

In my understanding, the decision-making process of Saudis in contemplating going into business, hearing from new and budding Saudi entrepreneurs themselves has proved most revealing. Next, I offer summaries of several conversations I have had with several notable Saudi business people concerning their experiences.

MR. SAUD AL-SUHAIMI, CEO OF JAWLAH TOURS

The story of Saud Al-Suhaimi's is illustrative and informative of the journey many Saudis undertake in establishing themselves as entrepreneurs and successful business people in the Kingdom. What struck me about Saud's entry and development in business is the display of several singularly important qualities that greatly assist new and budding business people in the success of their endeavors. From the beginning, and throughout his life as a business-man so far, Saud's trek in business has been marked by his ability to retain and put to use knowledge gained, adapt to and be guided by convictions on his own best perceived career paths, identify and capitalize on available resources, and to discern critical market trends.

Saud Al-Suhaimi is the founder of Jawlah Destination Management Company (Jawlah DMC). It is the first Saudi specialized travel and tour operator in the Kingdom. The company specializes in the meticulous preparation and offering of incentives, meetings, conferences, and events related to travel throughout Saudi Arabia. The depth of local resources and expertise, extensive industry knowledge and creative approaches to handling logistical challenges have facilitated a meteoric rise of what was at one time just an idea in the mind of Saud to run one of the most successful tourism companies in the Middle East. The roots of Jawlah's success is traced to the first of those singularly important entrepreneurial qualities mentioned earlier, *the ability to retain and put to use knowledge gained.*

Saud began his studies at King Fahad University of Petroleum and Minerals (KFUPM) in 1999 with the intention of earning his degree in computer engineering. His aspirations at that time were to gain as much knowledge about computer technology and engineering so as to enable him one day to establish his own computer manufacturing plant. Saud says even after beginning his undergraduate studies, he knew his real passion was business, not engineering. Although his ultimate goal was to start his own business, from 1999 to 2003 he continued four years with his elected degree major in computer engineering. Toward the end of that period, Saud realized that he began encountering some ephemeral difficulties with his education. The process and routine of gaining and retaining the content of his course work at KFUPM was being bogged down by an encroaching realization that his heart wasn't in it. "Computer engineering was not my passion. It is a very precise area of study and a somewhat rigid way of thinking. I was definitely having serious reservations about my work at KFUPM," Saud recalls.

So, after four years of studying the science of computer technology, Saud found himself at a crossroad. Still yearning to start his own busi-ness, yet having invested so much time in the study of computer science, Saud felt conflicted over how he should proceed with his education and vocational pursuits. At the time, Saud thought: "I found myself lost after studying computer engineering for four years. I didn't think it was a waste of time, because through that course work I gained keen analytical abilities and grounded knowledge in problem solving. Nevertheless, I felt myself drifting and knew I needed to step away from the concentrated course work to take a break."

So, as he finished his 2004 spring semester at KFUPM, Saud decided to apply to King Saud University (KSU) in Riyadh to add some courses and seek part-time employment in the capital city. He landed a part-time sales job at the Nike Sportswear store located in the Al-Faisaliah Mall in Riyadh. "It was one of the best things I did at that time. Through this opportunity at Nike, I discovered that I possessed really good skills in sales. I was very much impressed by the money to be made in sales and was able to earn good wages over the summer." The sales experience at Nike served to reignite Saud's passion for business and he resolved to return to KFUPM and shift his major from computer science to marketing.

Having spent a few years studying engineering acquiring an arsenal of analytical skills, he was ready to put to use the knowledge gained. In demonstrating the second of those singularly important entrepreneurial traits, the ability to *adapt to and be guided by convictions on his or her own best perceived career paths,* after his work experience at Nike, Saud redirected his life's energies to his real passion—business. Returning from his summer in Riyadh, in 2004 Saud began course work for a business degree in marketing at KFUPM. From 2004 to 2007 he studied marketing. Halfway through this period, in 2006, Saud recalled with particular savor his first work experience in marketing when he became a trainee in an advertising agency. "I gained invaluable work experience and became familiar with critically important and widely used advertising methods. I put this industry knowledge to work in real-world business situations," he said. After graduating from KFUPM, his next step was to go into business.

Saud graduated KFUPM with a burning desire to start his own business. He says, "I wanted to start my own business, but there was a problem ... I had no money and no idea on what business to start." Embarking upon the path of entrepreneurship, Saud manifested the third enterprising quality enumerated earlier, *the ability to identify and capitalize on available resources.* In formulating his thoughts on deciding on a course of action toward his startup, Saud turned to the closest and most valued resource most of us have ... family.

Surveying business activities in his hometown of the Holy City of Medina, Saud knew the core business engine there is the tourism industry, which revolves around the great religious role the City of Medina plays in Islam. Initially, he thought of starting a business as an authorized religious travel agent, a designation that requires official state licensure and minimum startup capital of US$266,640 (SR 1,000,000). He also thought of starting a hotel. At that time, however, the required capital to enter that business was also beyond his reach. Describing his initial difficulty with his startup decisions, Saud said:

> *I relied on the problem-solving techniques I learned at the university (KFUPM) to examine how best to decide on what type of business to start. As I moved through the door of religious tourism, I knew I should try to find a window to the industry. In other words, I thought perhaps there were some small service areas not currently being covered by the current industry. I began my market research. I met with tourists and spoke with them about their experiences and their needs. I soon realized there was a segment that was missing from the tourism market. That was the professional side of touring Islamic landmarks of Medina. That is where my decision to start a professional tour operator came from.*

After more than seven years in business, Saud can look back on what was a firm and reasoned decision to start his professional tour operations company. The skill sets he acquired during his years at KFUPM and the real-world experience in business working for the Nike retail store and the advertising agency are still being put to good use. The risks that he assumed and the family and local resources he employed in Medina in starting his business in hindsight demonstrated his keen entrepreneurial intellect. Saud's ability to identify the characteristics of the tourism market in Medina and to adjust the perimeters of his startup while settling into an unoccupied niche of the Saudi commercial landscape is equally impressive. It has also been profitable.

Saud sold a 51 percent stake in his company to Al-Tayyar Travel Group Holding Company (ATG) as Jawlah Tours Establishment for Tourism (JTET).[31] JTET is now a subsidiary of one of the largest travel and tourism companies in the Middle East. With more than 20 offices worldwide, including Europe and the United States, ATG has benefited from Saud and JTET's unique ability to contribute a dimension of the tour business ATG did not possess before investing in Jawlah. As Saud put it: "Of course, Al Tayyar had clients, with 400 branches and 7,000 corporate accounts, however, they did not have that particular arrow in its quiver—the capability of offering socio-cultural organized tours from A to Z. Jawlah had that ... as well as the ability to cater to "extreme travelers." Jawlah is one of only a few companies showing Saudi Arabia to primarily corporate travelers visiting the Kingdom. Ninety percent of Jawlah's business comes from corporate travel planning.

Within only a few short years of starting his business, Saud and Jawlah experienced remarkable success in business. In 2011, *Gulf Marketing*

Review featured Jawlah Tours Company as the recipient of the "Best Tour Operator" award at the "Excellence in Tourism Awards (SETA) presented at the Saudi Travel and Tourism Investment Market (STIMM), held in Riyadh in March 2011. The STIMM was held under the auspices of HRH Prince Sultan Bin Salman Bin Abdulaziz Al Saud, president of the Saudi Commission for Tourism and Antiquities (SCTA). Jawlah's "Best Tour Operator" award was one within eight categories and a high honor within one of the 26 subcategories covering all aspects of Saudi Arabia's tourism market.[32]

When I interviewed Saud for this book, he was quite sanguine about Jawlah and the future of Saudi Arabia's tourism industry. The travel and tourism industry in the Kingdom is valued at US$45.3 billion, and with all of the planned construction in the country, the industry is poised for long-term and robust growth. SMEs can and will play an important role in that market sector's growth as well as the expansion in many other industries. Saud offered some insightful and poignant views on the environment for entrepreneurism, however, and what it takes to be a successful entrepreneur in the Kingdom.

Saud's comments concerning entrepreneurship in the Kingdom introduced a healthy bit of realism to the research I was conducting on the environment for new and would-be businesses people. "It's not easy to be an entrepreneur when you look at how government encourages young people to get into business almost as a type of panacea for life's challenges. It's not easy. I think it is a dangerous thing to persuade young Saudis to shift their interests on what would otherwise be a focus on having a decent job to starting a business and all the risks that are attendant to that," Saud professed. He was somewhat critical of institutions that encourage people to start up their own businesses without first providing the minimal requisite tools to do so, such as a safe and nurturing environment.

What Saud was alluding to is the disappointing failure rate of most startups. Most experts peg the startup failure rate for all businesses at around 75 percent. Some have estimated that 9 out of every 10 business startups fail for one reason or another.[33] "I have seen Saudis begin their businesses, and after three or four years, and then leaving their businesses or selling 50 percent of their companies because of a variety of challenges they are not able to meet. I have a lot of friends that are selling their businesses." Saud said. "I'm telling you, the environment for entrepreneurs in the Kingdom is a lot more challenging than what has been portrayed in the media," he added.

There are many issues entrepreneurs face in Saudi Arabia that present challenges for the long-term success of their businesses. These include access to operational capital, acquiring critically important knowledge of how to run a business, learning and successfully applying winning marketing strategies, finding competent human resources, successfully funding and managing the scalability of a business, and many other uncountable aspects of being a profitable entrepreneur. It is hard for me to imagine someone or a group of people aggressively meeting these challenges without an enduring and potent desire to run their own business. It is not too difficult to understand how many are lured into the path of entrepreneurship on the promise of profits and success in life. This is particularly so when you have your government telling you that funding, training, and other support is readily available to you if you only take the plunge. As we will see in the next chapter, that government support is available. in his labor to grow Jawlah, however, Saud maintains he did not use much of it.

"I did not use much government support," Saud recalls. Many Saudis in business shun government support and go it alone. Saud believes there are basically two types of successful entrepreneurs in the Kingdom. The first, he says, are those who seemingly work in the shadows. "You don't hear about them," Saud says. "No one really knows about them and how they are building their businesses." They avoid the notoriety of the media. They make a great deal of money, however, without most knowing about it.

The second type of entrepreneur are those whose successes in business are well publicized and even politicized. The media, government, family, and friends hold them up as perfect examples of the Saudi entrepreneur. Their ingenuity, business prowess, and achievements are on full view for all to admire and marvel at their successes in business. Saud, numbering himself and Jawlah among this second type said, "We're in the light and receive a lot of the public's attention. We're followed by media and in turn we also follow the media and what is being said about us and other entrepreneurs."

Looking back on his own successes, Saud believes it is much better to be a traditional entrepreneur, the first type, in which one selects a growing industry and grinds away in virtual anonymity away from the public's attention. In his view, there is not as much creativity associated with business success in these industries as opposed to high tech, social media, or other newly invented areas of business. But, he believes this type of entrepreneur eventually finds the path more enjoyable and self-reassuring.

Saud believes it is easy for today's new entrepreneur in Saudi Arabia to become overwhelmed with the day-to-day tests that all business people must pass. Saud said when he began his startup, he believed he would grow his business and earn a decent income in the long term. He admits that rather than being eagerly engaged in the more enjoyable aspects of business such product development and marketing, he often finds himself bogged down with the more onerous facets of his business such as legal compliance and administrative brushfires. Saud admits: "When I started my business, I had no doubts about anything! And now, after seven years in business, I have doubts about everything!"

One other line of conversation with Saud that I found particularly helpful was his opinion on the question examined in this book: Whether second- and third-generational business people who are members of FOBs should be considered real entrepreneurs; the thought that subsequent generations of FOB members do not bear the same hardships, risks, and challenges a lone startup or individual businessperson manages when beginning or growing their enterprises. A number of Saudi business people with whom I spoke are of the opinion that the same accepted definitional standards of an entrepreneur does not apply to an FOB member. I asked Saud Al-Suhaimi whether he considered family-owned business second- or third-generation business people true entrepreneurs. His comments were insightful. He said:

> When I started my business and it began to pick up, as I began to get recognition, I found that I was a bit narrow-minded. When I would meet with some of my colleagues from some of Saudi Arabia's family-owned businesses that helped to grow their family's businesses, I thought they are not real entrepreneurs. I thought this because they started their business by having everything handed to them. Yes, they produced things, but they were able to make things out of resources they had made available to them. I said to myself, I am the real entrepreneur. However, over time, my opinions on this began to change. I found that it's not true these family business members are not true entrepreneurs. Like me, these people also have taken ideas and made a thriving business from that idea. You make resources out of the resources you have available. Regardless of where the resources come from, if I start from $0 and move the value of my business to $10 million, and a family businessperson moves from $10 million to $20 million in value, it is the same result. Like me, they are transforming a thing of lower to a higher value through their effort and creativity.

Saud's comments are in line with the beliefs of many, including those expressed by J. B. Say, which say that for someone to be considered an entrepreneur, there has to be a "transmutation" of the value of resources from a particular value to a higher one. Saud's Jawlah has certainly done this and continues to add value to the company and its investors.

MR. ABDULRAHMAN AL-OLAYAN, BUSINESSMAN, LECTURER, DOCTORAL CANDIDATE

Abdulrahman Al-Olayan possesses keen insight into some of the daunting challenges facing Saudi entrepreneurs. Abdulrahman Al-Olayan is a lecturer at Taibah University. He received his undergraduate degree in business from Taibah University in Medina, Saudi Arabia, and obtained his master's degree in business administration (MBA) from Bloomsburg University of Pennsylvania in the United States. He is currently a doctoral candidate at Morgan State University in the United States and works for their research department. During his business studies and having also trained at Imam Muhammad Ibn Saud Islamic University in Riyadh, he also began to pursue his own interests in business.

Saud started his own real estate business while he was studying at KAU. His business grew successfully, however, while running his business. Abdulrahman also assisted his Saudi compatriots in pursuing their own aspirations in starting and running successful businesses. He began to teach small business courses at Imam University. As he explained, "I wanted to assist aspiring business people to transform their lives and help them move up the socio-economic ladder by providing them basic entrepreneurial skills so they could launch their own businesses."

Ten years ago, Abdulrahman began teaching and working with both new and would-be entrepreneurs, both men and women. He has designed and taught university courses, seminars, and workshop lectures. He has acquired valuable experiences in providing career advisory programs and workshops as well as establishing career counseling centers benefiting men and women from various circumstances and geographical locations throughout the Kingdom. He has also provided course instruction to government employees. When one teaches people, one not only imparts information but one also gains knowledge from those one teaches concerning their beliefs and experiential realities related to their economic, social, and cultural station in life.

Abdulrahman has worked with young Saudi entrepreneurs in helping them realize their dreams. As he described the primary motivation of his work with budding business people, he said, "In beginning my work with the men and women looking to start their own businesses, I knew I wanted to help them transition from levels of lower economic means to a higher status. I wanted to help provide them with basic entrepreneurial skills so they could launch their own businesses." He holds definite opinions on the cultural, social, and economic influences experienced by most of today's Saudi entrepreneurial class.

Because of the particular challenges faced by women entrepreneurs, in recent years Abdulrahman has concentrated his efforts on organizing seminars and instructional workshops for Saudi women. His first workshop on teaching women the basics of successful entrepreneurship came in 2006. He believes that the obstacles for women in the creating and growing their businesses can be suppressive. The difficulties that women face in conceptualizing their business proposition, maneuvering through government bureaucracy and private business communities and influential circles and solving problems are more than what men face because of the gender-specific obstacles they face every day. Beyond this, during my interview with Abdulrahman for this book, he identified three main problem areas for Saudi entrepreneurs, education, social construction, and legal.

Education

After some time in the Kingdom, I learned that the Saudi educational system and how comprehensive examinations are administered to test student's proficiency on course curricula is different from that in the United States. To the learned follower of the Saudi educational system, particularly if you are Saudi and have successfully made your way through it, criticisms of how education is administered, delivered, and student performance assessed is common knowledge within the country. Complaints are frequently made by students that the system fails to adequately encourage individuality of opinions and reward personal preferences in their pursuit of greater knowledge within course disciplines. According to Abdulrahman, this perceived and often experienced rigidity in the system can be stifling to the entrepreneurial spirit and ambitions of matriculating Saudis. For Abdulrahman, this is a question of the proper development of an entrepreneur's character and behavior.

During my interview with Abdulrahman, he identified what he believes is one of the main weaknesses in how a curriculum is delivered and courses taught in Saudi Arabia. "There is a problem with the curriculum in the country. The system tends not to build free thinkers. Encouraging this dimension early and doing it throughout one's schooling is important in building as strong a character and indomitable behavior as possible," he said.

Course subject matter is uniform throughout Saudi Arabia virtually from kindergarten through twelfth grade to the university level. Until the seventh grade, all courses are taught in Arabic, after which English is injected into some courses. As opposed to the American practice, where students are tested throughout the year, often at the end of a quarter or trimester, Saudi students are tested on their accumulated knowledge only at the end of the school year. Teachers in Saudi Arabia customarily encourage and often require students to acquire and retain their course knowledge by rote. Memorization of course materials is prevalent locally, regionally, and nationally throughout the Saudi educational system.

Abdulrahman disapproves of this way of learning because, in his opinion, it holds a low tolerance for disagreement. When he views the student experience in the United States, he sees teaching predominately done through the Socratic approach, in which students are encouraged to challenge the validity of the theories upon which course materials are based and subjects presented. Through this teaching method, teachers prod their students to stretch their understanding and curiosities of the subject matter through expressing their opinions on what is being taught and even to articulate reasoned disagreement. Abdulrahman believes this method gives rise to the unrestricted spirit in the student, whereby he or she is eventually better equipped to identify, perceive, interpret, and ultimately deal with life's vexing dilemmas. As he put it: "In Saudi Arabia, you cannot argue with a teacher. Culturally, Saudi are predisposed to take what is being taught at face value and as a given. This molds the character of the Saudi entrepreneur at an early stage in development. It reinforces a lack of creativity. Only a strong personality and inner maverick streak will likely counteract this influence."

Others affirm Abdulrahman's belief. In an editorial for *The Harvard Crimson,* the oldest continuously published daily college newspaper in the United States, Talal Alhammad, a government contractor at Harvard University's Quincy House, recalled his educational experiences in the Kingdom. Drawing comparisons between what he views as an American educational system conducive to fomenting debate, dissent, and free thinking, and the Saudi system that he experienced in which dissent was suppressed, he stated:

> *[U].S. higher education helps students express their opinions, regardless of what stance students take or contrasting argument they might make. However, to criticize a teacher's arguments in a Saudi school is unimaginable. It is not uncommon in Saudi Arabia for students to be completely silenced if they question the validity of a professor's argument. I personally have been dismissed from the classroom countless times during high school for simply challenging the teacher's line of reasoning.*[34]

Mr. Alhammad went on to say:

> *Critical thinking is essential to a healthy and progressive education. Unfortunately, this type of instruction is not employed within the borders of Saudi Arabia at the high school or college level. Saudi schools do not emphasize the importance of independent thinking, opting instead to conveniently spoon-feed students information that does not test their mental capabilities.*[35]

Whether a nation's education system is more favorable to breeding more successful entrepreneurs than others would make for a long debate. Abdulrahman Al-Olayan's point is that how one approaches problems and obstacles as an entrepreneur is truly a definitional attribute. As we have seen earlier in this chapter, the businessperson who has the capacity for creative destruction, that ability to go forward uninhibited by the status quo of commerce, is a prerequisite to be an entrepreneur. For Abdulrahman and others, an educational system that fails to incubate disrupters is one that imposes artificial confines to the full development of the entrepreneurial spirit. But, for Abdulrahman, there is another problem area for Saudi entrepreneurs that must be considered.

Social Construction—Women's Issues

Business does not happen in a vacuum. As mentioned before, when starting a business in Saudi Arabia, one's social station, family and tribal identity, and social connections within Saudi society can weigh significantly on the support one receives during the often long struggle to make it. This is particularly true for women. As Abdulrahman has witnessed, the struggle for women in starting their own commercial enterprise and growing it is very much influenced by the socially enforced conformance to the established customs, mores, and laws governing gender interaction.

Abdulrahman made the point to me that by virtue of the social norms and legal regulations pertaining to gender in the Kingdom, a woman running her business, by and large must conduct her business through an experiential labyrinth. This maze is marked by a strict set of rules governing interaction with men, most family members, and government bureaucrats, who have considerable influence on the woman's ability to get things done. Abdulrahman believes that this is a system that does not afford women the opportunity to experience the running of a business first-hand as compared to the male entrepreneurial experience. In the male experience, the man faces a myriad of obstacles, problems, and challenges from a full frontal perspective. This means that men trying to run a business must bring to bear all of their abilities of problem solving to each obstacle confronted while running their business in the first and every instance without a filter in the form of gender interaction. Not so for the woman entrepreneur.

Abdulrahman looks upon the business environment for women in the Kingdom as one in which a woman trying to run a business must run a gauntlet of weigh stations or checkpoints wherein she must obtain the requisite "sign-off," permissions, approvals, or other approbations without which things just will not get done. He firmly believes that these socially imposed restrictions present significant inhibitors to the proper development of a woman entrepreneur's abilities to the solve problems that inevitably arise in running a business. Abdulrahman also thinks these barriers suppress the free stimulation of ideas that are the bedrock of creativity upon which a successful enterprise thrives. Empirical evidence supporting Abdulrahman's views on the limitations of women in the Saudi business world are scant because of the dearth of scholarly works on the subject. There have been surveys, research papers, and other reports, however, pertaining to the Saudi woman business experience worth citing.

"Doing business with impudence: A focus on women entrepreneurship in Saudi Arabia," a full research paper submitted by Muhammad Asad Sadi and Basheer Mohammad Al-Ghazali, and accepted by the King Fahd University of Petroleum and Minerals in Dhahran, and Naizak Global Engineering Systems[36] of Al-Khobar in 2009, examined the critical questions concerning Saudi women business owners. The purpose of the study was to look at the reasons why Saudi women choose to start their own business as well as examining some of the barriers they face in the Kingdom. Although the findings of the paper were based on a survey sampling of 350 participants, the study shed a rare light on the motivations and perceived limitations faced by women entrepreneurs voiced by women themselves.

The researchers, Mr. Sadi and Mr. Al-Ghazali, cited the usefulness of the study as identifying the factors that motivate Saudi women to start their own businesses and the barriers they face while doing so. The Sadi and Al-Ghazli study also restated an often presumed truism that there are significant differences between men and women in how they view aspects of starting a business and their motivations for doing so.

On the main motivation factors for women business startups, the study identified four primary motivators from the woman's point of view: (1) self-achievement, (2) independency, (3) self-confidence, and (4) profit motives. The study showed that both business men and women agreed that self-achievement is the most important factor that motivates Saudi females to start their own businesses.[37]

The study also cited the main barriers faced by women at the time of startup. According to Sadi and Al-Ghazali, the study survey's respondents listed the four main barriers as: (1) traditional restrictions; (2) lack of market studies; (3) lack of support of government; and (4) market domination by few investors.[38] Business women indicated that traditional restrictions are the most important barriers while business men indicated that a lack of market studies is the most important barrier facing Saudi women.[39]

The Sadi and Al-Ghazali study finally listed the four main operating barriers to starting a business identified by the study's respondent as: (1) lack of coordination between the various government departments; (2) lack of laws protecting her investment and customers; (3) lack of support of community, and (4) socio-cultural restrictions. Both business men and women study respondents agreed that the lack of coordination between the various government departments is the most important operating barrier facing business women.[40]

In a thesis paper written by Mariam Alhabidi in partial fulfillment of Arizona State University in a future award of Ms. Alhabidi's master's degree of science and technology, and approved in March 2013 by the university's graduate supervisory committee, she wrote on her research into Saudi women and their entrepreneurial pursuits. The thesis explored to what extent it is possible for Saudi women to start and grow their own businesses and through which their ability to "increase Saudi women's socio-cultural autonomy, financial independence, and overall well-being."[41]

The findings of the research Ms. Alhabidi conducted to arrive at her conclusions were based on surveys and actual interviews of Saudi business women. Her findings affirmed those of Mr. Sadi and Mr. Al-Ghazali in their paper concerning the barriers to women starting their own businesses and their chief motivations. Writing about several of the successful business women she interviewed, Ms. Alhabidi wrote:

> *These women were motivated to open their own businesses by a lack of employment opportunities as well as a desire for a higher wage or also a means to fulfill their dreams. Several of these women displayed a high level of self-confidence and self-reliance, something, which is not commonly displayed by the majority of Saudi women. Running their businesses also provided a source of increased self-confidence and self-reliance. These female entrepreneurs did face the usual business challenges of paying high rent or obtaining skilled employees. However, unlike women in Western countries, they also faced additional cultural and legal obstacles such as they were not allowed to deal directly with government agencies and required male drivers to travel about the country.*[42]

Women in Saudi Arabia are required to have male signatories, normally their husbands, close male family members or male guardians, to register a business or open a bank account. As Abdulrahman Al-Olayan pointed out during my interview with him, this places a buffer between the would-be business woman and the valuable experience of dealing with initial startup and other business matters. Women in Saudi Arabia are very much restricted in their dealings with government bureaucracies whose male clerks and desk personnel will not interface with them while executing their legal and regulatory responsibilities. These limitations are culturally and socially enforced and, according to Abdulrahman, will continue to present significant obstacles for women entrepreneurs.

Notwithstanding the significant barriers known to Saudi women in starting their own commercial enterprises, many of them still view entrepreneurship as a viable and inviting career path. A recent study by Glowork, the premier Saudi organization formed by young Saudi entrepreneurs that aims to empower women in the Saudi and GCC workforces and create equal opportunities for women reported that 33 percent of women in the city of Jeddah want to be entrepreneurs.[43]

Legal

Eminent Domain Abdulrahman Al-Olayan's last problem area for Saudi entrepreneurs pertains to the legal environment in the Kingdom that sometimes acts as an impediment for SME and new businesses. The two examples Abdulrahman cited were of policies and practices in eminent domain and the lack of a sufficient e-commerce infrastructure.

Abdulrahman recalled that when he started his SME consulting business and began organizing programs to assist Saudi men and women entrepreneurs in building their knowledge base and experiences in starting and running their own businesses, he related his own experience of raising capital to start his business and selected an office. Soon after opening his business in the Holy City of Medina, Abdulrahman was notified that land adjacent to the property upon which his business was located had become the a part of a tract of land over which the Saudi government would exercise its right of eminent domain to facilitate officially sanctioned development. The effect on his business and others more directly affected by the government's economic development plans was severely damaging. As Abdulrahman recalls, a grocery store owner affected by the government's move had to shut down as a result of a blocking of the public's access to his store for a year or more.

Eminent domain in the Kingdom is quite dissimilar to the public appropriation of privately held property in many other countries. In the United States, the right of the government to expropriate private property from its owners for its own purposes is well entrenched in law. It was first litigated in the U.S. Supreme Court case of *Kohl v. United States*.[44] In this case, a private landowner in the state of Ohio challenged the U.S. government's right to take privately owned property and convert it to the government's use. The U.S. Supreme Court ruled that the government's authority to take property for its own use was "essential to its independent existence and perpetuity."[45]

Further development of eminent domain law in the United States pertaining to compensation for the grieving landowner whose property is the subject of government seizure centers squarely on the Fifth Amendment of the Constitution. The Fifth Amendment expressly states: "...nor shall private property be taken for public use without just compensation."[46] The rights of the landowner in formally challenging the government's appropriation is firmly rooted in U.S. jurisprudence. Those rights extend to the landowner's enforced claim on the government to receive the "fair market value" of the property being deprived the landowner from government action. Although the procedures to be followed by aggrieved landowners affected by eminent domain actions vary widely throughout U.S. jurisdictions, there are clear paths of recourse available to them. Abdulrahman laments that such policies and landowner remedies are not as developed in Saudi Arabia.

Indeed, instances of Saudi commercial landowners being deprived of their properties, in whole or in part, have been well publicized in the country. The most notable cases have involved private landowners in the Holy Cities of Mecca and Medina where land prices are among the most expensive in the world. A few years ago, land in the Holy City of Mecca ranged between US$133,000 and $400,000 per square meter.[47] Land prices in Mecca and Medina are constantly being projected upward, with only short periods of price dips. With land prices so high, the Saudi government, central and municipal, rarely stop at the doorstep of disgruntled property owners in preventing their acquisition of land required for the construction of government-sponsored project developments related to an expansion of the holy pilgrimage.

It is the absence of predictable and firmly rooted avenues of recourse for a business owner whose property is subject to eminent domain in Saudi Arabia that Abdulrahman cites as a considerable legal hindrance to business people in some cases. He notes that businesses, particularly retail and client counseling establishments, can be severely affected when properties they own and count on to receive their customers are summarily shut down or access restricted.

Although not cited as an impediment by Abdulrahman Al-Olayan, another legal issue affecting the growth of entrepreneurism in has been the lack of modern bankruptcy laws. When considering the bright future of a startup or business person struggling to get an enterprise off the ground, it may seem counterintuitive to seek relevancy in laws that protect against business failure. The state of bankruptcy laws in the Kingdom, however, has long been a subject of interest for the Saudi private sector. Bankruptcy laws, particularly as they pertain to commercial bankruptcy, has been of continuing interest to the Saudi government as well.

The issue of how the Kingdom addresses the subject of bankruptcy is of such importance to the creation of an enabling environment for the growth of entrepreneurship, a brief and separate discussion of the topic follows.

BANKRUPTCY IN SAUDI ARABIA

As noted earlier in this chapter, the specter for an entrepreneur of failure of his or her business in Saudi Arabia is financial ruin and a personal failure that may have long-term social and cultural ramifications. Given the current state of how insolvency is settled in Saudi Arabia, many Saudis hoping to start their own businesses subscribe to the commonly held fear that once one experiences a business failure, it is highly unlikely that a bank or other lending institution will extend them additional funds to capitalize a new beginning. The potential stigma from failure in business is real and the lack of a substantive reformation of Saudi insolvency laws is often cited as discouragement of entrepreneurism. In contrast to the static nature of the state of bankruptcy laws in Saudi Arabia, like the doctrine of eminent domain in the United States, American bankruptcy laws are strongly rooted in the founding of America, the U.S. Constitution, and the ongoing development of U.S. common law on the subject.

In establishing laws governing insolvency at the beginning of the new nation, the authors of the U.S. Constitution borrowed from British laws on bankruptcy and gave the legislative branch of the new government power over the declaration, management, settlement, and ultimate disposition of insolvencies in the United States. Article I, Section 8, of the United States Constitution authorizes Congress to enact "uniform laws on the subject of bankruptcies."[48] Through this Constitutional authority, the U.S. government has developed its bankruptcy laws, making them deliberative and incessant. These laws are as rich and as colorful as the history of the United States itself and closely tracks the many milestones it has experienced during its journey as a nation.

In *Debt's Dominion: A History of Bankruptcy Law in America*, a book written by David Arthur Skeel Jr., law professor at the University of Pennsylvania Law School, Professor Skeel offers a panoramic view of the origin and development of American bankruptcy law.[49] From the incipient tussle between the federal government and the states, the dawn of the nation's railroads, to the Great Depression, and the rise of the American consumer economy, Professor Skeel delineates the development of a body of law that has been both dynamic in its growth and adaptive in its application. Throughout its development, bankruptcy laws and regulations were adopted that varied between their service of debtor or creditor rights.

As Professor Skeel noted in *Debt's Dominion*, based on its constitutional authority, the U.S. Congressed enacted its first bankruptcy law in 1800. That law only covered the involuntary bankruptcy of traders. The 1800 law was repealed and was followed by the passage and subsequent abrogation of several other bankruptcy laws and amendments governing insolvency. This eventually led to the first modern and permanent bankruptcy law in the United States with the passage on July 1, 1898, of the Bankruptcy Act of 1898, also known as the "Nelson Act."[50]

From the early origins of American bankruptcy law, whenever new legislation was crafted, there was usually a firmly established nexus connecting the interests of the debtor, creditor, and the nation's economy and society. The question as to whether a proposed piece of legislation would have bankruptcy imposed on the insolvent by force through creditor action or sought voluntarily by the bankrupt was one of the most hotly contested issues prior to the passage of the Nelson Act. In fact, the Bankruptcy Act of 1898 was a product of conferenced bills, each turning on whether it allowed for voluntary or involuntary declarations of insolvency. Professor David Skeel, in a scholarly paper for the University of Pennsylvania Law School Legal Scholarship Repository before his *Debt's Dominion* book, noted: "The House passed a voluntary bill (the 'Bailey Bill') in 1894, and the Senate Bill (the 'Nelson Bill') that was reconciled with its very different House counterpart (the 'Henderson Bill'), which permitted involuntary bankruptcy only in limited circumstances, such as fraudulent behavior by the debtor."[51] As Professor Skeel observed in his paper, there were some who wanted no bankruptcy law at all.[52]

Leading up to the passage of the Nelson Act, named for Minnesota Senator Knute Nelson the author of the archetypal legislation, the "Upper Country Bill" was dropped in the congressional hopper in 1875. This bill was the legislation from which the Bankruptcy Act of 1898 derived its origin. As Professor Skeel notes at significant length in his book, the nation's railroad companies and the expansion of the country's rail system was one of the most potent factors feeding the attention given to the development of the nation's bankruptcy laws.

The existence and growth of the nation's railway system was of enormous importance to the expansion and security of the country's boundaries. A constant obstacle for railroad companies were the incessant conflicts with landowners arising from the company's need to acquire land so they could expand the length of railway track. Land laws varied from state to state, and it was often the case that a rail company's ability to successfully expand its network hinged upon how deftly it maneuvered state and local politics and wrestling land away from recalcitrant landowners.

This was certainly the case with Senator Knute Nelson. Of paramount importance to Senator Nelson at the time was his work in extending rail track through northern Minnesota. The ability of the state and railroad companies to secure land for railway track through purchase, eminent domain, and the sale of property through the forced bankruptcy of landowners was part and parcel of the political cauldron brewing over the creation of permanent bankruptcy laws in that era. The Bankruptcy Act of 1898 finally settled this matter and provided for both voluntary and involuntary insolvencies. Of significance here for our discussion of corporate bankruptcy, however, the 1898 law did not permit corporations to voluntarily declare bankruptcy.

Numerous amendments and changes to U.S. bankruptcy laws followed the Bankruptcy Act of 1898. The next major change came in 1926 when

Congress amended the law to allow for the voluntary declaration of bankruptcy by corporations. There were other amendments that favored creditors. The totality of American insolvency laws, however, remained, on balance, more favorable to debtors.

It is important to note that up until the Bankruptcy Act of 1898, insolvency laws in the United States and most of Europe were decidedly pro-creditor. In many instances, debtors were not permitted a discharge of their debts without the consent of their creditors. In Great Britain between the thirteenth and mid-nineteenth centuries, debtors were routinely punished by imprisonment and other harsh punitive measures for their personal financial failures. Even during the early days of America, debtors were thrown in debtors' prison for failing to satisfy their debts. So, the Bankruptcy Act of 1898 was seen as a distinct change in the treatment of both personal and corporate insolvencies.

Further developments of bankruptcy law in the United States during the 1900s witnessed major revisions of the Bankruptcy Act of 1898 with revisions of all of that law's provisions in the 1938 Chandler Act; the Dischargeability Act of 1970 (Pub. L. 91–467, October 19, 1970, 84 Stat. 990); which greatly enhanced debtors' rights concerning the discharge of their debts; and most importantly, the Bankruptcy Reform Act of 1978. The Bankruptcy Reform Act of 1978, codified as Title 11 of the United States Code, was the most comprehensive revision of insolvency laws since the Chandler Act of 1938 and greatly facilitated the filing of bankruptcies for people and corporations. The Bankruptcy Reform Act of 1978 has been credited with greatly contributing to the United States becoming known as one of the world's most litigious countries. Significant amendments to the nation's bankruptcy laws were adopted and made law throughout the 1980s and 1990s, further strengthening the procedural, administrative, and substantive structure of U.S. law governing corporate and personal insolvencies.

After more than 117 years of permanent bankruptcy laws, American jurisprudence persists in honing the relevancy and utility of its system of adjudicating insolvency in the country. Although not even slightly approaching the maturity of U.S. law on the subject, bankruptcy in Saudi Arabia is also viewed as a work in progress.

As it currently stands, the bankruptcy laws of Saudi Arabia are antiquated and do not approach the standards of most commercially competitive nations. The basis of the Kingdom's regulations governing insolvency can be found in two laws that lack the kind of procedural or substantive specificity one would expect to find in modern bankruptcy laws. The Commercial Court Law (CCL), promulgated by royal decree No. 32 and issued on June 1, 1930, established the procedural regulations and subject jurisdiction of Saudi Arabia's early national court system. Under the law, all commercial disputes, except for those related to the insurance business, were declared to be settled by a "committee for commercial disputes" comprising two Shariah judges and one legal advisor. On January 24, 1996, the Bankruptcy Preventive Settlement Law (BPSL) was promulgated, which essentially removed the adjudication of commercial bankruptcies from the committee system set up by the CCL and gave such disputes between business debtors and creditors to the Board of Grievances. The law allowed debtors the option of arbitrating their financial disputes with creditors through the Council of Saudi Chambers of Commerce and Industry or the Board of Grievances.

The Board of Grievances, established by royal decree No. M/51 on May 10, 1982, created an independent administrative judicial commission responsible directly to His Majesty the King of Saudi Arabia. Although its administrative seat is in the Saudi capital city of Riyadh, it basically operates as a circuit court and hears cases from throughout the country. Since its creation in 1982, the Board of Grievances has grown significantly in its subject matter jurisdiction. On June 24, 1987, pursuant to Resolution No. 241 of the Council of Ministers, the chief consultative body to the King, consisting of his cabinet, settlements of commercial disputes were transferred to the Board of Grievances. Article 8 of its 1982 enabling law gave the Board of Grievances jurisdiction over deciding requests for the implementation of foreign judgments. Its decisions are rendered through a dependence on the Holy Quran. Foreign companies that have had to litigate trade and other business disputes with the board have historically complained of board decisions that have on occasion lacked impartiality, objectivity, and precedential reasoning. In recent years, however, those accusations have diminished.

The absence of comparably modern bankruptcy laws in the Kingdom that facilitate the efficient and uncomplicated discharge of debt works against the economy's need to preserve or reallocate the resources of failed businesses. They should be either saved or left derelict, respectively. A revealing study on where Saudi Arabia stands with its bankruptcy laws appears in the twelfth edition of the World Bank's flagship "Doing Business 2015" Economic Profile of Saudi Arabia.[53] This World Bank publication reports on how easy or difficult it is for Saudi entrepreneurs to open and run small- to medium-sized businesses while complying with relevant regulations. It measures and tracks 11 distinct areas in the business life cycle. Among those 11 areas is "resolving insolvency." In its introduction to resolving insolvency, the report made note of the utility of efficient laws on insolvency, stating:

A robust bankruptcy system functions as a filter, ensuring the survival of economically efficient companies and reallocating the resources of inefficient ones. Fast and cheap insolvency proceedings result in the speedy return of businesses to normal operation and increase returns to creditors. By improving the expectations of creditors and debtors about the outcome of insolvency proceedings, well-functioning insolvency systems can facilitate access to finance, save more viable businesses and thereby improve growth and sustainability in the economy overall.[54]

In the Resolving Insolvency section of the World Bank "Doing Business 2015" report, the Kingdom scored low in several important areas pertaining to the administration and procedural management of bankruptcies. In the reported data, the Kingdom took an average of 2.8 years and 22 percent of costs from the debtor's estate to resolve its insolvency. The report noted even then the most likely dispositive outcome would be the debtor company being sold piecemeal to satisfy the discharge of its debts. In the scored indices on subjects pertaining to "management of debtor's assets," "reorganization proceedings," and "creditor participation," the Kingdom failed to register any points in the rankings.[55] Among the 189 countries ranked in the "Doing Business 2015" report, Saudi Arabia ranked 163rd overall on the ease of resolving insolvency.[56]

The significance of such low rankings in the national experience of handling insolvencies have real consequences for failed business people who struggle to reestablish themselves commercially. In addition to the societal and cultural attitudes on business failure, which translate into a very personal stigma, commercial debtors also have to run a gauntlet of laws and regulations historically favoring creditors and the safeguarding of their interests against the assets of the insolvent. In a March 2011 policy research working paper for the World Bank titled "No Way Out, the Lack of Efficient Insolvency Regimes in the MENA Region." Mahesh Uttamchandani underscored these points when writing: "One of the main shortcomings is the approach to debtors as wrongdoers, even criminals, rather than economic actors in distress."[57] Commenting on the lopsided approach some MENA countries have taken in handling insolvencies, Mr. Uttamchandani goes on to say:

Several countries in the region have laws that punish debtors with civil penalties such as loss of the right to manage a company, restriction of movement (seizure of passport), and even prison. The approach to a debtor as an entity to be rehabilitated is rare in spirit, and still more rare in practice, as across the region, reorganization is rare, even when legal provisions may allow it. Such reorganization provisions tend to be heavily creditor-driven, providing little flexibility to debtors. Even liquidation procedures, which are perhaps better understood, are considered ineffective. Provisions in the laws are dated. Many of the laws have not been revised and modernized for a decade, or several decades.

Circumstances in the Kingdom may be changing. After a prolonged period of the private sector expressing their dissatisfaction with the current lack of updated bankruptcy laws, His Excellency, Minister of Commerce and Industry (MCI), Tawfiq Al-Rabiah has taken the lead in moving the needle forward on reform.

In March 2015, the MCI announced it was soliciting public comment on a draft of new bankruptcy laws for Saudi Arabia. In its announcement and articulation of the drafting of the proposed new regulations, the ministry touched on most of the problems arising from antiquated bankruptcy laws and economic interests served in facilitating reorganization of failed businesses and discharge of debt. The ministry stated:

> *MCI pointed out that the new draft of bankruptcy seeks to create a systemic environment that may contribute to expand the private investment base in terms of number and volume, through the preservation of the private economic value, to be added to the overall economy. Therefore, the new draft of bankruptcy would give priority to conciliation procedures or reorganizing the debtor's situation, who is in financial troubles and there is still a real and true chance to regain his trade activity to a level where he could add values to the overall economy and fulfill his obligations toward the creditors, as well as the new draft aims at liquidating the assets of the commercial institutions, which may fail to regain their trade activity in a regular and fast way.*[58]

Once adopted, this new law will be a definite step in the right direction. It also reaffirms the Saudi government's willingness, particularly the continuing improvement-mindedness of the MCI to change the business regulatory environment for the better—for both those regulated and for those whose benefit regulations are in place, that is, the Saudi people.

Establishing the regulatory framework that would constitute a safety net for failing entrepreneurs is a meaningful and markedly different approach in cultivating the kind of undaunted spirit successful startup communities around the world have achieved. Apparently, at least in part, this is what the MCI wants to achieve. In its announcement, it stated: "MCI stresses the importance of the new draft of bankruptcy for small and medium enterprises. Therefore, the new draft would contain a number of provisions that take into account the nature of these enterprises and stimulate entrepreneurs to start their business. These provisions would include simplified and swift remedial action to deal with the small and medium enterprises in case of financial troubles, in addition to some of the detailed provisions that might help stimulate the private sector to finance these enterprises."[59]

The absence of up-to-date bankruptcy laws has been cited by some of the interviewees for this book as a hindrance to developing the kind of creative entrepreneurial environment Saudis want to see. There is a question, however, if the concern for the prospects for recovery of failed Saudi businesses, particularly startups, is being somewhat overstated.

In a January 2014 press conference, Mr. Sherif Elabdelwahab, former chief executive officer of Riyadah, stated that the failure rate of Saudi entrepreneurs was quite low compared to their counterparts around the world. The National Entrepreneurship Institute, or Riyadah, as it is more commonly known, is a nationally funded program launched in 2004 and offers training, consultations, mentorship, incubation, and financing to SMEs. We discuss Riyadah in more depth in the next chapter. It is important to note at this point, however, that Riyadah's former CEO, Mr. Elabdelwahab, gave the vitality of Saudi entrepreneurship a big vote of confidence when in January 2015 he announced to the Saudi press that 84 percent of Saudi entrepreneurs have succeeded in their business ventures, while only 16 percent failed.[60] This is a strong showing for Saudi entrepreneurs, when we consider that most experts place the global startup failure rate at between 75 and 90 percent.[61]

However much the development of insolvency laws evolve in the Kingdom, I believe there has to be much greater levels of the accommodation of failure in business among Saudis. The failures at business and innovation among Saudi entrepreneurs must find much wider degrees of social and cultural acceptance in the Kingdom. I believe this is gradually happening in Saudi Arabia. However, as with many things in the country, a more accepting adjustment to the phenomenon of bankruptcies will take time.

NOTES

1. *New Republic*, "The Brutal Ageism of Tech," March 23, 2014, www
.newrepublic.com/article/117088/silicons-valleys-brutal-ageism.
2. Ibid.
3. Richard Cantillon, "An Essay on Economic Theory," English translation of
Cantillon's "Essai sur la Nature du Commerce en General," translated by
Chantal Saucier, edited by Mark Thornton (Ludwig von Mises Institute, Kindle
Edition, Auburn, AL) 2010, 20.

4. Ibid. 20.
5. Paul Reynolds, *Entrepreneurship in the United States: The Future Is Now* (Springer, 2007).
6. *Arab News*, "Entrepreneurship Is Becoming a Buzz Word in Saudi Arabia," December 12, 2014, www.arabnews.com/economy/news/673081.
7. Ernst and Young, "EY G20 Entrepreneurship Barometer," www.google.com/url?sa=t&rct=j&q=&esrc=s&source=web&cd=9&ved=0CFQQFjAI&url=http%3A%2F%2Fwww.cdmn.ca%2Fwp-content%2Fuploads%2F2014%2F01%2FEY-G20-main-report.pdf&ei=3FjzVJjqKo7msASj7IDgCQ&usg=AFQjCNH1SDdj7TuPnUkTI5QUGC0obeH1Ug&sig2=fRJOld3fbInsyh9sXHDx8A, 10.
8. Peter F. Drucker, *Innovation and Entrepreneurship: Practice and Principles* (HarperCollins e-books Kindle Edition, Reprint edition, March 17, 2009), 21.
9. Ibid. 22.
10. Joseph A. Schumpeter, *Capitalism, Socialism, and Democracy* (First Start Publishing, e-book Edition) October 2012, Chapter 7, "The Process of Creative Destruction."
11. Ibid.
12. Schumpeter, *Capitalism, Socialism, and Democracy*, Chapter 11, *The Civilization of Capitalism*.
13. www.businessnewsdaily.com/2642-entrepreneurship.html.
14. *Arab News*, "Saudi Graduates Still Prefer Government Jobs," January 17, 2014, www.arabnews.com/news/510581. (Accessed May 9, 2015).
15. *Al Arabiya News*, "Job Security Top Concern of Saudis in their 30s," November 8, 2015, http://english.alarabiya.net/en/business/economy/2015/11/08/Job-security-top-concern-of-Saudis-in-their-30s-.html.
16. Bayt.com and YouGov, "Bayt.com Entrepreneurship in the MENA Survey," November 2015, http://img.b8cdn.com/images/uploads/article_docs/bayt-entrepreneurship-survey-2015_27262_EN.pdf.
17. Ibid.
18. *Saudi Gazette*, "Few Takers for 10,000 jobs Offered by Riyadh Firms," June 16, 2014, www.saudigazette.com.sa/index.cfm?method=home.regcon&contentid=20140616208599.
19. *Arab News*, "Why Young Saudis Turn Down Blue-Collar Jobs," April 26, 2015, www.arabnews.com/news/737901.
20. Ibid.
21. *Arab News*, "New Taxi Company to Employ Saudi Drivers," July 11, 2014, www.arabnews.com/news/600006.
22. *Arabian Business*, "Saudi Healthcare Grads Snub Private Sector Jobs," January 3, 2012, www.arabianbusiness.com/saudi-healthcare-grads-snub-private-sector-jobs-438199.html.
23. *Saudi Gazette*, "682,000 Saudi Women Say No to Pvt. Sector Jobs." December 29, 2014, www.saudigazette.com.sa/index.cfm?method=home.regcon&contentid=20141230228965.
24. *Arab News*, "Saudis Shocked by Fatwa Banning Women Cashiers." November 1, 2010, www.arabnews.com/node/359330.

25. *Arab News,* "Women Cashiers 'Centrepoint' of Jobs," September 16, 2010, www.arabnews.com/node/355280.
26. *Arabian Business,* "Saudi Retailers Claim They've Lost $160m under Rules to Hire Women," March 11, 2014, www.arabianbusiness.com/saudi-retailers-claim -they-ve-lost-160m-under-rules-hire-women-542122.html#.VWuHaH3bKKk.
27. *Arab News,* "Feminization of Shops Creates 65,000 Jobs," August 8, 2014, www.arabnews.com/news/saudi-arabia/613241.
28. Rasem N. Kayed and Mohammed Kabir Hassan, Islamic Entrepreneurship, Durham Modern Middle East and Islamic World Series (Routledge Taylor and Francis Group, London and New York, 1st Edition, 2011), Kindle Edition, Chapter 6, "The Attitudes of Saudi Entrepreneurs."
29. Ibid.
30. Ibid.
31. Al Tayyar Travel Group Holding Company (A Saudi Joint Stock Company) and its Subsidiaries Interim Condensed Consolidated Financial Statements (Unaudited), for the three month period ended March 31, 2014, together with Review Report, www.google.com/url?sa=t&rct=j&q=&esrc=s&source=web& cd=10&ved=0CE8QFjAJ&url=http%3A%2F%2Fwww.tadawul.com.sa%2F Resources%2FfsPdf%2F378_2014-04-22_15-01-34_Eng.pdf&ei=LUmEVdya MYvdsAW_voC4Dg&usg=AFQjCNEygT3rVjn72m1HG7n3AgRUo1mLpw& sig2=YV1gqwonkvLru8JLnLJLOQ&bvm=bv.96042044,d.b2w.
32. *Gulf Marketing Review,* May 2011, No. 198, "Sector Analysis—Local Attractions, http://issuu.com/trendsmagazine/docs/gmr_may_2011, 66.
33. *Fortune,* "Why Startups Fail, According to Their Founders," September 25, 2014, http://fortune.com/2014/09/25/why-startups-fail-according-to-their-founders.
34. Talal M. Alhammad, "The Education Dilemma in Saudi Arabia," *The Harvard Crimson,* February 12, 2010, www.thecrimson.com/article/2010/2/12/saudi-education-students-school/.
35. Ibid.
36. Naizak Global Engineering Systems, Al-Khobar, Saudi Arabia, established in 1998, is an engineering and IT conglomerate providing specialized services to the oil and gas, petrochemical, electrical, power, and IT companies. It is a subsidiary of Al-Abdulkarim Holding Group and has a wide coverage in the Middle East, Asia, and Europe in conjunction with its partner companies. It is a valued member of the U.S.-Saudi Arabian Business Council. Its president, Mr. Khalid Al-Abdulkarim, is also the chief executive officer of Al-Abdulkarim Holding Group and a long-time supporter of public affairs issues that favorably impact the Saudi and U.S. business communities.
37. Sadi, Muhammad Asad, Al-Ghazali, and Basheer Mohammad, "Doing Business with Impudence: A Focus on Women Entrepreneurship in Saudi Arabia," King Fahd University of Petroleum and Minerals, Dhahran, Saudi Arabia, September 7, 2009, *African Journal of Business Management* 4, no. 1 (January 2010): 1–11, www.academicjournals.org/AJBM, www.academicjournals.org/ article/article1381762855_Sadi%20and%20Al-Ghazali.pdf.

38. Ibid.
39. Ibid.
40. Ibid.
41. Mariam Alhabidi, "Saudi Women Entrepreneur Overcoming Barriers in Al-Khober." A thesis presented in partial fulfillment of the requirements for the master of science and technology degree, Arizona State University Repository, March 2013, http://repository.asu.edu/attachments/114415/content/Alhabidi_asu_0010N_13058.pdf.
42. Ibid. 53–54.
43. *Saudi Gazette,* "33 Percent of Jeddah Women Want to be Entrepreneurs," July 29, 2015, www.saudigazette.com.sa/index.cfm?method=home.regcon&contentid=20150729251774.
44. *Kohl v. United States,* 91 U.S. 367 (1875).
45. Ibid. 371.
46. U.S. Const. Amend. V, Sec. 2.
47. *Overseas Property Professional,* "Mecca Home Sales Quadruple in 2013," January 14, 2014, www.opp.today/mecca-home-sales-quadruple-in-2013/.
48. U.S. Const. Art. 1, Sec. 2.
49. David Skeel, *Debt's Dominion: A History of Bankruptcy Law in America* (Princeton University Press: e-books Kindle Edition), 2001.
50. "An Act to establish a uniform system of bankruptcy throughout the United States," United Statutes at Large of the United States of America, from March 1897 to March 1899, and Recent Treaties, Conventions, Executive Proclamations, and the Concurrent Resolutions of the Two Houses of Congress, Volume 30, Chapter 541, July 1, 1898.
51. Skeel, David A. Jr., "The Genius of the 1898 Bankruptcy Act" (1999). Faculty Scholarship Paper 720, www.google.com/url?sa=t&rct=j&q=&esrc=s&source=web&cd=1&ved=0CB4QFjAAahUKEwj7h8TN55zHAhVJ2R4KHelND_g&url=http%3A%2F%2Fscholarship.law.upenn.edu%2Fcgi%2Fviewcontent.cgi%3Farticle%3D1719%26context%3Dfaculty_scholarship&ei=9bPHVbu5D8mye-mbvcAP&usg=AFQjCNEhxabiDJVjHrb_xmpYxUngb2s8pg&sig2=NqccKPseqT098RWNLluZ1w&bvm=bv.99804247,d.dmo; http://scholarship.law.upenn.edu/faculty_scholarship/720.
52. Ibid. 324.
53. The World Bank, "Doing Business 2015, Going Beyond Efficiency—Economic Profile 2015 Saudi Arabia," October 2, 2014, www.google.com/url?sa=t&rct=j&q=&esrc=s&source=web&cd=6&ved=0CD0QFjAFahUKEwi4p_So8_nGAhUJkg0KHTPkBkQ&url=http%3A%2F%2Fwww.doingbusiness.org%2Fdata%2Fexploreeconomies%2Fsaudi-arabia%2F%2Fmedia%2Fgiawb%2Fdoing%2520business%2Fdocuments%2Fprofiles%2Fcountry%2FSAU.pdf&ei=nma1VbjgMomkNrPIm6AE&usg=AFQjCNG6pnEl5MvJ-cwHJfWvIZ0Bj4jxvQ&sig2=Lr530BIrvYygS9_0_pGv4w, WB Report No. 92119.
54. Ibid. 75.
55. Ibid. 76.
56. Ibid.

57. Mahesh Uttamchandani, "No Way Out, the Lack of Efficient Insolvency Regimes in the MENA Region," Policy research working paper 5609, March 2011, 1, https://openknowledge.worldbank.org/handle/10986/33751.
58. Ministry of Commerce and Industry, Media Center, Ministry News, "MCI Requests Opinions of the Public on the New Draft of the General Policies of Bankruptcy," http://mci.gov.sa/en/MediaCenter/News/Pages/17-03-15-01.aspx (Accessed August 23, 2015).
59. Ibid.
60. *Arab News*, "Saudi Entrepreneurs Achieve High Success Rate, Only 16% Fail," January 1, 2015, www.arabnews.com/news/692806.
61. *Forbes*, "Entrepreneurs—The Little Black Book of Billionaire Secrets," Neil Patel, Contributor, "90% of Startups Fail: Here's What You Need to Know About the 10%," January 16, 2015, www.forbes.com/sites/neilpatel/2015/01/16/90-of-startups-will-fail-heres-what-you-need-to-know-about-the-10/.

CHAPTER 5

Exploring Saudi Entrepreneurism and Opportunities for Business

ENTREPRENEURSHIP AS A CATALYST FOR ECONOMIC GROWTH—SAUDI REALITIES

Entrepreneurship has long been recognized as a catalyst for economic growth. The economic consequences of creating a vibrant and healthy entrepreneurial class within a country can pay dividends to society well into the future. These dividends, although often not immediately perceived or seen, may include sustained job creation, foundational support for new industries and technologies, improved workforce skill levels, and the eventual creation of significant built wealth. The motivational factors leading governments or a nation's private sector to support commercial and industrial projects, particularly as they relate to SMEs and the pursuit of innovation, differ from country to country. Saudi Arabia's great push to diversify its economy by fostering broader private-sector participation in the expansion of its technological and industrial bases has led to new programs supporting Saudi entrepreneurs. Before discussing the Kingdom's efforts to support its entrepreneurs, however, the difference between how government and its institutions view their roles in investing in entrepreneurship and innovation and how the private sector weighs in on such areas should be noted.

Orthodox economic analysis views business development projects as being motivated by profits and the avoidance of losses. The reasoning goes something like this: investment decisions are most often taken and capital deployed by companies in projects that hold comparatively low risk and reasonably high assurances of profitable returns. This is particularly true for companies that must spend significant capital investment to fund the research and development of new products and technological advances. Economists theorize that once the decision to fund new product development and related R&D is made and work is undertaken, there may be unforeseen and unintended benefits that inure to a nation's economy and society at large. These potential economic or R&D "spillovers" may, over time, if experienced consistently and quantitatively, have transformative effects on a country's economic and societal well-being.

Established economic theory postulates that as private industry inevitably follows the profit motive, it will usually devote only those quantities of resources to projects that will likely lead to a significant return on its investment. From private industry's perspective, it is this reasonable rate of return as well as the potential for the development of profitable and new products, technologies, and services that form the basis of their investment decisions. Economists have dubbed this favored outcome of business as "private rates of return." This outcome, the theory goes, often falls short of the greater economic and social good to be realized by a nation at-large if the private sector had committed higher levels of capital resources and investment in the first place. This higher economic and social benefit potentially realized by society is referred to by economists as the "social rate of return." When the social rate of return is not realized through a disconnect between higher levels of private-sector spending desired by the government or "the people" so as to secure the optimal national outcome, the occurrence of a "market failure" is recorded.

Until very recently with the onset of government and private-sector initiatives to help small business and entrepreneurship, there has been a "market failure" in the lack of an institutionalized approach to support and promote SMEs and entrepreneurs. As observed earlier and as noted by several business people interviewed for this book, the biggest concerted government effort to support entrepreneurship in the Kingdom occurred during the early days of development of the Kingdom's modern economy and early stages of the Saudi oil industry when the government fed the nation's burgeoning Saudi contractor and vendor and supplier chain a steady diet of contracts and new business.

As noted in Chapter 1 under the section titled "The Private Sector's Role in National Development and Non-Oil GDP," many of the Kingdom's largest and best-known FOBs experienced their modest beginnings through the award of increasingly larger contracts from Aramco and government-controlled procurement entities. As these companies gained more business, their experience and productive capacities ascended ever steeper. The more these companies grew, the more public tenders they would win and government contracts awarded them. The ability of these large and increasingly diversified Saudi companies to win contracts by consistently demonstrating their proficiency in delivering was often enhanced by teaming up with global Western and later Asian firms making them even more formidable competitors.

Over decades, the tendency in the Kingdom has been for smaller companies with much less experience and capacity to be persistently squeezed out of significant and large government-funded project opportunities by the big companies. Many Saudi SMEs continue to voice scant hope in breaking into the highly competitive heavy industrial contracting business because of the high up-front capital costs as well as the commonly held belief that the big contracts always go to the big companies. To be fair, one may observe that when a country has faced such extreme pressures to modernize with breakneck swiftness as Saudi Arabia has over the last five decades, it would be somewhat unjust to criticize it for invariably selecting companies of size in order to get the job done on large and mega-industrial projects. The Kingdom cannot be faulted, however, for having the right intentions. It has always touted the need for an all-inclusive private-sector participation in spurring economic growth.

The Kingdom's development planners have been criticized for what has been perceived by some as a perennial neglect of its emerging entrepreneur class as it is claimed they have lurched from one national economic development strategy to another. Most of the current and serious government-sponsored entrepreneurship development entities and their programs have been created within the last 10 to 15 years. Private-sector entrepreneurship promotion organizations are even newer. Endeavor, for example, to be discussed shortly, has one of the highest impacts of all the entrepreneur organizations in the Kingdom, and it only began activities in 2012 and was launched in May 2014.

For decades, there have been calls from the Kingdom's leaders to the private sector to "do more" to contribute to the diversification of the Saudi economy. As previously discussed in Chapter 1 of this book, since the start of its modern economy, the Saudi government, in public pronouncements, five-year development plans, and its discourse with the Saudi private sector, has strongly emphasized the importance of broad-based private-sector engagement in the country's development. It is worth repeating that the First Five-Year Development Plan stated: "Only by continuously encouraging private enterprise—and small companies, family businesses, and individuals—to pursue those activities that they can undertake more effectively than government agencies, will the economy be able to benefit to the full from the ability and initiative of all its people."[1] Further on in Chapter 1, Objective 11 of Article 1 of the royal decree creating the Supreme Economic Council, stated its goal of: "Increasing the participation of the private sector in developing the national economy through the government's privatization program."[2]

The call from Saudi leaders continues today. Under the able leadership of the Custodian of the Two Holy Mosques, His Majesty King Salman Bin Abdulaziz Al-Saud and His Majesty's ministers, the Saudi government continues to enjoin the private sector to heighten their level of participation in the development of the Saudi economy by spending more investment capital inside the Kingdom that will create jobs and economic opportunities for SMEs. On May 27, 2015, His Majesty King Salman met with a large group of business leaders, including chairmen of the nation's chambers of commerce, heads of banks and Saudi FOBs in order to stress the Saudi government's eagerness to work with the private sector to resolve issues and encourage an increase in their investments in the country. His Majesty was quoted as saying to the businessmen gathered: "Our doors are open and we are ready to listen to your problems and proposals at any time.... Our main concern is the Kingdom and its people and you are part of it."[3]

The lack of greater success in having the Saudi private sector take on a greater share in investments within the Kingdom is the "market failure" constantly being scrutinized by public officials. It is one proposition to advocate for broad-based private-sector engagement in the development of the country's economy, and it is, of course, quite another when the reality is that those predominantly engaged in capital spending on industrial development projects are large family-owned companies or the country's largest quasi-state entities. The curing of this "market failure" of less-than-optimal private-sector participation must include the substantive involution of Saudi SMEs. One is to be reminded that most SMEs began as start-ups. The Kingdom must find more accelerated methods of getting SMEs involved in the growth of the economy through an expansion of available commercial opportunities for this critically important part of the nation's citizenry.

Saudi Arabia's leaders have often recognized the need for a more national commercial engagement more inclusive of the country's SME participation. In March 2014, lamenting the high number of SMEs in the Kingdom owned and run by expatriates, His Excellency, Saudi Finance Minister Dr. Ibrahim Al-Assaf, was quoted as saying, "These establishments [SMEs] are still owned by expatriates, which confirm that we still have a long way to go before these establishments can have an active contribution to employment and the domestic national product. We need to push these establishments to be owned and managed by nationals."[4] The minister went on to say, "There should be more support for small and medium-sized establishments, and stronger funding opportunities. The business environment should be improved to strengthen these establishments' role in the national economy, because small and medium-sized establishments are a rich source of employment opportunities, income, consumption, and growth."[5]

More than a year later, in October 2015, the Saudi Council of Ministers approved the creation of a government entity to combat the Kingdom's intractable long-term unemployment situation and drastically reduce the high composition of foreigners. Commenting in an *Arab News* article reporting on the creation of the entity, economist Fahd Bin Juma was quoted as stating, "... the labor force in the Kingdom is 11,912,209-strong, but of that number, only 47 percent are Saudis (5,591,563) while 53 percent (6,320,646) are foreigners."[6]

Executive leadership farming in Saudi Arabia is in its third real developmental decade. Cultivating tomorrow's business leaders optimizes the possibilities of yielding successful businesses and in turn ensures a steady flow of potential private-sector investors in the domestic economy. Neglect of propagating tomorrow's business leaders will come at the expense of diminishing returns for a nation's economic development schemes. Although some would disagree, I believe the Kingdom's leadership is not only well aware of this but it is doing its best to promote entrepreneurial leadership in the country to foster greater participation in and contribution of SME to the Saudi national economy. The most promising recent development in the Kingdom for entrepreneurship and SMEs has been the overhaul of Saudi government-sponsored SME-focused policies, programs, and institutions.

On Monday, October 26, 2015, the Council of Ministers adopted multiple measures designed to greatly strengthen and support SME growth in the Kingdom and bring the country in line with world standards concerning best practices for SME programs and institutions. His Majesty King Salman approved the creation of an entity called the Public Authority for Small and Medium Enterprises (PASME).[7] This new entity will exercise financial and administrative independence over its affairs but be overseen by a board of directors chaired by the Saudi minister of commerce and industry.[8] It has been known for some time that the MOCI has been studying the feasibility of establishing an SME-focused entity akin to the U.S. SBA, which exists to support and promote SMEs in the United States. PASME looks to have very similar attributes.

To further the purpose of this new institution, Saudi Minister of Culture and Information, His Excellency Adel Al-Turaifi was quoted by the Saudi *Gazette* as stating: "The authority aims at regulating SMEs in the Kingdom as well as in supporting, developing, and taking care of them in line with the best international practices."[9] Minister Al-Turaifi went on to say: "This will be done to achieve the objective of raising their productivity, increasing their contribution to gross domestic product (GDP), raising their capacity to play a role in the national economy in order to generate more jobs for Saudis and the nationalization of technology."[10]

PASME will also take on the enormous responsibility of guiding the establishment of a greater national framework to manage the growth and funding of SMEs in the Kingdom. The Council of Ministers directed that PASME subsume supervisory powers over SMEs previously held by the Coordination Council of SMEs sector within the Saudi Credit and Savings Bank (SCSB) and the National Center for SMEs within the MOCI. The entity tapped to fund Saudi SMEs by having transferred to it responsibilities previously held by the SCSB is the Saudi Industrial Development Fund.

For many Saudi SMEs, especially startups, perhaps there is no more important issue than their access to financing their businesses. Many complain about what they view as the onerous documentary hurdles they must surmount to secure loans from Saudi banks and other financial institutions. In a Bloomberg article on the Kingdom's SMEs and the reduced funding levels of Saudi banks to SMEs, Hasan Al-Hazmi, co-founder of Supply and Logistics Solutions, a 2014 start-up providing storage and cargo services located in Riyadh, summed up the frustration of many Saudis with startups when he was quoted as saying: "Banks are not lending to any startups without providing annual financial statements audited by licensed entities in Saudi Arabia ... [H]ow would I be able to provide a bank with statements if I just started?"[11]

The Kafalah program, established in 2006 and managed by the Saudi Industrial Development Fund (SIDF) of the Saudi Ministry of Finance, offers financial institutions in Saudi Arabia guarantees up to 80 percent of loans made by those institutions to SMEs. The thought behind the program was that banks were not lending to SMEs, particularly new ones, because of the inherent risk of lending to unproven commercial ventures. By shifting that risk to the Saudi government, the thinking goes that financial institutions would be more likely to lend capital to Saudi businesses' skimpy bank and financial statements. The Kafalah guarantees to the lender can last up to seven years. Another related program called Taqeem allows banks to secure important credit information on potential loan applicants in order to better adjudge repayment abilities.

For the year 2013, the SIDF reported it had approved 2,515 guarantees in comparison to the 1,670 guarantees approved the year before. It reported that the value of guarantees issues that year totaled US$342,000. Direct loans to approved SME Kafalah applicants from participating Saudi commercial banks rose from US$471,428 in 2012 to US$625,986 in 2014.[12] Purportedly, since its inception in 2006, a total of 4,082 enterprises have been funded at a cost of US$1.8 billion.[13] The Kafalah program offers more than just SME corporate financing. Training and SME preparedness is also a part of their service function. The SIDF states on its website:

> *Another impressive aspect of the Program's activities is the fact that they are not limited to the issuing of guarantees for SMEs, but also embrace training, education, and awareness-raising of SME owners and Kafalah stakeholders. These training exercises are conducted in collaboration with the International Finance Corporation (IFC), a member of the World Bank Group; the Institute of Banking [established by Saudi Arabian Monetary Agency (SAMA)], together with the participation of Saudi banks and chambers of commerce and industry. Efforts are under way in coordination with the World Bank to develop appropriate training strategies for SME owners.*[14]

However, as reported in the Bloomberg article quoted in footnote 208, there are signs lending under Kafalah could be slowing, owed to a variety of reasons. As the article states: "Lending under the nation's SME Loan Guarantee Program, also known as Kafalah, plunged 76 percent to 572 million riyals ($153 million) last year as banks tightened rules, according to data from the Saudi Industrial Development Fund. That compares with a 12 percent increase for total bank credit last year to 1.25 trillion riyals, according to Saudi central bank data."[15]

The need to invest in tomorrow's leaders is not only a Saudi challenge, but it is also one requiring the attention and resources of the GCC as well. According to a study done by the Leadership Circle, the GCC nations are under-spending on the development of future crops of its business leaders. The Leadership Circle, a global leadership development company with a community of certified coaches and consultants and committed to nurturing transformative changes in the thinking and action patterns of entrepreneurs, has concluded that organizations in the GCC region are not living up to international benchmarks for how to develop future business leaders. On October 8, 2015, news outlets reported the Leadership Circle's findings quoting the organization as saying: "The lack of leadership development is a serious issue in Saudi Arabia. With the largest population of the GCC countries and a government ambitiously committed to the Nitaqat program, increasing significantly the involvement of its nationals in the private workforce, there is a growing need for qualified leaders."[16]

The Leadership Circle further noted that: "An internationally accepted rule of thumb is that professional development should consist of 70 percent on-the-job learning, 20 percent coaching from the line manager or a coach, and 10 percent classroom training. The gap in coaching has negative repercussions on the entire leadership development."[17]

There is no shortage of organizations, programs, funds, and other initiatives that seek to foster greater growth of entrepreneurs and small businesses in the Kingdom. Let us look at the public- and private-sector contributions to the development of entrepreneurship and the development of SMEs in Saudi Arabia.

PROMOTION AND SUPPORT OF SAUDI ENTREPRENEURS AND SMALL AND MEDIUM-SIZED BUSINESSES

There are numerous SME and entrepreneurship promotion organizations in Saudi Arabia today. Some are government-funded; others are private-sector originated programs that are supported by Saudi companies large and small. Some of these programs and initiatives focus on individual business people with innovative technologies and ideas for inventions, while others concentrate on developing an individual's business practice acumen and successful and proven entrepreneurial skills sets. The end game for many engaged in the proliferation of new enterprises and SMEs encompass goals often articulated by both government and business: the growth of the private sector, increased investment of Saudi capital inside the Kingdom, greater non-oil sector job growth and an expansion of the country's knowledge-based economy. A look at the existing organizations promoting entrepreneurship and the SME community reveals a diverse group of entities serving the Kingdom.

In Table 5.1, "Organizations Associated with Entrepreneurship in Saudi Arabia," you can see a listing of both public- and private-sector entities offering programs and services designed to grow the capacity and number of startups and SMEs in the Kingdom.

These organizations vary in the number of startups and SMEs they serve, their size in terms of funding and staffing, and also in regard to the amount of notoriety and frequency of recognition they receive within and outside the Kingdom for the work they perform. Virtually every organization offers training and training support. All but three entities out of the 35 listed offer some type of counseling services to aspiring and accomplished business people. Out of the 35 SME-focused entities listed, 23 offer some type of loan package or financial assistance. Let's examine a number of these organizations and their impact on Saudi entrepreneurship and SMEs.

ENDEAVOR GLOBAL INCORPORATED (ENDEAVOR) AND ENDEAVOR SAUDI ARABIA

Endeavor is a global entrepreneurship support organization that promotes itself as "leading the high-impact entrepreneurship movement around the world."[18] It is an organization whose mission is not only to accelerate the growth of "high-impact entrepreneurs," but to spur fundamental change in the positive growth of economies in which these special types of entrepreneurs are found as well. Endeavor Global, Incorporated, the worldwide parent company, was conceived and founded by Linda Rottenberg and Peter Kellner in 1997 and is headquartered in New York City. The organization had its initial launches in Chile, Argentina, Brazil, Uruguay, and Mexico. By 2001, Endeavor had selected 100 high-impact entrepreneurs, and in the following year the first Harvard Business School case study about Endeavor was taught at the university. Since that time, it has grown to an organization that operates in 19 locations around the world, including North America, Latin America, Europe, Africa, the Middle East, Asia, and, of course, in the Kingdom of Saudi Arabia.

Table 5.1 Organizations Associated with Entrepreneurship in Saudi Arabia

Name of Organization	Organization Type	Role							
		Consulting	Follow-ups	Loans	Facilitate Procedure for Startups	Training Support	Training	Standard Testing for Acceptance	Receiving Application for Entrepreneurs
1 The Centennial Fund	Private non-profit	✓	✓	✓	✓			✓	✓
2 Saudi Credit & Savings Bank	Government owned	✓	✓	✓				✓	✓✓
3 King Salman Institute for Entrepreneurship (KSU)	Government owned	✓	✓			✓			✓
4 Badir Program for Technology Incubators	Government owned	✓	✓		✓				✓
5 Chambers of Commerce (all regions)	Government owned non-profit	✓		✓		✓			✓
6 Bab Rizq Jameel	Private non-profit	✓✓	✓	✓✓		✓		✓	✓✓
7 Prince Sultan Fund for Women Development	Private non-profit	✓	✓	✓✓			✓		✓✓
8 Knowledge and Business Alliance	Government owned	✓	✓		✓	✓			✓
9 Saudi Commission for Tourism & Antiquities	Government owned	✓	✓			✓		✓	✓
10 National Entrepreneurship Institute	Private non-profit	✓	✓		✓	✓			✓
11 King Khalid Foundation	Private non-profit	✓	✓	✓		✓	✓		✓
12 Riyadh Valley Company	Private non-profit	✓	✓	✓	✓	✓	✓		✓
13 Wadi Jeddah	Private non-profit	✓		✓	✓	✓		✓	✓
14 Dahran Techno Valley Company	Private non-profit	✓		✓			✓	✓	✓
15 Mubader Program (Riyadh Chamber of Commerce)	Government owned non-profit	✓			✓			✓	✓
16 King Salman Youth Center	Private	✓	✓			✓	✓		✓

#	Organization	Ownership								
17	Waed Company (Saudi Aramco Center for Entrepreneurship)	Government owned	✓		✓	✓	✓	✓		✓
18	STC Ventures	Private for-profit	✓	✓	✓		✓	✓	✓	✓
19	SABIC center for small and medium enterprises	Government owned	✓		✓		✓	✓		
20	Madina Institute for Leadership & Entrepreneurship	Private non-profit	✓	✓	✓		✓	✓	✓	✓
21	i2 Institute for Imagination and Ingenuity	Private	✓		✓		✓	✓	✓	✓
22	Innovation and Entrepreneurship Program at Umm Al Qura University	Government owned	✓		✓		✓	✓		✓
23	Makkah Techno Valley Company	Private for-profit	✓		✓		✓	✓	✓	✓
24	Entrepreneurship Center at KAUST	Private	✓		✓		✓	✓		✓
25	Entrepreneurship Center (Princess Nora University)	Government owned	✓		✓		✓	✓		
26	Endeavor Saudi Arabia	Private non-profit	✓✓		✓✓		✓	✓	✓	✓✓
27	N2V - National Net Ventures	Private for-profit	✓✓		✓✓		✓	✓	✓	
28	National competition to develop an action plan for PrinceSultan Center for Science	Private	✓✓				✓			
29	Social Charity Fund	Government owned	✓✓	✓	✓		✓	✓		
30	Saudi Fast Growth	Government owned	✓✓		✓		✓	✓		
31	SAGIA	Government owned	✓		✓	✓		✓		
32	Okal Group for Angel Investors	Private non-profit	✓	✓	✓		✓	✓	✓	✓
33	Verso Incubator	Private	✓✓	✓✓	✓		✓	✓		
34	Sirb Network	Private	✓✓	✓✓	✓✓		✓	✓	✓	✓✓
35	Intilaaqah Program (Shell)	Private non-profit	✓		✓✓		✓✓	✓	✓	✓✓

Endeavor enjoys a substantial worldwide network of business advisors, both individuals and organizations, who act as mentors, advisors, coaches, and as a "global board of directors" for entrepreneurs selected to join the program. The aim is to provide entrepreneurs access to and the ability to rely upon some of the most fundamental and critical elements to the successful entrepreneurial equation: talented individuals and organizations in the business world, proximity and open doors to financial and human capital, and entry to strategic markets. The example that Endeavor is setting in the area of support for high-impact entrepreneurs is without equal in regard to its global scope and constancy of analysis.

Endeavor's 61st international selection panel met in Morocco in October 2015 and chose 18 companies from 12 countries as their newest Endeavor entrepreneurs. The organization now claims to support 1,159 high-impact entrepreneurs from 735 companies in 24 emerging and growth markets.[19] Much of Endeavor's rate of success with the entrepreneurs it accepts into its programs seems to be traced to the rigorous and meticulous process of identifying, screening, and ultimately selecting its applicants. This process is conducted by Endeavor's international selection panel (ISP), a group of distinguished international business leaders, and is a 12- to 18-month multilayered operation that makes visible as much of a 360-degree, scrupulous, and exacting examination of aspiring successful entrepreneurs as can be found anywhere in the world today.

The world is Endeavor's universe from which it searches for qualified applicants. As its website states: "We select individuals of all ages, ethnicities, and educational backgrounds, delivering a meritocratic message to the developing world: through hard work, creativity, and values-driven leadership, individuals living anywhere, from any background, can turn an entrepreneurial idea into a world-class venture."[20]

Nominations of applicants can be made by the Endeavor network or the applicants themselves. All applications are thoroughly screened and scrutinized to determine if initial interviews will be granted. Candidates are given initial interviews to assess each candidate's practical abilities to successfully go through the Endeavor program. A second review is then conducted by senior-level members of Venture Corp, a trademarked and branded service group of Endeavor Global, Inc., which provides education services such as seminars, workshops, speaker event series, and individual mentoring programs in the fields of venture capital and entrepreneurial business leadership. Venture Corps members conduct multiple interviews during this second phase in which the candidate's business's strategy, innovation, growth-potential, and entrepreneurial personal qualities meet Endeavor's program standards.[21]

In the next stage managed by the local selection panel, consisting of a group of 10 to 15 Venture Corps and local Endeavor board members, conduct additional candidate interviews, debate the merits of each candidate and then ultimately select those candidates who are recommended to the ISP for the final phase of consideration. As finalists, candidates are then interviewed and judged by the ISP and from that group of finalists the ISP names those to be included in the new class of Endeavor entrepreneurs.

Besides the credit to Endeavor's outstanding organization leadership, vision, and selection process, its stand-alone status as the most-recognized and accomplished entity championing the interest of high-impact entrepreneurs is due in large part to the nature of the "high-impact entrepreneur." They are a breed apart in regard to their propensity for exponential business growth rates and the reverberating positive effects they have rippling through their host economies. But to understand Endeavor and its mission, one must understand the meaning of "high-impact entrepreneur."

High-impact entrepreneurs constitute the vanguard in the advancing army of new and successful businesses. In many ways, they are an elite group within business possessing superior abilities that yield consistent and predictable beneficial multipliers that resound throughout an economy. They create the most jobs, experience the highest growth rates, are among the greatest creators of wealth, and become the best role models for aspiring SMEs. In a commentary for CNBC.com, Linda Rottenberg, co-founder and CEO of Endeavor, and one of the most-renowned experts on entrepreneurship in the world, once described "high-impact entrepreneurs" by saying: "High-impact entrepreneurs are visionaries who generate the highest returns, create the most high-value jobs, have the most significant impact on their communities, and inspire the most people to follow their lead—saying, 'If she or he can do it, I can do it too.'"[22] Endeavor's proposition to global economic development policy and decision makers is that if you are going to devote resources to investing in SMEs, a strong case is to be made to have a significant portion of that capital spent on the highest-yielding segment of that business group ... high-impact entrepreneurs. In a revised edition of his book *The World Is Flat,* well-known author and *New York Times* columnist Thomas Friedman extolled the virtues of Endeavor by referring to it as operating under a "mentor capitalist" model and calling it "the best anti-poverty program of all."[23]

Other key attributes of the high-impact entrepreneur were articulated in a 2011 report authored by Rhett Morris of Endeavor's Center for High-Impact Entrepreneurship and the Global Entrepreneurship Monitor (GEM). The report was sponsored by Ernst and Young. In surveys of entrepreneurs, conducted by GEM for the report, it was reported that "only three out of every 1,000 respondents to the GEM surveys had founded a business that achieved high rates of growth, as defined to be an average of 20 percent or more estimated annual growth in the number of individuals employed."[24] Other cited attributes of the high-growth entrepreneurs: "High-growth entrepreneurs represent only 4 percent of the total entrepreneurs who responded to the GEM surveys, yet the businesses they have founded or co-own created close to 40 percent of the total jobs generated by all entrepreneurs who responded to the survey. [And] high-growth entrepreneurs are more likely to have started their businesses to increase their incomes."[25] High-impact entrepreneurs are outperformers in every sense of that term. Endeavor has shown that this special breed can be found in every part of the world. It should be no surprise that they have been found in the Kingdom of Saudi Arabia.

Endeavor Saudi Arabia was founded in 2012 by a visionary group of young Saudi business people, a group well-experienced in knowing what success looks and feels like in the Kingdom. Endeavor Saudi Arabia lists its founding board of directors as: Rami K. Alturki, president and CEO of Khalid Ali Alturki & Sons (Alturki Holding); HRH Princess Banderi; A. R. Al-Faisal, director general, King Khalid Foundation; Mohammed A. Hafiz, CEO; Al-Sawani; Musaab S. Al-Muhaidib, CEO; Al-Muhaidib Technical Supplies; Abdulaziz A. Al-Omran, VP, Khalid & Abdulaziz Al-Omran Co.; Hossam Radwan, CEO of Abraaj Saudi Arabia; Faisal Tamer, managing partner at the Tamer Group; and Abdulla Al-Zamil, CEO of Zamil Industrial. Rami Alturki serves as the board's chairman.

Endeavor Saudi Arabia has a range of programs and activities designed to identify, prescreen, and select high-impact entrepreneurs into an intense program that prepares each entrepreneur for successfully continuing upon and accelerating on the path of high growth and sustained positive impact. The aim is not only to remove the well-known barriers to successful entrepreneurship but to provide each Endeavor selectee a catalyst to an optimal environment enabling him or her to grow and resonate his or her success to fuel wealth creation, more jobs, and stronger macroeconomic conditions.

I sat down with the chairman of Endeavor Saudi Arabia, Rami Alturki, to discuss the state of entrepreneurship in the Kingdom and Endeavor Saudi Arabia's work in promoting the high-impact entrepreneur. We discussed the historical barriers to successful entrepreneurship that Endeavor Saudi Arabia sees SMEs facing every day in the Kingdom: (1) fear of business failure; (2) lack of role models; (3) limited management expertise; (4) lack of contacts and mentors; (5) lack of trust; and (6) limited access to "smart capital." Rami said that all of these inhibiting factors can have a stifling effect on SMEs overall. However, in his view, what is particularly damaging to the prospects of increasing employment and growing the economy is having these barriers keep the high-impact entrepreneur from reaching his or her business goals. This is because high-impact entrepreneurs have been shown many times by Endeavor's research to be the SMEs that yield the greatest impact by creating 100 times more jobs than most startups.

For Rami and his involvement in founding Endeavor Saudi Arabia, the attraction was being able to position himself and other key business leaders in the Kingdom with the abilities to make a difference within an organization possessing the structure and unique programs to in turn make a difference in the lives of entrepreneurs and their high-growth businesses within the entire country. For Rami and his fellow Endeavor Saudi Arabia board members, these special entrepreneurs constitute essential elements in the Kingdom's drive to create the new and innovative jobs the country needs. The role Endeavor Saudi Arabia plays in mentoring and guiding Saudi high-impact entrepreneurs is proving successful in the creation of new wealth and projecting these businesses into becoming global competitors.

I asked Rami Alturki for some of his thoughts on the direction of entrepreneurship in the Kingdom and his insight into some of the more harmful impediments facing today's Saudi SME.

"There are numerous challenges facing Saudi SMEs today. Some of the specific challenges faced can ultimately prove fatal to a business just starting or attempting to scale up. The lack of reliable and routine access to professionals such as lawyers, accountants, bankers, and successful business peers can constitute a considerable drag on a company trying to grow. In today's increasingly global regulatory environment, a lack of knowledge of how to establish and maintain satisfactory corporate governance and compliance policies may be quite detrimental if sound advice is not secured," Rami stated.[26]

Expanding his comments on the common lack of knowledge by many SMEs, Rami said: "A lot of Saudis are sitting around at bigger companies with many great ideas. Taking that leap into entrepreneurship for many Saudis can be quite a daunting prospect. There are so many talented and smart entrepreneurs in the Kingdom. Many find it difficult, however, to surmount many of these obstacles going it alone. In the area of corporate finance, for example, many Saudi start-ups and SMEs find themselves in a quandary when they find their access to needed capital blocked because they are not prepared to meet the financial disclosure requirements of most lenders, investors, and financial institutions. Most of the time, that's why many entrepreneurs fail because they don't have the proper appreciation for financial disclosure.[27]

During my interview with Rami, I asked him about comparisons made between today's Saudi entrepreneurs and the first-generation FOB founders, he offered some interesting observations.

Rami believes that when most aspiring Saudi business people consider the well-known first generation big businessmen of decades ago, they view those times as very different from today's environment. Because the environment was different, younger Saudis find it challenging to view older generation business leaders as role models in a practical sense. As others have, Rami makes the point that during the foundational times of some of the Kingdom's largest and better-known Saudi businesses, those companies received significant government support through readily available contracts as the country sought to build its modern infrastructure.

Moreover, the kind of coaching and business guidance provided those young, essentially Saudi, startups on a daily operational basis were prevalent and accessible when working contracts for some of the first Saudi industrial entities of the 1960s, 1970s, and 1980s such as Aramco, Saudi Arabian Fertilizer Company (Safco), Saudi Iron & Steel Company (Hadeed), and Saudi Yanbu Petrochemical Company (Yanpet). To be sure according to Rami, young Saudis respect and admire these older generational business leaders, but it is a struggle for them to find relevance in the decades-old experience of these firms to their daily challenges in growing their businesses in the Kingdom today.

I posed one of the more material questions of this book to Rami when I asked him whether he believed today's Saudi entrepreneur has the same kind of "fire in the belly" that propelled Steve Jobs to achieve unequaled heights in the fields of computers, information technology, and innovation. The question as to whether Saudis have the requisite will to work, grind it out, and enthusiastically pursue entrepreneurial dreams is routinely speculated upon. This question goes to a critically important social issue among Saudis concerning the Saudi work ethic.

There is no shortage of Saudis, among them Saudi business people, who believe that young Saudis have yet to become conscientious and dependable workers. I have witnessed some Saudi businessmen eschew the hiring of more Saudi workers than required by law because of their reputed undependable performance on the job. Although I believe this is very far from the norm, I have heard numerous stories concerning Saudi workers who routinely show up for work late and leave for the day significantly shy of the full set of hours they are required to be on the job. Many believe there is a kind of malaise or mild disaffection among many Saudi youth when it comes to the level of participation in any kind of daily laborious pursuits. Some have offered very blunt comments suggesting the lack of assiduousness, industry, and drive on the part of some younger generation Saudis stems from a social and familial cultivation of their sense of entitlement and privilege.

Rasheed Abou-Alsamh, a Saudi-American journalist, writer, and blogger, wrote: "The truth is that the Saudi generation born after the first oil boom ended around 1983 is an especially spoiled one. They have grown up with maids and drivers at their beck and call; they have been spoiled by parents who gave them everything from expensive clothes to cars to make them happy. This is a generation that hasn't known the deprivations of the pre–oil boom days when Saudi Arabia was a much poorer nation that did not have many luxuries."[28]

In stressing the importance of education in the growth of a knowledge-based society in an opinion editorial, editor-at-large of the *Saudi Gazette*, Khaled Almaeena, in part blamed the high unemployment rate in GCC countries like Saudi Arabia in part can be traced to Saudis graduating without the requisite skills sets saleable to private-sector jobs. Mr. Almaeena wrote: "According to statistics from the World Economic Forum, the GCC countries collectively have one of the highest youth unemployment rates in the world. To my mind, the reasons for this include the apathy of young people and their lack of work ethics in addition to their inability to master the job descriptions required by the private sector."[29]

In reply to my question concerning the "fire in the belly" for business and industry among young Saudis, Rami stated that he believed undoubtedly that there are many Saudis quite zealous in their pursuit of success for their businesses. He said he could readily give examples of Saudi entrepreneurs, in particular Endeavor Saudi Arabia's own candidates, who have achieved notable successes in entrepreneurship in the Kingdom. But, he added, he also laments over what he sees as a "crisis of aspirations" afflicting many Saudi youth. Rami stated:

> *For many Saudi youth, what I see is there has been an "ease of affluence," "culture of entitlement" and a kind of enjoyed "welfare state" that have collectively possibly stunted the potential for the type of commitment required in order to start and build a successful business. Very few Saudis develop the kind of will and seriousness, make the sacrifices, and to acquire the skills and knowledge needed to start and run their own businesses. Moreover, even when a business has been created and has achieved an initial level of success, many find that they are ill-equipped to scale their enterprises to higher and sustained growth. Assisting high-impact entrepreneurs in correcting these deficiencies is what makes Endeavor unique in the Kingdom and around the world.*

Rami applauded the Saudi government, particularly the Ministry of Commerce and Industry for recognizing the challenges and obstacles faced by Saudi SMEs. He noted their willingness to listen and consider the views of organizations like Endeavor Saudi Arabia and acknowledged the government was working to address some of the problems. In addition to getting aspiring Saudi business people the help they need in filling in the knowledge and skills gaps with corporate governance, financial disclosure, and other best-business practices, Rami also believes another area that needs improvement is changing certain aspects of Saudi culture so as to nurture startups. Rami appreciates the cultural difference between the United States and Saudi Arabia when it comes to their tolerance for business failures.

"I certainly recognize that failure in business here in Saudi Arabia, particularly the financial aspects of failure, can be devastating for a Saudi," Rami said. "It can have potentially long-lasting consequences. Culturally and legally, the United States is much more experienced in absorbing failed businesses than Saudi Arabia. No doubt, there is a need here to promote a "cultural accommodation of failure" to reduce much of the fear factor in starting up new businesses in the Kingdom. But it will take some time to make this cultural shift," he said.

Endeavor Saudi Arabia continues to identify and select high-impact entrepreneurs from the Kingdom. Many of these Saudi high-impact entrepreneurs are today's Saudi business disrupters. A prime example of this new breed is Saudi inventor and entrepreneur Ms. Lateefa Alwaalan, founder and general manager of Yatooq, the creation of Ms. Alwaalan. A beneficiary of close contacts of Endeavor's network of dedicated entrepreneurs as well as the guidance and support of Saudi incubators, she used her own funds and took out bank loans to pursue her entrepreneurial dreams. Ms. Alwaalan was supported by KACST's BADIR incubator in developing a portable electric brewer of Arabic coffee. Good and authentic Arabic coffee, one of the daily pleasures I miss about living in the Kingdom, requires attention to the details in a traditional and fairly involved brewing process. Ms. Alwaalan's creativity and use of Saudi initiatives to which she had access from partnerships allowed her to patent, produce, and sell into international markets the Yatooq Arabic coffee maker.

Ms. Alwaalan has become a role model for many aspiring Saudi entrepreneurs, especially Saudi women, and continues to receive accolades for her accomplishments. She received the 2015 Ernst and Young (EY) 2015 "Entrepreneur of the Year" award. It is the example of Ms. Alwaalan and those others set by many of today's Saudi entrepreneurs that affirm the value of support organizations such as Endeavor.

THE NATIONAL ENTREPRENEURSHIP INSTITUTE (RIYADAH)

One of the most impactful and effective entrepreneur support organizations in Saudi Arabia is the National Entrepreneurship Institute, or "Riyadah," as it is more commonly known. The story of Riyadah, from its creation through development and onto the achievements it has recorded over the years, is one of true appreciation and care for the spirit of Saudi entrepreneurism.

The essence of Riyadah is the recognition that teaching Saudis from all walks of life and socio-economic status the life-changing experience of starting one's own business and providing them with the tools and knowledge to earn a living doing so releases the very best in the individual.

One of the greatest tributes payable to Riyadah is that it has led the way in providing useful support to Saudis in transitioning them from unemployment and a life of dependency on the state to real self-reliance and self-determination through successful entrepreneurship. It is an organization that continually evaluates its effectiveness and relevance and adjusts its focus and the application of Riyadah's unique program processes for aspiring entrepreneurs to optimize its value proposition. I had the distinct opportunity to interview the former chief executive officer of Riyadh, Dr. Sherif Elabdelwahab, for this book. He provided me with an abundance of insight into Riyadah's operational structure and thorough applicantion and evaluation processes.

Having assumed the position of CEO in 2011, Dr. Elabdelwahab's education and background could not have been more suited to the responsibilities he fulfills at Riyadah. He earned two master's degrees in public services administration and TESOL (Teaching English to Speakers of Other Languages), and was awarded a PhD from Ohio State University in foreign and second language education with an emphasis in workforce development. Beyond his educational achievements suiting him to shepherd the aspirations of budding Saudi business men and women has been his work experience in the areas of human resources youth empowerment programs. He has been an ESL (English as a Second Language) instructor, designed and delivered curricula instructional programs for a number of public- and private-sector institutions inside and outside the Kingdom. He has also written and presented, regionally and internationally, many esteemed papers on the subjects of EFL, independent learning and human resources development. Within Dr. Elabdelwahab's able hands, along with the experienced staff upon which he relied at Riyadah, the organization has gone from 22 branches and 1,400 entrepreneurs served in the Kingdom to 39 branches and 3,000 entrepreneurs out of 9,500 trainees.

In recounting the origins of Riyadah, Dr. Elabdelwahab noted for me how the importance of entrepreneurship in Saudi Arabia made its early impressions in the Kingdom earlier than the eighteenth century. It hit its long stride during the decades of the 1970s and 1980s and the country's oil boom. Dr. Elabdelwahab's recollection of this commercial expansionary period is in accordance with what I have learned from that foundational period of early Saudi entrepreneurs and FOB founders. It was a fast-paced, kinetic, unpredictable time in business when mavericks worked day and night and abounded and flourished in their craft. The energy and enthusiasm of these first-generation startups resonated throughout the Kingdom and seemed to telegraph (and eventually telex) the "new frontier" nature of business opportunities there on behalf of the country to the entire world. As Dr. Elabdelwahab put it: "In those days, Saudis started businesses with absolutely nothing and would walk for miles and miles in search of opportunities. Initially, there was little government support for developing their aspirations and growing their businesses. Eventually though, the expanding oil sector hit the global big leagues and Saudi Arabia's petroleum revenue waves raised all boats. And, according to Dr. Elabdelwahab, that is when entrepreneurship in the country began to change.

Dr. Elabdelwahab noted that with the onset of the oil boom of the 1970s and 1980s, there was a shift in the Kingdom in which the entrepreneurial pursuits of Saudis in their own businesses was gradually replaced by white-collar jobs. The kind of new frontier mind-set was replaced by a reliance of younger Saudis on their parents' personal largess and the growing availability of government jobs as the size of the public sector continued to grow. This dependency, said Dr. Elabdelwahab, created a bubble in which younger generations of Saudis forsook the higher risks associated with starting one's own businesses and surviving on their own life skill sets for the relative comfort of a salaried paycheck or even less strenuous daily pursuits. Government policies were not focused on the promotion of entrepreneurship. Government's emphasis on entrepreneurship began to take hold around 2000 and grew during that decade. That was the time when Riyadah was created.

At its beginning, Riyadah was one of the Technical and Vocational Training Corporation's (TVTC) strategic partnerships. The TVTC is the pre eminent government-sponsored technical and vocation training program in the Kingdom. Formerly known as the "General Organization for Technical Education and Vocational Training" (GOTEVOT), it has established itself as the leading provider of technical and vocation training in Saudi Arabia. With more than 100 locations throughout the Kingdom, the TVTC serves more than 120,000 trainees in disparate fields. It was the demonstrable successes of the TVTC within its small and medium businesses development center (SMBDC) that led the Kingdom's Ministry of Petroleum and Mineral Resources (MOP) to start a national entrepreneurship initiative. Riyadah was soon to become one of its most important and effective partners. There was an ever-increasing recognition by the Saudi government of the importance of entrepreneurship to the individual and the nation's economy.

In 2004, with an initial grant of US$8 million, the MOP partnered with the founders the Japan Saudi Arabian Methanol Company, SABIC, Saudi Aramco, STC, Alinma Bank, SCSB, and TVTC to establish Riyadah as a strategic partner of the TVTC. All of these entities are represented on Riyadah's board of directors. It is notable and commendable that it was the Japanese who stepped up as the only foreign entity to officially support Riyadah's founding. The creation of Riyadah was more than just a triumph for SMEs business owners and those who aspire to become them. It was a victory for the notion that occurs to many unemployed Saudis that they can equip themselves with the knowledge that can start them on their own paths toward financial self-determination. The fear factor has been discussed in this book and its insidious, inhibiting, and harmful effects on the determination of Saudi entrepreneurs to succeed in the face of repeated defeats and disappointments. The creation of Riyadah and the development of its entrepreneur development training system has successfully contributed to a lowering of the high failure rate of Saudis starting their own businesses.

After its start as a strategic partner in the TVTC's SMBDC in 2004, the organization produced its first batch of entrepreneurs in 2006. As it experienced and executed on the delivery of its training program, Dr. Elabdelwahab said Riyadah learned much about its program, processes, and about the Saudis matriculating through the program. The regular monitoring and assessments of the SMBDC partnership program and its entrepreneurs fostered a re-engineering within the entity.

"During this re-engineering phase, we learned a lot about the applicants and those accepted into the program. Many of the success indicators that we look for in the individual appear or do not. A percentage of those accepted do not show up when they are required to. We learned about a person's ability to problem solve and what aspects of our program best tested an individual's ability to troubleshoot their way past obstacles or existential threats to their businesses," Dr. Elabdelwahab said. "What do you do when the person has absolutely no experience or knowledge in the business they want to start? How do you adjust and fine-tune the program to make it better not only in substance and delivery but make it a better experience for the entrepreneur?" This is some of what was involved in the re-engineering of Riyadah.

In the middle of 2010, after the re-engineering of the organization, Riyadah had its official start as a stand-alone organization distinct from the SMBDC program function it had with TVTC. In 2011, Riyadah had achieved full operations with programs and activities eventually being offered at 25 male and 14 female branches and three liaison offices in the Kingdom. Those who benefit from the full range of Riyadah's training programs, support services, and award activities occur in 68 cities within the Kingdom of Saudi Arabia. Besides helping the prospective entrepreneur drill down on critical skills and developmental understandings of how to successfully administer and grow one's own business, Riyadah also provides instruction and insight on other crucial aspects of starting a business in

Saudi Arabia. Training on these aspects include promoting one's own business ideology, building positive beliefs toward small businesses, and promoting awareness of the importance of cultural values in developing one's business.

The branch and liaison offices are run by Riyadah local branch coordinators who are in charge of managing the delivery of the programs, administration of the local offices, and, in most instances, instructing Saudi trainees. Dr. Elabdelwahab refers to them as Riyadah's "soldiers" without whom the fight for entrepreneurial advancement through the use of the organization's program systems would not be possible. Riyadah is able to maintain a bank of knowledgeable and capable professionals as its coordinators through an active "train-the-facilitator" program. In this way, Riyadah has been able to multiply their number and activity level of each branch office opened in the Kingdom.

In 2012 and 2013, Riyadah created e-training and e-solutions training programs for existing entrepreneurs with active businesses that lack the time to make their way through extended Riyadah course materials, but want to enhance the management and growth of their companies. The growth of Riyadah's Internet-based services and training solutions to Saudi entrepreneurs is impressive and reaches any aspiring or current business person with an Internet connection along with a computer, tablet, or smartphone. Riyadah understands and is taking full advantage of the phenomenal growth in mobility occurring within the Kingdom.

Dr. Elabdelwahab further related that the use of Riyadah's e-portal platform is also used to train aspiring entrepreneurs through the 24-step program of Riyadah's entrepreneurship program. Saudi entrepreneur-trainees, in over 81 Saudi cities across two million square kilometers have the ability through Riyadah's e-training platform to complete 20 of the 24 steps necessary to meet Riyadah's requirements for successfully matriculating its course materials.

Riyadah's relationship with the TVTC remains quite active. Thirty-four percent of business start-up applicants to Riyadah program come from the TVTC. The TVTC has an extensive reach and access to all of the Kingdom's universities. since its beginnings, however, Riyadah has expanded its collaborations beyond its linkage with the TVTC. Riyadah has an active collaboration with the International Labor Organization (ILO) and is one of the ILO's strategic partners in delivering the ILO "Know About Business" (KAB). The ILO, an esteemed and multi lateral global institution that serves the interests of working men and women by fostering the cooperation and coordination between governments, its private sector, and workers together in order to set labor standards, develop policies, and create programs, promote social and economic growth and well-being. It is headquartered in

Geneva, Switzerland, and has its International Labor Office, the permanent secretariat of the ILO, located in Geneva. It has offices around the world.

The ILO's KAB entrepreneurship awareness training program is being offered in the Kingdom through Riyadah and is run by local certified trainers in optional practical training (OPT). OPT is a period during which undergraduate and graduate students with a specific designated immigration status who have completed or are pursuing degrees for a specific period are allowed to work and thereby gain practical experience in their chosen fields.

The ILO KAB program was established in the 1990s and is meant to benefit "teachers in general secondary education, trainers in vocational and technical training institutions, and higher education professors trained to deliver KAB course content and be certified as KAB national facilitators."[30] The KAB program has been an invaluable tool in Riyadah's toolbox and has been allowed to supply an adequate stream of qualified entrepreneur instructors in each new office it opens in the Kingdom. It is this "training the facilitator" feature of Riyadah in multiplying those that offer instruction of aspiring entrepreneurs that is a distinguishing feature of the organization among business promotion entities in the Kingdom.

The 10 modules offered in the ILO KAB program curriculum are: (1) What is enterprise? (2) Why entrepreneurship? (3) Who are entrepreneurs? (4) How do I become an entrepreneur? (5) How do I find a good business idea? (6) How do I organize an enterprise? (7) How do I operate an enterprise? (8) What are the next steps to become an entrepreneur? (9) How does one develop one's own business plan? and (10) a social entrepreneurship module.[31] The ILO touts the strengths of the KAB program as: "Interactive, learner-centered, and participatory methodology of teaching and materials; step-by-step training for teachers/trainers/professors; adaptability to requirements of national curricula; can quickly achieve scale and sustainability, being implemented through national educational structures; transfer of re-training potential to national constituents through building core groups of KAB key facilitators inside the education system (often at training of trainers institutes); [and] KAB methodology being updated every two years."[32] I think it is the thoroughness of the KAB program delivered by Riyadah combined with the reach the organization has through its branch offices and cooperation with the TVTC that accounts for its actual results and success.

Riyadah has complete training packages in six critical areas of entrepreneurial development:

- Training
- Consultations
- Mentorship

- Incubation
- Financing attainment
- Permits assistance

Riyadah's unique brand of entrepreneurship promotion and training and the effectiveness it has recorded over the years is institutionalized in its Erada services program. Erada is Riyadah's "Start Your Own Business" training service. (not to be confused with Erada Advanced Projects, a wholly owned Saudi company in Riyadh). Erada first measures the Riyadah trainee's aptitude for entrepreneurial pursuits. It next helps the trainee develop his or her idea for the business. Next, providing the requisite skills to start and run his or her own businesses, Riyadah instructs and guides the aspiring entrepreneur through a series of lectures and challenges that show the trainee what entrepreneurship means and the life significance of starting one's own business. Riyadah and its skilled workforce help trainees explore alternative sources of financing for starting their business. They assist the trainees with acquiring required licenses, permits, and authorizations for legally running their business. They also assist the trainees in obtaining any equipment necessary to operating their business. Once up and running, Riyadah provides consultation services and mentoring throughout their first year of operation in order to optimize their chances for success.

There is no "come one, come all, accept all" sign outside Riyadah's door. I believe the reason why Riyadah has achieved such levels of success has much to do with the amount of attention and examination it takes in assessing each Riyadah trainee applicant. The process of making it into Riyadah is relatively involved and rational in its structure. With the exception of indigents or the financially distressed applicants, all applicants must pay a fee of US$266 (SR1,000) before they can engage in the simulation training Riyadah provides. According to Dr. Elabdelwahab, this application fee not only covers the cost of developing the business plan, but it also provides some level of confidence on the part of Riyadah that their applicants are fairly serious in their aspirations.

The application fee, evaluation, matriculation, and support process of Riyadah's Erada program is presented graphically in Figure 5.1.

The process begins with an application. Most applications are filed online through their e-application system. The application is evaluated during the approval process with additional information sometimes requested. A thorough interview is conducted of the applicant and a decision is made whether to send the applicant directly to simulation training or to an ancillary training assessment session called "ideation training." Before joining with Riyadah's intense simulation training modules, plan development, and support programs, the ideation training helps fill in some of the blanks an

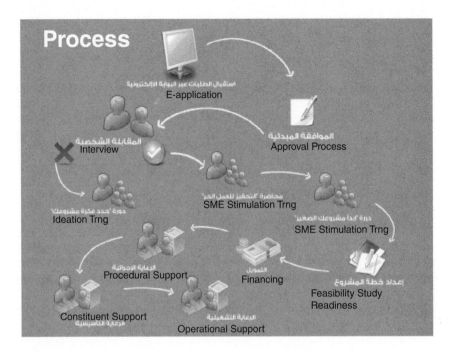

Figure 5.1 Riyadah Trainee Application and Matriculation Process

entrepreneur trainee may have in the full development of his or her ideas for their business and clear identified paths toward the implementation of the idea.

Riyadah then takes trainees through a series of program exercises in which they go through a one-day simulation in which they are confronted with multiple problem-solving and trouble-shooting exercises. After the one-day simulation program there are other simulations that follow. The process is a rigorous system to identify and test a trainee's existing abilities and strengths to cope with the many obstacles and challenges that arise in a new or growing business. Trainees spend at least four hours a day for six weeks creating and developing a viable business plan. With the help and guidance of Riyadah staff members, trainees are able to improve and polish their business plans. After final submission of authenticated business plans are made by trainee, a committee reviews each plan's feasibility and readiness for the next phase in the Riyadah system. The committee either approves it or declines each plan. After approval and its being judged ready, the trainee and the Riyadah team then move the plan to the financing phase. The plan goes to the SCSB for review and a determination as to whether it will be funded. The financing review process normally takes approximately

45 days. Following final notification that his or her business plan has been approved for financing, the trainee then has 90 days within which to start the business.

After the successful launch of their businesses, graduates of the Riyadah program receive support and counseling months after starting their own companies. This kind of "cradle-to-cash" care Riyadah devotes to each of its trainees has allowed it to experience exceptionally high success rates.

In January 2015, reporting 2014 end-of-year results, Dr. Elabdelwahab reported to the press that by December, Riyadah had trained 9,447 out of 10,000 targeted trainees. Seventy-nine hundred Saudis were approved for loans from among the 10,000 who had completed their business plans and another 1,000 businesses had been in the process of opening their operations. Forty-seven hundred and twenty young Saudi entrepreneurs have started their own business enterprises in 181 business categories.[33] Riyadah's successful track record resonates well past its own corporate halls. The organization continues to work with partners and collaborate with government institutions to transmit its message that entrepreneurship for the individual is life-transforming and a meaningful livelihood.

Riyadah has contributed to the awareness of Saudi graduates of the King Abdullah Scholarship Program by offering entrepreneurship training from Riyadah's "Develop Your Business Idea" (DYBI) program. Riyadah has also offered over 8,000 young Saudis selected for the Saudi Arabian Ministry of Education's summer camps program throughout the Kingdom the opportunity to learn about entrepreneurship and the rewards from a life in business. I believe this will be one of the most enduring and most laudable legacies for Riyadah, the spirited encouragement to greater number of Saudis for them to think in a different way. They're leading Saudis, through actual instruction and training, how to conceptualize the source of sustenance for their lives extending beyond a future of government jobs or publicly dispensed dole.

THE CENTENNIAL FUND (TCF)

From the very beginning, the Centennial Fund (TCF) has had the highest support acquirable from Saudi Arabia's royal rulers. In July 2004, with the greatest interest in and recognition of the importance of the Saudi private sector and its development to the national economy, His Royal Highness Prince Abdulaziz Bin Abdullah Bin Abdulaziz Al-Saud, fifth-born son of His Majesty, the late King Abdullah Bin Abdulaziz Al-Saud, founded the Centennial Fund. HRH Prince Abdulaziz Bin Abdullah serves as TCF's chairman of the board of trustees. On July 8, 2004, the late King Fahd Bin Abdulaziz Al-Saud approved the formation of TCF and it was legally established by royal decree No. 190/A.[34] It was and continues to be an initiative supporting the wishes of King Fahd, late King Abdullah Bin Abdulaziz Al-Saud and Saudi Arabia's current King Salman Bin Abdulaziz Al-Saud contribute to equipping young Saudi entrepreneurs with the foundational knowledge, relevant skill sets, coaching, and financial resources to start and grow their own small and medium-sized businesses in the Kingdom. The vision of the founders of TCF was to facilitate the impact young Saudi entrepreneurship would have on the positive economic trends in the Kingdom and in turn for those entrepreneurs to gain from those trends.

At its creation, the TCF had the most influential and powerful leaders of the Saudi Arabian government and private sectors behind it, supplying advice, financial resources, and direction so it could fly off the ground when it began operations. In fact, one of the most revealing facts about the entity's beginning is its collaborative relationship with the General Investment Authority of Saudi Arabia (SAGIA).

SAGIA is the Kingdom's one-stop shop for preinvestment and postinvestment assistance. On paper, SAGIA was established on April 10, 2000, on the authority of Resolution No. 2 of the Saudi Arabian Council of Ministers. It was created to aid in implementation of the Saudi Arabian government's newly minted Foreign Investment Law of 1999. It is promoted and recommended as the first resource and assistance consultation any potential foreign investor should make as it may begin the process of capital investment within the Kingdom. That is what SAGIA is on paper. It has grown, however, to become much more than a consultation resource and paper mill.

As in most countries from the private sector's perspective, government bureaucracies often present special challenges to a company's intention to enter a host country's market, satisfy local law requirements, hire the necessary human resources, get its offices, plant, or operations up and running, and subsequently achieve profitability. Even a country possessing world-class and transparent investment policies and enforced laws and regulations will often encounter complaints from foreign investors as to how laws and rules are interpreted and applied.

While serving in the commercial section of the U.S. embassy in Riyadh and having assisted hundreds of American companies seeking to do business in Saudi Arabia, I can attest to SAGIA's reputation as an effective resource for foreign investors as they seek to navigate some of Saudi Arabia's bureaucratic thickets, solve seemingly inconsistent procedurally applied rules, and deal with the occasional thoroughgoing and unequivocal riddles that would confound even the most astute and erudite local and international commercial law attorneys. SAGIA's able leadership and the competent cadre of staff professionals that run SAGIA's Investor Service Center and Government Relations Unit continue to serve as invaluable resources to foreign investors into the Kingdom. SAGIA has the authority to license foreign investment projects, coordinate with other government ministries and agencies, and provide critical information required by investors in following through with their investment decisions. SAGIA has representatives from multiple ministries and agencies in-house to provide quick answers and procedural facilitations during the investment application process.

SAGIA has been led and continues to be led by a group of most able leaders. SAGIA's first governor was His Royal Highness (HRH) Prince Abdullah Bin Faisal Bin Turki Al-Saud, who served from 2000 to 2004. HRH Prince Abdullah Bin Faisal now serves as Saudi Arabian ambassador to the United States, having assumed his ambassadorial posting at the royal Saudi Arabian embassy in November 2015. SAGIA's next governor was Amr Al-Dabbagh, who served in that capacity from 2004 to 2012.

SAGIA's current governor is His Excellency Abdullatif Bin Ahmed Bin Abdullah Al-Othman. A former senior vice president of Saudi Aramco with over 30 years of experience in planning and managing oil and gas projects, H.E. Governor Al-Othman succeeded Amr Al-Dabbagh in May 2012 with the rank of minister. A Massachusetts Institute of Technology (MIT) graduate, Governor Al-Othman is a man of formidable intellect and fully satisfies his reputation as an exceedingly competent planner and organizational tactician. I have had the opportunity to work closely with Governor Al-Othman and SAGIA. The USSABC collaborated in the organization and planning of the Washington, D.C. September 4, 2015, "U.S.–Saudi Investment Forum" held in conjunction with the visit of His Majesty King Salman Bin Abdulaziz Al-Saud[35] and that evening's dinner in honor of His Majesty King Salman. Along with Saudi Aramco, I worked with Governor Al-Othman and had the opportunity to observe a sampling of his capabilities at close range. Undoubtedly, SAGIA continues to be well served by the governor's exceptional leadership.

What is most revealing about SAGIA and TCF is how quickly after the TCF's creation was it placed in a collaborative relationship with SAGIA. As mentioned, TCF was established by royal decree on July 8, 2004. On July 20, 2004, TCF signed a collaborative agreement with SAGIA "to work together in helping Saudi entrepreneurs to translate their commercial ideas into projects."[36] Then SAGIA governor, Amr Al Dabbagh, signed the SAGIA-TCF partnership agreement with the founder of TCF, HRH Prince Abdulaziz Bin Abdullah. Mr. Al-Dabbagh currently serves as chairman of the board of directors of the Al-Dabbagh Group, a 50-year-old family conglomerate headquartered in Jeddah, Saudi Arabia. This FOB was founded in 1962 by His Excellency Sheikh Abdullah Al-Dabbagh, former Saudi Arabian minister of agriculture. When he served as SAGIA's governor at the time of TCF's establishment, Amr Dabbagh served as chairman of TCF's board of directors. Former Governor Al-Dabbagh was a strong supporter of the July 2004 partnership agreement and named numerous initiatives between SAGIA and TCF during his tenure. Mr. Al-Dabbagh sits on TCF's board of trustees and served just beneath HRH Prince Abdulaziz Bin Abdullah as the board's vice-president.

The Centennial Fund describes its aims as: "... to enable the new generation of Saudis to achieve financial independence through starting their own businesses through training, mentorship, government support and soliciting loans, transforming them from job seekers to job providers."[37] The TCF operates a number of initiatives and international collaborations in its mission to bring more Saudis into the world of entrepreneurship and sustain them in their successes. It actively seeks to expand the Saudi entrepreneur ecosystem through these initiatives and partnerships. This work includes offering business networking opportunities, supporting entrepreneurs through general and specialized training, securing legal advice for the entrepreneur, assisting in feasibility studies, marketing advice, counseling and educational services, supplying financial help, providing assistance to entrepreneurs in dealing with government, and assisting entrepreneurs with developing their technologies.[38]

One of TCF's most interesting initiatives is called "international academy for entrepreneurs." The Centennial Fund has created an international academy for entrepreneurs in order to broaden the proposed training and empowering programs for youth. Several courses on the fundamentals of technology entrepreneurship, with global partners like Robotics Centre, Microsoft, the Intel Program for Innovation, Blackberry Academy, and the 3-D Printing Center, provide the process technology entrepreneurs use to start technology-based companies, or to use it. It involves taking a technology idea and finding a high-potential commercial opportunity, gathering resources, such as talent and capital, figuring out how to sell and market the idea, and managing rapid growth. To gain practical experience alongside the theory, entrepreneurs form teams and work on start-up projects in those teams. A lot of students and young Saudis participated in these programs.

The Global Entrepreneurship Forum (GEF) is an annual event that gathers international leaders in business and entrepreneurship in one location for the purpose of sharing insights, exchanging best practices, and generating exposure for the latest trends and innovations in the global community of entrepreneurs. The Centennial Fund (TCF) launched this initiative in 2013 as an extension of the annual HRH Prince Abdulaziz Bin Abdullah International Award for Entrepreneurship.

The theme of this year's forum is Innovation in Social Enterprise, as the GEF explores the viability of solving a variety of social issues, both locally and globally, through the vehicle of entrepreneurship.

The annual awards were launched by His Royal Highness Prince Abdulaziz Bin Abdullah Bin Abdulaziz as an initiative of the Centennial Fund, under the supervision of the advisory council. The aim of the program is to encourage entrepreneurial projects and to celebrate the owners of such projects in the Kingdom through commendations and awards.

One of TCF's initiatives is called "Business in a Box," which basically constitutes a "plug and play" approach to launching a young Saudi who wants to start his or her own business. It is a start-up process TCF says is completely automated and provides all of the "tools, documents, and steps along with the idea of a successful and an innovative enterprise."[39] Essentially, these are ready-made businesses "in a box," already created by TCF in 26 fields, waiting for someone to plug in and start a company.

The Centennial Valley (CV), another TCF program that is a catalyst for business incubators supplying an array of integrated services. The first CV was established in King Abdullah Economic City (KAEC). Since then, CVs and their incubator services have been established and operate within Imam Muhammad Ibn Saud Islamic University, Al-Sharq University, Hail University, Al-Qassim University, Taiba University, King Abdulaziz, Al-Jouf University, and Jazan University.

TCF maintains an impressive array of international collaborations, quality control systems, and accreditations with world-renowned organizations. Although not an exhaustive listing, the following are organizations with whom TCF has active collaborations: Gulf Cooperation Council of Entrepreneurs (GCC UE); Young Entrepreneur's Alliance G20; Asian Entrepreneurs of Alliance; World Alliance of Young Entrepreneurs; the Clinton Global Initiative; Youth Business Singapore; United Nations for Industrial Development Organization (UNIDOBahrain); Microsoft; and Shell.

One of the distinctive attributes of TCF is that its approach to assisting entrepreneurs is often guided by the best practices and model systems it is exposed to through the international collaborative agreements it maintains. This is important to the organization because one of TCF's bedrock principles of operation. Its mission is to constantly look at ways in which to diminish the barriers to entrepreneurship for aspiring or existing Saudi business people. TCF Director General Dr. Abdul Aziz Bin Hamoud Al-Mutairi recently adopting new methodology aiming to change the culture of the local community. These perspective changes are supported by the government's new objectives of using new business models such as Education for Entrepreneurship and Employment (E4EE) in addition to another of TCF's new initiatives called childpreneurs. After the Centennial Fund's studies and experiments in addition to access to the world's best experiments, we found that the best model is to provide integrated services that contribute to the reduction and limitation of these challenges.[40]

Similar to Endeavor, TCF has its own management system for the induction of entrepreneurs into its programs and their care during the process of bringing their business dreams to life. Its course of care is called the "Entrepreneur Management System" (EMS). TCF's EMS protocols begin with intake procedures requiring registration and verification of the applicant's data. Next, the applicants will go through an education phase (academy) depending on his business idea to give the applicant the required skills and knowledge to start a business. In recognition that acquiring funding for one's business venture is one of the most challenging blocks for an aspiring entrepreneur, TCF works with the entrepreneur in submitting loan applications for their proposed business project.

After undertaking the business and obtaining funding, TCF's EMS takes the entrepreneur through its integrated web-based system, which matches them up with mentors, and having multi-continuous follow-up and in addition to giving the applicants the chance to access all given support for the SMEs through many of TCF's strategic partners. At any time, the TCF entrepreneur is able to submit service requests and check his or her status online. TCF EMS protocols include online reports and performance charts that inform the entrepreneurs, trainers, mentors, and others on the risk of the entrepreneur's performance and fledgling business, needed adjustments to executing the plan, and monitoring the entrepreneur. This integrated approach in TCF's EMS, as well as the other initiatives of TCF, are indicative of the organization's approach of scanning the globe for the best practices in delivering impactful entrepreneurship empowering structured programs. As within any organization that purports to support and counsel would-be entrepreneurs, the proof of its effectiveness is usually quantitatively measured in some way. I've met with TCF Director General Mr. Abdul Aziz Bin Hamoud Al-Mutairi to discuss TCF and its successes in getting more young Saudis into their own businesses. Director General Al-Mutairi credits TCF's positive impact, growth, and continuing recognition to the enduring support of its founder, HRH Prince Abdulaziz Bin Abdullah. Mr. Al-Mutairi pointed to the fact that throughout its existence, HRH Prince Abdulaziz has taken great care to safeguard and advance the founding principles of TCF in all of its initiatives and any of the organization's new directions of expansion. It has been the appreciation of youth projects to the economy, the importance of equipping young Saudis with the tools to surmount the many obstacles faced by the entrepreneur, and the constant search for best practices in supporting the entrepreneur that, the director general says, has kept the TCF effective and relevant.

Director General Al-Mutairi believes, as others have voiced to me, that there are many challenges faced by today's Saudi entrepreneur. I asked him about the issue of how failure in business is faced by Saudis in the Kingdom.

He said: "This subject of business failure and the impact on the failed business person is a serious one. It can be the kiss of death for any entrepreneur in the Gulf due to cultural influences. Yes, the cultural challenges are strong. And, the government, private sector ... everyone should do more to handle this problem." The director general pointed out that Gulf entrepreneurs come from a heritage of trading and merchant businesses. For this reason, he said, the same culture that presents challenges for business failure at the same time has the potential to give the Saudi entrepreneur an advantage.

I also discussed the recurring question in this book, that of the existence or even prevalence of the "fire in the belly" of Saudi entrepreneurs. Director General Al-Mutairi said he does find evidence of the passion for business that many Saudis have when they comes to TCF for support and guidance. He said he believes it is the support from TCF and other entrepreneur support organizations in the Kingdom used in nurturing and growing this passion for business by young Saudis that will lead to the positive economic impact all Saudis want to see coming from more and more Saudis with their own successful businesses.[41]

SAUDI TECHNOLOGY DEVELOPMENT AND INVESTMENT COMPANY (TAQNIA)

The Saudi Technology Development and Investment Company, or TAQNIA as it is commonly known, is one of the Kingdom's best examples of a Saudi public institution that combines a focus on advanced technology and entrepreneurship. It places high priority on all three. It is the Saudi Arabian government-owned investment arm that works to contribute to the diversification of the country's economy and the Kingdom's push toward knowledge-based industries. Established by royal resolution No. (M/47) on June 22, 2011, and based on action taken by the Council of Ministers through Resolution No. 217, dated June 21, 2011. It is a joint stock company fully owned by the Kingdom's Public Investment Fund (PIF). From its inception, TAQNIA's objectives included securing the transfer of strategically important technologies, commercializing its developed innovations and technologies, supporting growth of the country's GDP, diversifying the economy, and contributing to the creation of high-quality jobs.

TAQNIA's vision is: "to drive accelerated diversification of the Kingdom's economy through knowledge-based industries, thereby creating value-adding jobs, and to help create an innovative ecosystem in the Kingdom."[42] Its mission is to: "[a]chieve its vision by investment in local and global technologies and actively engage in the development and growth of those technologies into economically sustainable enterprises."[43] TAQNIA states that key inputs to its operational goals and agenda are the goals and guidelines of the National Industrial Strategy (NIS), discussed in Chapter 2, and the National Knowledge Economy Plan.

TAQNIA's chairman of the board of directors is His Highness Prince Dr. Turki Bin Saud Bin Mohammad Al-Saud, who also represents King Abdulaziz City for Science and Technology (KACST) on TAQNIA's board. His Highness is truly a towering figure within Saudi Arabia among those who purport to be champions of innovation, entrepreneurship, and the development of advanced technologies. His Highness has been the author and at the forefront of major initiatives and programs within the Kingdom, and his background is worth noting.

His Highness received his PhD in aeronautics and astronautics from Stanford University, and joined KACST in 1997. Dr. Turki Bin Saud became the director of the newly established space research institute within KACST. In 2004, Dr. Turki became the vice president for research institutes of KACST and the chairman of the science council. He is chairman of the supervisory committee of the national science and technology plan; the boards of several joint nanotechnology centers set up in collaboration with leading world universities and companies; and the board of the National Technology Incubation program, BADIR. Dr. Turki was also one of four team members that translated the vision of the late King Abdullah Bin Abdulaziz Al-Saud and wrote the charter for KAUST. He has been a driving force within KACST and the Saudi science and technology community for collaboration, innovation, creativity, and effectiveness in policy development and execution. It has been under His Highness's leadership that KACST and TAQNIA experienced a deepening of the support structure for Saudi entrepreneurship.

TAQNIA Chairman Dr. Turki Bin Saud is ably served by the other board of directors of TAQNIA, and they are: Mr. Abdullah Bin Ibrahim Al-Iyadi, TAQNIA vice chairman and representative of the Public Investment Fund; Dr. Mohammad Bin Abdulaziz Al-Ohali, representative of the Ministry of Higher Education; Dr. Ibrahim Bin Abdulaziz Al-Hinaishill, general manager of Saudi Credit and Savings Bank; Dr. Ammar Adennan Alnahowi, representative of Saudi Aramco; Dr. Fahad Bin Abdulaziz Al-Shuraihi, representative of Saudi Basic Industries Corporation; and Dr. Abdullah Bin Hassan Al-Abdulqadir.

TAQNIA is actively developing and acquiring scientific and technological expertise through collaborations, strategic alliances, and technology licensing arrangements in order to present industrial opportunities to the Kingdom. TAQNIA has kept up a blistering pace of accomplishments and their work centers on 29 industrial categories from which they promote opportunities to local and foreign companies and institutions. TAQNIA has achieved the initial phase of success in 17 of the 29 categories. The organization is experiencing ongoing successes in launching joint ventures with local and global technology leaders and investors. This has burnished their reputation and their own goal of swiftly moving the Kingdom within reach of being a knowledge-based-dominated economy. The main areas for which TAQNIA seeks out joint ventures and collaborations around the world are: life science and health; security and defense; information, communications and technology (ICT); material science, energy and environment and water technology.

TAQNIA has established a number of subsidiaries to support its mission. They are as follows: TAQNIA Cyber, a government-owned company specializing in information security, communication security, and signals intelligence; TAQNIA Space, pursuing the manufacturing of satellites, providing secure satellite communications and high-value remote sensing data; TAQNIA Defense, which is to develop and deliver defense and security technology solutions, build, develop, and produce defense and security technologies through local and global strategic partnerships; TAQNIA Services, a domestic service provider in the fields of technology management and commercialization and engineering and technical services; TAQNIA Services, a firm offering consulting and management advice in technology strategies, technology and innovation programs, commercialization of R&D outputs, and high-quality engineering and technical services; Technovia, a national center for translational R&D in Saudi Arabia with a focus on building technology innovation and commercialization capacities, bridging the gap between research outcomes and successful industries; and advanced water technology (AWT), which develops affordable water solutions throughout the entire water value chain by using innovative technology and excellence.

TAQNIA is active on several fronts in the support of entrepreneurism within the Kingdom. Its TAQNIA Services subsidiary has a strategic alliance with KACST, Saudi Aramco, KAUST, KFUPM and RTI International, which serves to scale R&D activities within the Kingdom to ensure the fruits of those projects are ready for commercialization. The non-Saudi partner, RTI, is one of the world's leading research institutes. An American research institute, RTI, is headquartered in North Carolina and has a staff of more than 3,700, and provides research and technical services to governments and businesses in more than 75 countries. RTI is located in North Carolina's Research Triangle Park, one of the largest research parks in the world. RTI's areas of service excellence and expertise are: health and pharmaceuticals, education and training, surveys and statistics, advanced technology, international development, economic and social policy, energy and the environment, and laboratory testing and chemical analysis.

The TAQNIA Services alliance has been set up to actually use some of the intellectual properties produced by all Saudi research centers. It will scale them up to be ready for consumption by Saudi industrial activities.[44]

Besides facilitating the commercialization of IP out-turns, TAQNIA Services also aids technology startups by providing support in areas such as investment finance, legal, technical assistance, advisory consultancy, marketing and strategy, and business development.[45] The support role TAQNIA was given in the area of financing entrepreneurship was directed soon after TAQNIA was formed. In October 2012, His Highness Prince Dr. Turki Bin Saud Bin Mohammad Al-Saud announced a venture capital fund would be established by TAQNIA to support startups and other projects that serve the interests of the Kingdom's objectives of diversifying the economy, broadening the Saudi industrial base, and adding to its intellectual property stockpile of advanced technologies.

I had the opportunity to interview the chief executive officer of TAQNIA International, Mr. Fahad Alhussain. He also serves as a consultant to the board of directors of TAQNIA Holding. Through TAQNIA International and TAQNIA Holding, the parent, TAQNIA, is building a powerful and growing portfolio of investment holdings and IP assets reflective of the range of technologies it continues to pursue around the world. Mr. Alhussain is the right combination of businessman, financial capitalist, able administrator, and deal hunter.

Since 2012, when he assumed the role of CEO with TAQNIA, Mr. Alhussain has built TAQNIA from a start-up to a holding company with more than 16 subsidiaries. He is a prominent member of the business community and widely known within the Kingdom's ICT sector. Before joining TAQNIA, Mr. Alhussain was CEO of International Systems Engineering (ISE), an economic offset company in Saudi Arabia specializing in the provision of technological solutions and support of large-scale defense projects. Under Mr. Alhussain's leadership, ISE grew 600 percent. Before ISE, he was tapped to manage the Saudi Internet service provider (ISP) industry's major merger of AWALNET, NASEEJ, and ALALAMIAH. While Mr. Alhussain was at AWALNET, the company's revenues doubled and he engineered the company's acquisition by Saudi Telecom Company (STC), the largest provider of telecommunications services in the Kingdom. He was also on the team that brought about the launch of Saudi Arabia's first satellite, SAUDISAT 1. He holds numerous board positions, including BADIR ICT.

During my interview, I spoke with the TAQNIA CEO and discussed a number of subjects, including the importance of innovation and technology to the Kingdom's future, the promise Saudi startups and entrepreneurship hold for the country, and the role of SMEs in the Kingdom's future economy.

During my discussion with him, Mr. Alhussain highlighted the role of TAQNIA in the promotion of entrepreneurship. He outlined the history of TAQNIA, which began with its chief mandate of contributing to the diversification of the Saudi economy. Specifically, he said, at the time our slogan was to have TAQNIA be "the SABIC of technology." After the usual parade of consultants and in-depth studies in preparation for the creation of TAQNIA, what emerged were the three main areas of subject concentration for the organization, which were: (1) investment attraction and promotion; (2) industrial development; and (3) the R&D developmental services.

In terms of investment attraction and promotion, TAQNIA Holding was the first entity in the Kingdom established by the Saudi government to function as a venture capital firm. Mr. Alhussain said, "In this business line, we initially threw a rock in a pond whose waters were quite still and caused a ripple effect resulting in such an impact that today, everyone in the Kingdom is talking about venture capital. TAQNIA was the first." He said that to see the establishment of TAQNIA, the first government-funded Saudi venture capital firm, in an investment environment historically considered to be very conservative was quite a momentous occasion. It took much effort to gain the trust of TAQNIA's prospective shareholders.

One of the first important steps in this direction was to gain Riyadh Capital Bank as a shareholder. This backing eventually led to the formation of TAQNIA's first venture capital fund. On December 22, 2015, His Highness Prince Dr. Turki Bin Saud Bin Mohammed Al Saud, president of KACST and chairman of TAQNIA, inaugurated the Riyadh Taqnia Venture Capital Fund, with an initial capitalization of US$120 million. In announcing the fund, His Highness emphasized that "the establishment of this fund is one of the essential tools to achieve the Kingdom's transformation into the knowledge economy, which is adopted by the government of the Custodian of the Two Holy Mosques King Salman Bin Abdulaziz Al-Saud, to turn the Saudi economy into a knowledge-based one through securing robust organizational and technological infrastructures as well as the efficient resources to provide support and encouragement to small- and medium-sized enterprises (SMEs) so as to invest in high value-added technological areas.[46]

Mr. Alhussain pointed to how the new investment strategy by the PIF is to seek out investment opportunities that have a strategic value returns regard to serving the development goals of the Kingdom as opposed to purely monetary returns. Riyadh Taqnia Venture Capital Fund will operate within the Kingdom and internationally. The fund's strategy will focus on investing in startups and other companies for which there is a huge upside for the development and industrial growth and expansion priorities of Saudi Arabia. An example, Mr. Alhussain stated, was in the area of water desalination. He said, "Today, the Kingdom is now the largest producer of desalinated water in the world, satisfying approximately 20 percent of global demand. If we had invested and taken equity position in the leading technology companies in this field years ago, we would have not only benefited financially, but we would have proprietary rights in a technology that has high use and value inside Saudi Arabia."

Seventy-five percent of the new fund will focus on investments in the United States, Europe, and technology investments from other developed countries, while 25 percent will be devoted to investments emanating from within the Kingdom. So, Mr. Alhussain pointed out, there is a two-pronged investment approach. When a technology startup or existing enterprise has attractive technologies in areas of developmental priority for the Kingdom, and the enterprise has a high promise of profitability inside the Kingdom, it is then that the prospective investment would be a target for the new fund. So, Mr. Alhussain stated: "We are not a silent investor but rather an investor that would need to grow the company actively while pursuing its ultimate profitability, thereby exacting our returns on investment."

Of no less importance, but less commented on by Mr. Alhussain was the second and third areas of industry development and R&D developmental services. Concerning industry development, he said this can be described as mimicking the petrochemical giant SABIC, but in TAQNIA's case, for the area of technology. In the R&D developmental services area, it is TAQNIA's responsibilities to help in the commercialization of technologies. Normally, TAQNIA would come in as a late-stage investor. TAQNIA Holding's subsidiary, TAQNIA Services, is engaged in this area of commercialization facilitation.

During the interview, Mr. Alhussain graciously provided me with his opinions on the important themes of this book. Specifically, when I asked him about his opinions on how an entrepreneur should be defined, he expressed great interest in the question. He related how when BADIR was established, he served on its board. He served on a committee to evaluate the first entrepreneur applicants to BADIR. These applicants came to BADIR seeking funding for their ventures. The committee faced the question of who should be considered an entrepreneur and receive acceptance into the BADIR program. As Mr. Alhussain recalls, there were 108 applicants. Some of them were seeking to start old or existing businesses. So, he said, out of the 108 applicants, the committee ultimately accepted eight for admission into the BADIR program. The elimination of the unselected applicants was primarily based on whether the applicant was starting some type of business other than that which was based on a new idea, technological solution, or new-to-market technology. What Mr. Alhussain was saying is that the committee was looking for creative destruction among the applicant's venture ideas.

Another question on which Mr. Alhussain offered his opinion was whether the third- or fourth-generation FOB executives should be considered entrepreneurs. Mr. Alhussain sees the dichotomy of the issues when you view a third- or fourth-generation FOB family member in the family business with little at stake, yet he or she is trying to do something different in an entrepreneurial spirit. He told me that in this regard, the BADIR experience is quite useful. To many who have dealt with BADIR or those who have pursued access to its programs tend to believe entrepreneurs can be produced swiftly with little effort. However, he pointed out, it takes a whole ecosystem with all of its support functions to produce successful entrepreneurs. This is where he sees the useful function of the type of entrepreneurial ecosystem within an FOB. Those family members and FOB working environments tend to act as an ecosystem that would nurture the new ventures attempted by that third or fourth generation FOB business executive. BADIR's incubation program is one of the best that Mr. Alhussain has been close to and he said he saw the real benefits of having a 360-degree support system within which the growth of an entrepreneur is tended to on a daily basis.

The last question posed to Mr. Alhussain to which he responded related to his opinions as to the general environment for the Saudi entrepreneur. He expressed considerable optimism for the entrepreneurial ecosystem in the Kingdom. He sees great support from the government these days, particularly when it comes to the Saudi government's initiatives to change the Kingdom's laws pertaining to startups and the area of bankruptcy.

What also inspires Mr. Alhussain's optimism is the changing mentalities on the part of Saudis when it comes to starting their own businesses. He attributed some of this to the tens of thousands of Saudi students coming back to Saudi Arabia after having studied abroad. Mr. Alhussain sees them coming back with a heretofore-unseen enthusiasm to start their own businesses and new ventures. In a generally risk-averse society, Mr. Alhussain sees considerable reason for optimism when he views the changes in Saudi attitudes on this subject.

NOTES

1. Kingdom of Saudi Arabia, Central Planning Organization, Riyadh, the Development Plan for the Kingdom of Saudi Arabia, 1970–1975 (1390–1395 AH), 21.
2. Royal Decree No. A/111 dated August 29, 1999 (17/5/1420 AH), Article (1), Objective (11).
3. *Arab News,* "Kingdom 'Means' Business," May 28, 2015, www.arabnews.com/saudi-arabia/news/753236.
4. *Arab News,* "SMEs Still Run by Foreigners," March 15, 2014, www.arabnews.com/news/540496.
5. Ibid.
6. *Arab News,* "Cabinet OKs Body to Create jobs for Saudis," October 21, 2015, www.arabnews.com/saudi-arabia/news/823431.

7. Saudi Press Agency, "Custodian of the Two Holy Mosques Chairs Cabinet's Session," October 26, 2015, www.spa.gov.sa/english/details.php?id=1412407.

8. *Arab News,* "New SME Body 'Will Generate Jobs for Saudis,' October 28, 2015, www.arabnews.com/saudi-arabia/news/826951.

9. *Saudi Gazette,* "SMEs Get a Boost," October 27, 2015, http://saudigazette.com .sa/saudi-arabia/smes-get-a-boost/.

10. Ibid.

11. Deema Almashabi, *Bloomberg News,* "Saudi Banks Pull Welcome Mat From Startups Seeking Loans," February 25, 2015, www.bloomberg.com/news/ articles/2015-02-26/saudi-banks-pull-welcome-mat-for-smes-seeking-loans-arab-credit.

12. Saudi Industrial Development Fund, "Small & Medium Enterprises Loan Guarantee Program," www.sidf.gov.sa/en/Achievements/Pages/SmallandMedium Enterprises.aspx (Accessed December 8, 2015).

13. *Arab News,* "Kafalah Helps Young Entrepreneurs to Succeed in Business," February 7, 2014, www.arabnews.com/news/521901.

14. Ibid.

15. Almashabi, "Saudi Banks Pull Welcome Mat."

16. *The Saudi Daily Record,* "Development of Business Leaders in KSA Does Not Live Up to the Global Standards," October 8, 2015, http://saudidailyrecord.net/ story-z4796309.

17. Ibid.

18. Endeavor, www.endeavor.org/(Accessed October 31, 2015).

19. Endeavor, http://endeavor.org/entrepreneur-feature/our-newest-entrepreneurs/ (Accessed November 6, 2015).

20. Ibid.

21. Ibid.

22. Linda Rottenberg, "Why High-Impact Entrepreneurship Matters," Guest Commentary for CNBC.com, November 14, 2012, www.cnbc.com/id/49822816.

23. *Business Wire,* "Tom Friedman Calls Endeavor's Model "The Best Anti-Poverty Program of All," July 25, 2007, www.businesswire.com/news/home/ 20070725005902/en/Tom-Friedman-Calls-Endeavors-Model-Anti-Poverty-Program. (Accessed November 4, 2015); and Thomas Friedman, *The World Is Flat 3.0: A Brief History of the Twenty-first Century,* 3rd ed. (New York: Picador, 2007).

24. Rhett Morris, Ernst & Young, Endeavor Center for High-Impact Entrepreneurship and Global Entrepreneurship Monitor, "2011 High-Impact Entrepreneurship Global Report," www.sosyalinovasyonmerkezi.com.tr/yayin/2020110002 .pdf (Accessed November 4, 2015).

25. Ibid.

26. Interview with Rami Alturki, president and CEO, Alturki Holding, Alturki Holding HQ, Alturki Business Park, Al-Khobar, April 7, 2014.

27. Ibid.

28. Rasheed Abou-Alsamh, "Why Taking a Maid on Vacation Is Absurd," *Rasheed's World,* August 25, 2007, www.rasheedsworld.com/wp/category/work-ethic/.

29. Khaled Almaeena, "Why Don't Saudi Graduates Have the Skills Necessary for Employment?," *Saudi Gazette*, November 8, 2015, http://saudigazette .com.sa/saudi-arabia/why-dont-saudi-graduates-have-the-skills-necessary-for-employment/ (Accessed November 11, 2015).
30. The International Labor Organization, ILO, "Rural-Relevant Tools, Know About Business-KAB," www.ilo.org/wcmsp5/groups/public/@ed_emp/ documents/publication/wcms_159163.pdf (Accessed November 27, 2015).
31. Ibid.
32. Ibid.
33. *Arab News,* "Saudi Entrepreneurs Achieve High Success Rate, Only 16% Fail," January 1, 2015, www.arabnews.com/news/692806.
34. The Royal Embassy of Saudi Arabia, Information Office, "Political and Economic Reform in the Kingdom of Saudi Arabia," www.saudiembassy.net/files/ PDF/Reports/Reform.09.20.04.pdf.
35. U.S.-Saudi Arabian Business Council, "U.S.-Saudi Investment Forum," Program Agenda, September 4, 2015, www.us-sabc.org/i4a/pages/index.cfm? pageID=4298.
36. Ibid.
37. The Centennial Fund, Presentation: "Our Initiatives in Entrepreneurship for the Shift to a Knowledge Society," 2014, 7.
38. Ibid. 13.
39. Ibid. 29.
40. Mr. Sultan Al-Shuwayeb, GM Assistant, Sector Head of Non-Financial Services, the Centennial Fund, Abstract: "The Centennial Fund's Business Model to Support Entrepreneurs in Saudi Arabia and Abroad," December 16, 2014, www .insme.org/files/abstract_sultan-al-shuwayeb.
41. Ibid.
42. TAQNIA "TAQNIA, an Overview," www.taqnia.com/2014/EN/about.html (Accessed December 11, 2015).
43. Ibid.
44. TAQNIA "TAQNIA Services," www.taqnia.com/2014/EN/services.html (Accessed December 13, 2015).
45. Ibid.
46. King Abdulaziz City for Science and Technology, Dr. Turki Bin Saud launches Riyadh Taqnia Venture Capital Fund, www.kacst.edu.sa/en/about/media/news/ Pages/news748.aspx (Accessed January 6, 2015).

CHAPTER 6

New Horizons for the Kingdom and for Its Domestic and Foreign Businesses

A NEW ERA IN U.S.–SAUDI COMMERCIAL RELATIONS

As mentioned in the preface of this book, His Majesty King Salman Bin Abdulaziz Al Saud's September 4, 2015, visit to the United States was historic. It was his first official state visit to meet with his American counterpart, President Barack Obama. It was the first official visit by a Saudi Head of State to the United States with an accompaniment of His Royal Highness Deputy Crown Prince Mohammed Bin Salman Bin Abdulaziz Al Saud, an entourage of so many high-ranking Saudi cabinet members, including Defense Minister Deputy Crown Prince Mohammed Bin Salman; the Saudi Minister of Foreign Affairs, His Excellency Adel Bin Ahmed Al-Jubeir; the Minister of Finance, His Excellency Dr. Ibrahim Bin Abdulaziz Al-Assaf; Minister of Health, His Excellency Khaled Bin Abdulaziz Al-Falih; and Minister of Commerce and Industry, His Excellency Dr. Tawfiq Al-Rabiah. The governor and chairman of the board of directors of SAGIA, His Excellency Abdullatif Al-Othman, was also a part of King Salman's delegation from the Kingdom and one of the main causal agents for the commercial interchange associated with the King's visit.

The visionary authoritative statements made by Deputy Crown Prince and Defense Minister Mohammed Bin Salman concerning the opening of a new era of cooperation between the Kingdom of Saudi Arabia and the United States were well publicized during and after His Majesty King Salman's visit. The deputy crown prince articulated the Kingdom's plans for a dizzying array of collaborative areas of investment for the two historic trading partners in which U.S. companies stand to gain from hundreds of billions of dollars of projects in Saudi Arabia. In what was termed a "New Strategic Partnership for the 21st Century," His Royal Highness Deputy Crown Prince Mohammed Bin Salman briefed U.S. President Barack Obama on the

Kingdom's views on ways in which to elevate the relationship between the two countries to much higher levels of cooperation and, more to our point here, higher levels of bilateral trade and investment.

Most significant for U.S. businesses, pronouncements of this new era of bilateral U.S.-Saudi commercial relations is the impressive list of industry sectors in which American companies might pursue trade and investment opportunities. Reporting extensively on the Kingdom's new strategic initiative with the United States announced during the September 4, 2015, visit, *Al Arabiya News* reported the value of expected investments as cited by economists it sourced as US$2 trillion spread across 12 industry sectors. Of this amount, the news source said, over US$700 billion in business opportunities is expected to be business done in partnership between Saudi and American firms.[1]

In sector-specific terms, US$300 billion is anticipated from the oil and gas sector and its exploration, refining and distribution subsectors. The mining sector is expected to generate US$200 billion in such areas as phosphate and aluminum exploration. As Saudi Arabia is one of the world's top spenders on national defense products and services, the sale of U.S. military equipment and services also are predicted to be on the rise. Included in the sector opportunities will be an estimated $150 billion from the financial services industry opening the doors to commercial ventures for all-sized companies seeking to do business in the Kingdom.[2]

The Saudi housing market, which on an annual basis generates a shortfall in affordable housing of between 160,000 to 200,000 homes, is predicted to produce U.S.–Saudi partnership opportunities valued at more than US$100 billion. The list of sector-specific market bilateral commercial and investment opportunities continues beyond these areas. US$100 billion in U.S.–Saudi commercial and investment opportunities are estimated for the health and medical sector over the next five years, and another US$100 billion for technical and vocational training in the Kingdom. The Saudi retail market is expected to generate US$75 billion in investment opportunities.[3]

It would be quite a coup to have the Kingdom make a wholesale shift toward the United States as the preeminent and dominant source for its trade and investment needs. To say the least, it would be unperceptive to view His Majesty King Salman's U.S. visit and the announced "New Strategic Partnership for the 21st Century" initiative as U.S. business vanquishing its European and Asian competitors in the Kingdom for the foreseeable future. In fact, although Saudi Arabia has more corporate investments from the U.S. corporate community than investments from companies from any other nation, in recent years the United States has seen a decline in its overall share of foreign direct investment (FDI). Nevertheless, with investments in the downstream petrochemical industry such as the Dow Chemical Company's (Dow) US$20 billion "Sadara" JV investment with Saudi Aramco, the United States is not likely to lose its top spot anytime soon.

The mention of the Sadara JV is worth expanding upon because it is indicative of the nature of investments the Kingdom seeks to attract from foreign investors. It is the first chemical company in the GCC to use naphtha as a liquid feedstock. The project is a win-win for Dow and the Kingdom. The Sadara JV will contribute to Dow's aim to achieve strategic growth in the Middle East through the production of cost-efficient high-performance petrochemicals. The sequenced start-up process will begin with the production of polyolefins, thereby maximizing the timing in the ethylene cycle. Later production phases will include the production of ethylene oxide/propylene oxide and its derivatives, followed by polyurethanes.[4]

The volatility of global commodity prices for petrochemicals aside, with offtake agreements in hand from Dow's global customer base, the project's success seems to be in little doubt. The petrochemical installation will allow Dow and Saudi Aramco to sell to key growth markets, including domestic sales inside the Kingdom, in areas such as packaging, construction, and building materials, electronics, furniture, and bedding, automotive, and transportation.[5] Most importantly for Dow and Saudi Arabia, there are 18,000 jobs associated with Sadara—high-end jobs that will benefit the Saudi economy in many ways.

For Saudi Arabia, the Sadara JV adds to the Kingdom's already formidable petrochemical production complex. The JV's location is uniquely geographically situated in close proximity to the critically important regional markets of Europe, Asia, and Africa. The Dow–Saudi Aramco Sadara JV has afforded the Kingdom the ability to offer a prime example of how global investors can position their investment capital to projects in the country with the strong promise of excellent returns through their access to Saudi Arabia's abundant mineral resources and close proximity to the world's high-growth global markets.

In addition to the JV production facility, the Sadara JV has collaborated with the royal commission of Jubail and Yanbu (RCJY) to establish an advanced manufacturing industrial park adjacent to the Sadara petrochemical plant. PlasChem Park, located in the industrial city of Jubail on the Arabian Gulf, is situated on a 12-square-kilometer site and will be devoted exclusively to chemical and conversion industries that make direct or indirect use of the Sadara JV's products and raw materials from other suppliers. PlasChem Park has two sections, the Chemical Park and the Conversion Park and its tenants will manufacture a wide variety of products in the following areas: automotive industry applications; construction chemicals and products; home and personal care products; pharmaceuticals; paints and coatings; alternative energy; water, power, oil and gas chemicals; and consumer goods and appliances.

Dow is not the only American company with billions invested in Saudi Arabia. General Electric (GE) has committed an investment of US$1 billion to the Kingdom to be invested in energy, health care, and the pursuit and promotion of innovation. The GE Innovation Center, part of this investment, opened in November 2015 and is part of the Dhahran Techno Valley. It was created to be a collaborative think place where universities, think tanks, private sector and government can come together and share ideas, new thinking and approaches, and participate in the development of new technologies. The US$1 billion investment by GE in the Innovation Center is a part of the company's "Vision 2020," which "… creates a path for new initiatives in localization, technology innovation, and manufacturing to drive the country's digital transformation by 2020."[6] The GE investment will afford the Kingdom the opportunity to further its objectives to increase the localization in the energy supply chain from extraction to consumption. To the greatest extent possible, Saudi leadership wants to see the sourcing of raw materials, value-added products, finished goods, and contracting and vendor services in the Kingdom coming from domestic Saudi companies, especially SMEs. Through this preference of localization, the country aims to make significant gains in raising Saudi workforce numbers, strengthen local manufacturing, increase the capacity of the SME supply chain, and achiever gains in the training of Saudi professionals.[7] In the following section, there is more to say on the critically important issues of localization of manufacturing and SME capacity building and how Saudis and American corporations view their roles.

The prospects of attracting more U.S. capital into Saudi projects resulting from the "New Strategic Partnership for the 21st Century" is not the only bright spot in the U.S.–Saudi bilateral economic ties. The trade relationship between the two nations is trending upward.

In 2004, the total value of U.S. trade in goods with Saudi Arabia stood at US$26.2 billion.[8] In 2014, the total value of U.S. trade in goods with Saudi Arabia reached US$65.7 billion, over a doubling of the level of bilateral trade in the 10-year period.[9] During this period, with exception of years 2008 and 2014, the value of U.S. goods into the Kingdom increased. Although 2015 end-of-year figures were not available at the time this chapter was written, in October 2015, the total value of U.S. goods to Saudi Arabia stood at US$15.9 billion.[10] The month of December is historically the strongest month for U.S. exports. Using 2014 U.S. exports totals to the Kingdom for the months of November and December, year-end totals of U.S. exports to Saudi Arabia were expected to reach an all-time record high.

The balance of trade for the United States with Saudi Arabia has been trending in its favor over the past few years because of a decline in U.S. reliance on Saudi oil as a result of the rise of U.S. shale gas. Additionally, the level of Saudi exports to the United States from a dollar value perspective will likely decline because of the lower global oil prices. At the end of 2015, prices for West Texas Intermediate (WTI) is down year-on-year 30 percent. With greater U.S. investment destined for the Kingdom, however, it is predicted that American exports will follow those investments and the value of U.S. goods and services continue to increase.

I believe the future for greater levels of trade and investment between the Kingdom and the United States is very promising. Getting the broader U.S. business community engaged in the Saudi market is a great part of the mission of the U.S.-Saudi Arabian Business Council. The USSABC has viewed a decided uptick in the level of interest by American firms in the Saudi market. For U.S. exporters, Saudi Arabia is not the first market that companies turn their attention to naturally as compared to North American markets, Europe, or even Asia. There are geographical market consider-ations and some cultural subtleties than many American companies miss when strategizing over the Saudi market. Primarily, from an investment per-spective though, one of the most important overarching considerations in positioning a company's capital in projects within the Kingdom is how to build in the "give-back" to the country.

Those familiar with the history of business between the United States and Saudi Arabia know that there was a time during the 1970s and 1980s when one could find American business executives lining the reception areas of most Riyadh hotels closing lucrative business deals. During these boom years, Saudi Arabia quickly gained a reputation among many American business people as a market one could go into to gain quick and signif-icant profits. One did not have to live or have an office in the Kingdom to maintain a profitable business. So, they flew in from the United States or Europe to conduct their business and then leave. Even up until the first few years of the twenty-first century, Western companies routinely addressed the Saudi market through offices in Europe and Arabian Gulf neighboring cities such as Dubai, Doha, and Manama. Today, however, the situation is very different.

Saudis, both government officials and business people alike, want to see long-term commitments to the Saudi market by foreign companies seeking to do business in the Kingdom before agreeing to do business with them. This is becoming a standard approach Saudis are taking with foreign com-panies coming to market. There is much in the country that would attract competitive companies from around the world.

According to the U.S. Department of Commerce, International Trade Administration's U.S. Commercial Service, the "best prospects" for American companies in the Kingdom include the following industry sectors: agribusiness, automotive, construction equipment, defense industry equipment, education and training, electrical power systems, engineering and architectural services, health industries, information and communication technology, oil and gas field machinery, security and safety, and water resources equipment.[11]

As in the 1960s, 1970s, and 1980s, American companies have long established their market approach to Saudi Arabia by way of agency and distribution agreements. On occasion, this has led companies to establish successful joint ventures with reputable Saudi-owned companies. These ventures, by and large, have been mutually beneficial to both the U.S. company its Saudi counterpart. Some of these relationships, particularly between large Saudi FOBs and American companies, have lasted for decades and continue to prosper. As mentioned before, though, the best approach for most entrants to the Saudi market seeking long-term growth in market share is a strategic view of coupling market entry with establishing a permanent presence in the Kingdom through production, manufacturing, education, or training service facilities. Saudis are demanding more of their business relationships with foreign companies operating in the Kingdom.

Today's business relationship has to transcend the one-dimensional U.S. export sale of goods and services to Saudi Arabia, and it must have multidimensional transactional benefits that reach critically important subject matter for Saudis such as educating their citizens, building up capacity of their SMEs and improving the productive prowess and base competencies of local business so that those businesses can produce in Saudi Arabia more of what the Kingdom consumes in the country. This reoccurring theme of capacity building and localization of manufacturing and production is one that produced a very insightful gathering of some of the world's most recognized and respected chairmen and chief executive officers of some of America's largest corporations.

SAUDI AND AMERICAN GOODWILL AND RIGHT INTENTIONS—A HIGH-LEVEL DISCUSSION ON U.S.–SAUDI BILATERAL COMMERCIAL RELATIONSHIPS

On the sidelines of the September 4, 2015, visit of His Majesty King Salman Bin Abdulaziz Al Saud to Washington, D.C., there was an unpublicized, private meeting of some of the world's best-known C-suite executives of some of the world's largest U.S. companies with top Saudi government officials and business leaders. Although the U.S.-Saudi Arabian Business Council worked to get some of these distinguished corporate attendees to the meeting table, the organization and coordination of this meeting was firmly in the capable hands of the governor of the Saudi Arabian General Investment Authority (SAGIA), His Excellency Abdullatif Bin Ahmed Bin Abdullah Al-Othman.

The meeting, which took place in the late afternoon at the Westin Georgetown Hotel in Washington, D.C., was one of the headiest gatherings of top Fortune 500 chairmen and CEOs with whom I have ever had the privilege of being in a room. This list of attendees was almost dizzying. Although not exhaustive, the partial list of those in attendance included: Mr. Klaus Kleinfeld, chairman and CEO of Alcoa, Mr. Denis Muilenberg, president and CEO of Boeing, Mr. Ryan Lance, chairman and CEO of ConocoPhillips, Mr. John J. Hamre, president and CEO of the Center for Strategic and International Studies (CSIS), Mr. Andrew Liveris, chairman and CEO of Dow Chemical Co., Mr. David Seaton, chairman and CEO of Fluor, Mr. Jeffery Immelt, chairman and CEO of GE, Mr. David Lesar, chairman and CEO of Halliburton, Mr. Jamie Dimon, chairman and CEO of JPMorgan Chase and Co., Mrs. Marillyn A. Hewson, chairwoman, president and CEO of Lockheed Martin Corporation, Mr. Thomas Kennedy, chairman and CEO of Raytheon, Mr. Abdallah Jum'ah, chairman of Saudi Investment Bank, Saudi co-chairman of the USSABC and former president and CEO of Saudi Aramco, Yousef Al-Banyan, CEO (Acting) of SABIC, Mr. Thomas Donahue, president and CEO of the U.S. Chamber of Commerce, Mr. John S. Watson, chairman and CEO of Chevron Corporation, Mrs. Lubna Suliman Al-Olayan, CEO and president of Olayan Financing Company and principal of the Olayan Group, Mr. Arne Sorenson, president and CEO of Marriott International, Inc. and Mr. Steven J. Demetriou, president and CEO of Jacobs Engineering Group, Inc.

In addition to the master of ceremonies for this gathering, His Excellency SAGIA Governor Abdullatif Al-Othman, Saudi government officials in attendance were the Saudi Minister of Finance, His Excellency Dr. Ibrahim Al-Assaf, the Saudi Minister of Health, His Excellency King Khalid Bin Abdulaziz Al-Falih (as of May 2016 appointed Minister of the new Ministry of Energy, Industry, and Mineral Resources—replacing the old Ministry of Petroleum and Mineral Resources), and the Saudi Minister of Commerce, His Excellency Dr. Tawfiq Fawzan Alrabiah (as of May 2016 appointed Minister of Health).

I was fortunate enough to tag along with my Saudi co-chairman, Mr. Abdallah Jum'ah. Although I did not have a seat at the table, I was able to be in the room, which included no staffers or other personnel for either the corporate heads or the Saudi ministers. I took fairly meticulous notes from the entire meeting, which was difficult to do given the extraordinary composition of those giants of global industry in attendance and the substance of the dialogue. It was one of the most candid and insightful conversations between top Saudi public- and private-sector officials and American corporate leaders concerning the U.S.–Saudi commercial relationship that I have ever heard during my career.

Without attribution or ascription of commentary to any particular participant, I believe I can convey the salient features of the dialogue and important messages concerning the opinions of those around the table pertaining to the U.S.–Saudi bilateral economic and commercial relationship and the importance and esteem with which all around the table hold it. As opposed to ascribing one particular comment or line of remarks to one minister, I will simply describe the message conveyed by "the ministers" and offer other commentary as coming from the group. This will be done in the case of the corporate participants around the table as well, attributing their comments to the chairman, CEO or president.

After welcoming everyone to the table, Governor Al-Othman set the tone for the meeting by telling everyone the primary reason for getting everyone around the table is so that the Kingdom could hear from its important partners from the United States, those companies that have demonstrated long-term commitments to Saudi Arabia. Saudi Arabia wanted to hear from them, in an honest and open discussion, what in their opinion was going right and what needed to be improved upon. The Saudi ministers in attendance underscored how much they viewed the opinions of the assembled corporate leaders as important in knowing what they as a government was doing right or wrong in terms of facilitating and supporting the bilateral ties they share as trading and investing nations. I can say to a person from what I heard and witnessed, from the beginning to the end of the meeting, the corporate side expressed nothing but appreciation for their willingness to listen and a sincere desire for the Kingdom and its people to derive optimum benefit from their invested business interests in the country.

The Saudi government officials let the business audience know that it was their responsibility as a government to provide all of the tools business needed to continue to meet with success in the Saudi market. There was a strong message that despite lower oil prices, the economic stability of the Kingdom was not in question and that its fundamentals were in good shape. During this exchange, there was an extraordinary amount of candor and directness by the Saudi government officials around the table concerning the country's current fiscal circumstances and the well-publicized fiscal consequences to the Kingdom from lower global oil prices. The message from the officials was that the current situation with oil prices was actually viewed as an opportunity by the Kingdom to make necessary changes so that the Saudi economy would be able to maintain a healthy economy despite what may happen in the oil market.

Tightening fiscal pressures from lower oil prices means an opportunity for the Kingdom to double down on its efforts to diversify its economy and localize more and more its supplier sources to homegrown competitive internal suppliers. The ministers and the SAGIA governor wanted to get a clear message across to those American investors around the table that in its pursuit to empower its SMEs, build capacity of its own internal supply chain firms, and create additional engines of economic and market growth, there would be an even more decided shift toward localization and increasing its knowledge base. It was at this point when the ministers pointed to the advantage that many American firms, such as those around the table that have been engaged in the Kingdom's market for years, have a definite advantage in working with the country in pursuing its growth goals.

It was noted that although U.S. firms have been most aligned with the Kingdom's growth potentials in offering the necessary technologies, equipment, service offerings, and investment capital in the growth of key Saudi industry sectors, the Kingdom is looking for more from them. It was suggested that U.S. firms, and indeed any foreign competitor seeking to grow in the Kingdom, should find new and different service models through which they can aid the Kingdom in growth employment among Saudis, help to improve the capacity of local firms, especially SMEs, and assist government efforts to feed business to local and competent supply chain companies.

One of the chairman and CEOs at the table began his remarks by asking the Saudis at the table how his company and the rest around the table could help to create a better environment in the Kingdom. He advised that when you are trying to attract and support SMEs to the market, training is key. Government coordination with an investor like his company is also crucially important. He went on to say that for an investor such as his company, a system of "retail supply" in terms of locally sourced vendors may not apply. With the level of marketing and innovation it would have to rely upon in their operations, normally they would have to source their needs from within.

Another chairman and CEO stated that his company had experienced successes in sourcing their needs locally. His company has placed an emphasis on outsourcing a significant portion of their supply chain needs to local companies, particularly SMEs. He added that he was proud that a rising number of these firms, particularly pertaining to service providers, were women-owned businesses.

One chairman and CEO cited his own company's example of successes in training and hiring significant numbers of Saudi women engineers. This senior executive has had more than 20 years' personal experience in working in the Kingdom, and his company has been doing business there since the mid-1940s. He stated that indeed there were missing pieces to the local supply chain pool, and that in his opinion there certainly needed to be more done to strengthen the capacity and skills of SMEs that are potential participants among local vendors and suppliers.

What I found most interesting and refreshingly reassuring, is that these titans in the global corporate community were all expressing undeniable genuine and absolute rock-solid support and interest in helping the Kingdom achieve its most important development goals. Their companies, all multibillion-dollar worldwide organizations, were actively engaged in supporting and encouraging the local supply chain, increasing their hiring of Saudis, and in most cases contributing to the education and training of the younger generation of Saudi workers … the future of the Kingdom. For the future of Saudi–U.S. commercial relations and the work that I do, I found it inspiring that these ladies and gentlemen, with so many of their own company's global markets requiring their attention, were intimately aware of and thoroughly informed as to the details of their company's Saudi market presence.

And another chairman and CEO of a company that recently completed a US$3 billion project in collaboration with the Kingdom and has reached an 85 percent Saudi-hire rate, also stated his concern for the improvement of the environment for local outsourcing and fuller engagement of Saudi SMEs. One challenge he identified is that there are Saudi firms seeking contracting opportunities with his company, but lack the required level of capabilities normally preventing a company like his from doing business with them for the large projects undertaken. He urged a stronger emphasis within the Kingdom on not only expanding the technical knowledge upgrades needed by the younger generation and their own companies, but also ensuring that they receive the educational enhancements such as real-world business experience before pursuing contracting opportunities with a Global 500 company.

The challenges faced by the Kingdom in growing its local talent pool are quite significant. At the USSABC, a familiar refrain among our U.S. members is the lack of real-world business experience by young Saudis seeking employment and contracting opportunities with their companies inside the Saudi Arabia. This is an ongoing circumstance faced by both Saudis and foreign investors that tends to act as a detriment to full engagement in Saudi localization. Comments offered at the table by the Saudi government officials on this subject were not surprisingly aimed at strongly encouraging the American corporate investors present to do more in contributing to the education, training, and contracting of Saudi vendors and suppliers, particularly young Saudi business people. From the Saudi perspective, it is wholly understandable for the Kingdom's leadership to adopt a position in which after years of affording large-capitalized American companies profitably present in the Kingdom the opportunity to do business and gain from government tenders, they would expect these firms to step up their contributions in this area.

In summing up the September 4, 2015, CEO Roundtable, its bears mentioning that although the discussion was heavily weighted toward building up Saudi local talent pools, education and training, and capacity building of the Saudi supply chain, there were other areas of discussion. Although the United States has a variety of tax treaties with more than 40 countries, in terms of double taxation treaties, Saudi Arabia is not one of them. The lack of a double taxation treaty between the United States and the Kingdom places American investors at a distinct disadvantage and can be a high hurdle when it comes to U.S. investment capital finding its way to Saudi projects. Another issue brought up by one of the chairmen and CEOs at the table was the observation that although Saudi Arabia has done quite well in attracting energy-intensive companies to the Kingdom as investors, the challenge for the rest of this century and beyond is how the country will draw more non-intensive industries and companies to market. Other issues discussed were visas for company employees for entry to the Kingdom, import duties and regulations pertaining to industrial and construction equipment destined for Saudi Arabia, and improving the image of the Kingdom abroad and portraying a more accurate and welcoming picture of the country within investing nations around the world.

NEW FISCAL REALITIES AND RECURRENT DEVELOPMENT THEMES

During the first few days of 2016, the Custodian of the Two Holy Mosques, His Majesty King Salman Bin Abdulaziz Al Saud submitted his first budget to an expectant nation since he ascended the throne earlier the previous year. For more than a decade, on high oil prices the Kingdom of Saudi Arabia had followed robust budgets with plenty of expenditures benefiting most of its demographics. The Kingdom's military apparatus, the ranks of government workers, social welfare recipients and programs, health care providers and patients, students and teachers, and the consumer at large all had a stake in sustained high levels of government spending on the defense budget, public largess, and generous and long-provided subsidies for the necessities of life such as water, car petrol, and food.

So in June 2014, when global oil prices began a steep and precipitous dive, few were surprised when the ever-present predictions of doom and gloom from the Kingdom's naysayers gained momentum. Compounding the negativity were a host of geopolitical and fiscal occurrences that added to the pessimism.

The Kingdom's attempts to check Iranian hegemonic aspirations for greater influence in the region have been well publicized in the world press. These regional aspirations of Iran have been characterized by its support of Syria's dictator president, Bashar Al Assad; its support for Hezbollah, the Shi'a Islamist militant group and political party based in Lebanon; its meddling in Iraq; its support for the Al Houthis, a Zaidi Shi'a group based in northern Yemen, which began an insurgency in Yemen rebelling against Saudi-ally former Yemeni president Ali Abdullah Saleh; and a number of prickly incidents that repeatedly have seen Iran interfering in the domestic affairs of the Kingdom of Saudi Arabia and its regional neighbors.

It has been the Kingdom's military intervention in Yemen, launched in March 2015, codenamed "Operation Decisive Storm," which has caused the most concern among financial analyst over the Kingdom's fiscal situation because of the siphoning action from the nation's coffers dedicated to the conflict's prosecution.

For the Kingdom, the last straw followed their execution of a radical Shite cleric, a Saudi citizen who gained support inside Iran for his repeated attacks on the Saudi monarchy, inflammatory speeches, violent acts, and support for domestic terrorism. After this execution, Saudi-Iranian relations reached new lows with protestors in Tehran storming the royal Saudi embassy and setting it on fire. The Saudi government, having had enough of the Islamic Republic's belligerence and insults, severed diplomatic ties with Iran on Sunday, January 3, 2015. Quickly following suit, the Kingdom's allies, the United Arab Emirates, Sudan, and Bahrain, severed or downgraded diplomatic relations with Iran.

Beyond the geopolitical issues and the potential fiscal strain caused by its defense spending, another cautionary sign came when in July 2015 it was reported that to cover a budget deficit resulting from lower oil prices, the Kingdom had issued US$4 billion in sovereign bonds, the first time it had done so since 2007.[12] In March 2016, the *Wall Street Journal* reported that the Saudi ministry of finance asked foreign banks operating in the Kingdom to submit their proposals for a loan of between $6 billion and $8 billion in size.[13]

The sovereign debt issuance and the Kingdom's approach to the global debt market came on the heels of additional warnings from the International Monetary Fund (IMF). As a consequence of Saudi Arabia being a signatory to the IMF's Articles of Agreement, it conducts regular and required consultations with the Kingdom's leadership. IMF Article IV consultation discussions with the Kingdom began on May 28, 2015, and concluded on July 29, 2015.

In its report of the Article IV consultations, the IMF announced it projected a government fiscal deficit of 19.5 percent of GDP for the Kingdom in 2015, but that the country would return to surpluses during the 2015 to 2020 time period.[14] Moreover, the report stated that the lower trend in oil prices for the Kingdom underscored the importance of structural reforms to be instituted by the country. It suggested a number of measures the Kingdom should take to avoid dire fiscal future consequences. These recommendations included lowering or eliminating some subsidies, raising domestic consumer energy prices, reducing the employment levels of government employees, expanding its non-oil revenues by further diversifying its economy and instituting by way of land and a value-added- tax (VAT).

To provide even more fuel to the purveyors of Saudi doom and gloom, Bloomberg and other media reported delays in Saudi government payments to its contractors due as a result of lower oil prices and a growing deficit.[15] Further reports of the government suspending construction projects and slowing its spending on infrastructure only added to the speculation that needed structural reforms would soon be forthcoming as admonished by the IMF. In its year-end report, the ministry of finance stated that it had activated a budget support provision allowing it to redirect US$48.8 billion in capital and operating expenditures to meet obligations for projects of national priority and to meet emerging costs of projects instituted by royal decree.[16] Moreover, with the Saudi government running an annual budget deficit of more than US$100 billion, and having liquidated more than US$90 billion of its foreign assets in 2015 to pay its bills, the fiscal situation as of December 2015 was almost universally viewed as unsustainable. The recommended changes by the IMF constituted a fresh reminder of the stark realities faced by the Kingdom. As 2015 drew to a close, the question posed as to whether Saudi Arabia's leadership would heed the warnings from one of the world's foremost authorities on national fiscal realities would be answered within a few months after the IMF's Article IV consultation with the Kingdom was made public.

In December 2015, the task of signaling the Kingdom's intention to push forward with needed economic structural reforms fell to the new generational voice of the government, Deputy Crown Prince Mohammed Bin Salman. People familiar with the inner workings of the Saudi government and followers attest to a palpable and pervading new energy within the business of government these days. Many credit His Royal Highness Prince Mohammed's own energy, drive, and predilection for handling detailed work with this newly perceived reinvigoration. Whatever the case, when the Deputy Crown Prince, Chairman of the Council of Economic and Development Affairs (CEDA), addressed an audience of senior government officials, business people, and economists, he presented a mix of intended measures aimed at enabling the Kingdom's economy to withstand any adverse consequences from falling oil prices.

As a prelude to the budget, His Majesty King Salman would be expected to announce the following month, Deputy Crown Prince Mohammed Bin

Salman told those in attendance at the December 2015 meeting that the Kingdom would move toward instituting new spending reforms that would place more areas of expenditures under greater scrutiny and restrictions. The government would also be accelerating the pace of privatization of government-owned enterprises in order to spur economic growth, add more private-sector jobs, and reduce government outlays for maintaining such operations.[17] The deputy crown prince reportedly also told the audience that a new approach to the management of the government's business would be introduced, one designed to ensure that key performance indicators (KPIs) for government employees and agencies are pursued and for which accountability would be required. The probability is high that more responsibility for oversight for this new approach will be taken on by the CEDA.

The public did not have to wait much further beyond the deputy crown prince's pronouncements for His Majesty King Salman Bin Abdulaziz Al Saud's presentation on the Kingdom's new approaches to budgeting and fiscal management for 2016. On December 28, 2015, His Majesty King Salman announced a 2016 annual budget that would see expenditures projected at US$224 billion, down 14 percent from 2015 spending expectations, and revenues forecasted to reach US$137 billion, down from the US$162 billion forecast for 2015. The 2016 budget projects the Kingdom will run a US$87 billion deficit for the year. Although the final detailed budget document was not available when this chapter was written, multiple news outlets reported the Kingdom's 2016 budget revenue forecast was based on a projection of per barrel oil prices averaging US$29.

The changes for the Kingdom's 2016 budget represents developments that, in the eyes of its leaders and those who have urged a more fiscally responsible approach as dictated by their current and recent cost and revenue trends, are wholly required and that will serve the long-term economic health well. Under the 2016 budget, the Saudi government plans to rationally adjust the money it spends on subsidies for fuel for automobiles, water, and electricity over the next five years. As is historically the case, education, health, and social welfare programs will continue to receive a large share of budgetary expenditures. As usual, Saudi defense spending is off-budget and is expected to remain robust given the external neighboring security challenges it continues to face.

Just as intriguing and worth scrutinizing are the budget numbers presented by the Custodian of the Two Holy Mosques, His Majesty King Salman, and the underlying thought shifts in the budget's rationale by the Saudi leadership in the casting of the 2016 budget's fiscal accountability, public finance operational management and monitoring, and the long-standing emphasis on diversifying the revenues of the country.

As covered in Chapter 1 of this book, the goal of moving the Kingdom away from its near-total dependence on oil revenues toward an economy with more multifaceted revenue sources has been around since the First Development Plan in 1970. For the Tenth Development Plan, unveiled late in 2015, the drive toward diversification continues. Privatization, as it was viewed in the early Development Plans of the country as a catalyst for economic growth and diversification, is once again receiving gathering momentum.

In addition to the Kingdom's 2016 budget, part of the blueprint of the way forward for Saudi Arabia is the Tenth Development Plan. After the familiar and well-meaning objectives of maintaining the Kingdom's Islamic teaching, values, and national identity in its stated first objective, the next stated goal of the Plan states:

SECOND OBJECTIVE:
Enhancing economic diversification with its different dimensions, through:

Vertical Diversification:
2.1 *Raising utilization rates of mineral resources, diversifying perti-nent activities and encouraging expansion in local production, processing, and manufacturing of mining raw materials.*
2.2 *Developing production and service activities, which have strong linkages with oil and gas industries as well as upstream and downstream activities that depend on oil and gas.*

Horizontal Diversification:
2.3 *Expanding production capacities of the industrial sector, par-ticularly in fields covered by the national industrial strategy.*
2.4 *Developing the services sector and increasing its contribution to GDP with due emphasis on financial, tourism, transport, engineering, communication, and information technology (IT) services.*
2.5 *Diversifying economic activities in non-oil sectors with due emphasis on high-productivity, and promising comparative advantage activities.*
2.6 *Investing in projects related with diversification of energy sources.*
2.7 *Developing non-oil exports and increasing their contribution to the total value of exports.*
2.8 *Encouraging local and foreign strategic partnerships to imple-ment investment projects that contribute to diversification of the production base of the national economy.*
2.9 *Developing low-water-consuming agricultural products as well as fishing activities.*

Spatial Diversification:

2.10 *Making use of the comparative advantages of the provinces in boosting spatial diversification of economic activities along with expansion in establishment of industrial zones and business and technology incubators to improve utilization of these advantages.*[18]

There are other familiar refrains from previous development plans in the Tenth (Five-Year) Development Plan.

As discussed in other chapters of this book, innovation will continue to be an extremely important catalyst for long-term economic growth and future prosperity. The Third Objective, as stated in the Tenth Development Plan, lists a "Transition to a knowledge-based economy and a knowledge society, through: dissemination of knowledge; knowledge utilization; knowledge generation; and knowledge management."[19] Coupled with the Saudi leadership's articulated underscoring of its support for SMEs and the public- and private-sector institutions that serve them, there are great opportunities for American companies in collaboration and venturing within the Kingdom in the areas of technology development, transfer, and commercialization.

The privatization strategies identified as priorities will be pursued more aggressively. The Tenth Development Plan's Fourth Objective, "To expand the absorptive capacity of the national economy and enhance its growth, stability and competitiveness," and its stated goal lists under "Market absorptive capacity and regulation" one of its goals as: "Finalizing implementation of the privatization strategy in accordance with a specified schedule."[20]

One can debate the success of Saudi Arabia's economic development plans and achievements. I believe, however, the Kingdom's past and current plans have been developed by leaders taking the greatest care for Saudi religious beliefs and cultural values as well as the welfare of the Saudi people. Both incremental and, at least in the case of the initial revelations and buildup for the 2016 budget, expansive steps taken by the Kingdom since embarking on national development plans in early 1970s have real meaning for the country and its people. Saudi Arabia's journey toward full economic diversity has been a kind of progressive functional continuum upon which all previous actions and outcomes, whether completed, successful, adjusted, or abandoned, have contributed to Saudi Arabia's forward motion toward diversification.

There is a newfound sense of urgency among the Kingdom's current leaders for encouraging greater engagement by the Saudi private sector in contributing to the country's economic development goals. As discussed in Chapter 1, the goal of having the private sector shoulder more of the industrial development and expansion needs of the country is ever present. This message has been conveyed by the Custodian of the Two Holy Mosques,

His Majesty King Salman Bin Abdulaziz Al Saud and his senior government leaders to Saudi business with renewed vigor. As the Kingdom looks to reduce public expenditures for large development projects by placing them on hold or downsizing their scale, the pressure for the Saudi private sector to take up the slack will only grow. This is a question that bears watching over the next few years. Will Saudi businesses, especially the nation's large private companies and FOBs, meet the challenge by investing more of its capital into projects that grow the country's industrial base. Two indicators I believe may signal future progress in this direction will be how successful the Kingdom will be in attracting foreign institutional investors to the Tadawul and to what extent will the country persuade its businesses to spend more of their capital inside the country as opposed to Saudi direct investment in other markets.

In a sweeping five-hour interview with Bloomberg's editor-in-chief, John Micklethwait and five other Bloomberg journalists, His Royal Highness Prince Mohammed Bin Salman Bin Abdulaziz, Deputy Crown Prince, provided the first in-depth details of what many are calling the most substantial change in Saudi economic policy since the country's founding.[21] The deputy crown prince discussed a wide range of issues from the planned partial privatization of Saudi Aramco to the expanded role of Saudi Arabia's public investment fund (PIF). His royal highness stated that he expected that the vision for the Kingdom's economic future within a month from the interview. The National Transformation Plan, which the deputy crown prince stated would be a component of that vision, would come later.[22]

Some of the more salient features of the deputy crown prince's interview were the expectation that shares of Saudi Aramco (less than 5 percent) could be offered to the public as early as 2017; the post–Saudi Aramco IPO creation of potentially the world's largest sovereign wealth fund in an expanded PIF with a value of US$2 trillion; an aggressive shift toward reducing current government assets by relinquishing them to private-sector interests; and the strong relationship the Kingdom has with the United States.[23]

There is no question that these are momentous developments in the unfolding future of the Kingdom. In late April 2016, the Council of Ministers, under the chairmanship of the Custodian of the Two Holy Mosques King Salman, Saudi Arabia's vision for 2030[24] proposed a comprehensive articulation of the way forward for the Kingdom's economic growth. As stated in Vision 2030's foreward, it is based on three pillars: (1) The Kingdom of Saudi Arabia's status as the heart of the Arab and Islamic worlds; (2) the country's determination to become a global investment powerhouse; and (3) transforming the country's unique strategic location into a global hub connecting three continents. Vision 2030, a prelude to the

Kingdom's national transformation plan, will have long-term and profound implications for a number of critically important national industry sectors.

In the deputy crown prince's interview, fundamental structural changes in the Saudi health care industry was discussed. The oil and gas, transportation, energy, petrochemical, and consumer retail sectors have also been previously discussed by Saudi leadership as facing significant change. It is encouraging that the vast majority of public pronouncements by Saudi leaders all point to their expectation that American businesses will have ample opportunities to play strategic roles in the economic, commercial, and industrial development plans of the country.

In a dramatic sign of the Kingdom's resolve to transform Saudi Arabia's economy and leave behind its incessant economic dependence upon hydrocarbons, on May 8, 2016, global media reported a momentous shakeup by King Salman of multiple cabinet officials and reformation of various ministries and government agencies. Long-serving oil minister Ali Al-Naimi was replaced by Saudi Aramco's one-time CEO and then chairman, Khalid Al-Falih and the old Ministry of Petroleum and Mineral Resources was renamed the Ministry of Energy, Industry, and Mineral Resources and Mr. Al-Falih was put in charge. Mr. Al-Falih, who had been serving as the Kingdom's health minister, was replaced by Tawfiq Al-Rabiah as the new health minister. Minister Al-Rabiah had been serving as the minister of commerce and industry. That ministry was renamed the Ministry of Commerce and Investment. A number of other ministries, authorities, and agencies were affected by the King's restructuring and reshuffling. Besides the continuation of placing capable and competent people in positions of highest responsibilities in the country, a new trend is emerging: the faces of ministers and senior government officials are getting younger.

Lastly, on June 6, 2016, the Kingdom approved its National Transformation Plan, what many view as the government's principal executory tool for bringing into reality its Vision 2030. The plan sets forth ambitious goals in raising non-oil revenues, the imposition of taxes on "harmful products" and plans for the eventual levy of personal and unified income taxes, the reduction in government employment, the creation of 450,000 jobs by 2020, and the achievement of multiple economic, governmental and strategic industrial leaps into a better future for the Saudi Arabia.

As I have argued in this book, the key to the Kingdom achieving long-term prosperity and a sustained economic expansion trajectory is robust engagement and broad capital contribution from the Saudi private sector and their foreign investor partners in the country.

CLOSING THOUGHTS

Throughout most of my professional career, I have had the opportunity to travel around the world promoting U.S. business in foreign markets. I've easily flown more than several millions of miles doing so. To this day, one of the greatest pleasures and sources of job satisfaction I have is the ability to travel throughout the United States meeting businesses with interests in expanding internationally. I have visited thousands of companies, everything from small two-person start-ups to large-cap global competitors with tens of thousands of employees. I continue to experience a real sense of awe and high fascination with the strength, creativity, and intrinsic value of American business. I have seen in a multitude of sectoral varieties, product and service lines, and levels of executive and production-line talent what makes the great engines of American enterprise continually churn. Most important, for me, is having had the privilege of facilitating the global market entry and growth in country market shares for thousands of U.S. companies. I have done so as an individual counselor and a management leader for organizations in the business of assisting American companies with their international market strategies.

From these experiences, I have learned a very simple fact, almost too obvious but worth repeating. What I have learned is that regardless of the political, social, or economic circumstances with which a country may be facing, business will always get done and operate. If commercial entities exist within its borders, enterprising people will always make a buck, ruble, peso, or riyal. I say this to my American business audience in the context of Saudi Arabia to make two points. First, no matter what external or internal occurrences involving Saudi Arabia may be hitting today's headlines or media home page, you may be assured that the Kingdom's businesses are doing business and will continue to do so; and second, if you are a business competing in global markets and your products or services have market receptivity in the Kingdom, you may be equally certain that you have at least one or two foreign competitors adding to their global market girth by doing business in that country.

Historically, for American companies engaged in most U.S. industry sectors, domestic markets have been so large and satisfying that exporting rarely came naturally to them. When the world begins to get a bit smaller and diversifying the company's revenue streams becomes a priority and the search for welcoming international markets is the order of the day, Saudi Arabia is usually not the first market proposed. Moreover, with conflicts in the Middle East appearing to be almost serial in nature and hyperbole the norm in the portrayal of one's prospects for personal safety in the Kingdom, Saudi Arabia routinely appears low on corporate lists for new market development. America's foreign competitors count on this lack of market intelligence and lack of awareness in their gains of unchallenged footholds and shares in the Saudi market.

The Kingdom of Saudi Arabia is an open and competitive market. Its city streets are as safe if not safer than any city in North America, Europe, or Asia. American executives visiting the Kingdom for the first time discover this for themselves. Unlike the 1960s, 1970s, or 1980s, U.S. companies entering the Saudi market for the first time often find themselves surrounded by a plethora of foreign competitors with large and entrenched market shares. Unless such companies possess commanding competitive product or service advantages, as many U.S. firms do, it is often very difficult for new-to-market American companies to achieve swift market success.

The keys to business opportunities are those that have always existed. Make certain the required market research is obtained. Be knowledgeable of all legal issues and seek out competent advice, do your due diligence on all potential partners, and go strong into the market demonstrating a long-term commitment. Following these practices will ensure the optimization of the market potential.

Lastly, any strategy for the Saudi market must include the promise of long-term commitment. Corresponding with a long-term market commitment is the constant recognition of the promise of Saudi youth. I know the first-generation Saudi FOB owners were once young and ambitious entrepreneurs. There have always been obstacles for entrepreneurs anywhere and for those in the Kingdom there is no difference. What makes the potential for today's entrepreneurs so great is the unprecedented amount of innovation, incubation, and growth occurring in Saudi Arabia. With the kind of commitment from the Kingdom's leaders being witnessed today, I am excited about the future for Saudi business and fortunate to be in the business of promoting its prospects in the United States.

NOTES

1. *Al Arabiya News,* "Saudi, U.S. to Deepen Ties with Giant New Investment, Partnership Plan," September 5, 2015, http://english.alarabiya.net/en/business/economy/2015/09/05/Saudi-unveils-giant-U-S-partnership-and-investment-plans-.html.
2. Ibid.
3. Ibid.
4. Dow Chemical Company, "Sadara Joint Venture Now 94 Percent Complete—On Track for First Production Units to Start Up in 2015," Midland, Michigan June 23, 2015, http://www.dow.com/news/press-releases/sadara%20joint%20venture%20now%2094%20percent%20complete%20on%20track%20for%20first%20production%20units%20to%20start%20up%20in%202015.
5. Ibid.

6. General Electric, "GE's $1 Billion Investment in Saudi Arabia Creates a Path for New Initiatives in Localization, Technology Innovation and Manufacturing to Drive Country's Digital Transformation by 2020," November 3, 2015, www.geglobalresearch.com/news/press-releases/ges-global-research-center-in-saudi-arabia-to-drive-cutting-edge-innovation-and-digital-transformation.

7. Ibid.

8. United States Census Bureau, "Trade in Goods in Saudi Arabia," https://www.census.gov/foreign-trade/balance/c5170.html.

9. Ibid.

10. Ibid.

11. U.S. Department of Commerce, International Trade Administration, U.S. Commercial Service, "Doing Business in Saudi Arabia," http://export.gov/saudiarabia/doingbusinessinsaudiarabia/index.asp (Accessed December 31, 2015).

12. Thomas Reuters, Reuters U.S. "Update 2—Saudi Arabia Issues First Sovereign Bonds since 2007, More to Come," July 10, 2015, www.reuters.com/article/saudi-bond-idUSL8N0ZQ03F20150710.

13. Nicolas Parasie, "Saudi Arabia Seeks Up to $8 Billion Loan," *Wall Street Journal*, March 9, 2016, www.wsj.com/articles/saudi-arabia-seeks-to-raise-up-to-8-billion-loan-1457534170.

14. International Monetary Fund, "Saudi Arabia: 2015 Article IV Consultation—Press Release, Staff Report and Informational Annex," IMF Country Report No. 15/251, September 2015, https://www.imf.org/external/pubs/ft/scr/2015/cr15251.pdf.

15. Matthew Martin, "Saudi Arabia Said to Delay Contractor Payments as Oil Slumps," *Bloomberg Business*, October 19, 2015, www.bloomberg.com/news/articles/2015-10-19/saudi-arabia-said-to-delay-contractor-payments-after-oil-slump.

16. Kingdom of Saudi Arabia, Ministry of Finance, Riyadh, "Press Release, Recent Economic Developments and Highlights of Fiscal Years" 1436–1437 (2015) and 1438–1438 (2016)," December 28, 2015, https://www.mof.gov.sa/English/DownloadsCenter/Budget/Ministry's%20of%20Finance%20statment%20about%20the%20national%20budget%20for%202016.pdf.

17. Andrew Torchia and Marwa Rashad, "Exclusive-Saudi Deputy Crown Prince Draws Up New Economic Reforms," Thomas Reuters, Reuters U.K. Edition, December 18, 2015, http://uk.reuters.com/article/uk-saudi-economy-policy-idUKKBN0U127Q20151218.

18. Kingdom of Saudi Arabia, Ministry of Economy and Planning, Riyadh, "Objectives of the Tenth Development Plan (2015–2019)," 2, www.mep.gov.sa/themes/BlueArc/index.jsp;jsessionid=0565C99F9B869B6AA9823487E0E0BE09.gamma?event=View&ViewURI=/inetforms/themes/clasic/article/articleView.jsp;jsessionid=0565C99F9B869B6AA9823487E0E0BE09.gamma&Article.ObjectID=119 (Accessed January 5, 2015).

19. Ibid. 4.

20. Ibid. 5.

21. Bloomberg, "Saudi Arabia's Deputy Crown Prince Outlines Plans: Transcript," April 4, 2016, www.bloomberg.com/search?query=Saudi deputy crown prince.
22. Ibid.
23. Ibid.
24. *Al Arabiya* (English "Full text of Saudi Arabia's Vision 2030" April 26, 2016, http://english.alarabiya.net/en/perspective/features/2016/04/26/Full-text-of-Saudi-Arabia-s-Vision-2030.html.

Index

Note: Page references followed by "f" and "t" indicate an illustrated figure and table, respectively.